WATERCOLOR THIS BOOK

LEARN TO WATERCOLOR

20

Step-by-Step Beginner-Friendly Lessons
on Watercolor Paper

LACEY WALKER
of Rebel Unicorn Crafts

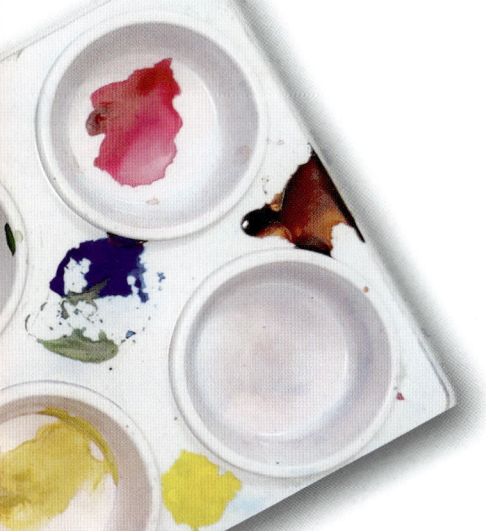

Walter Foster

CONTENTS

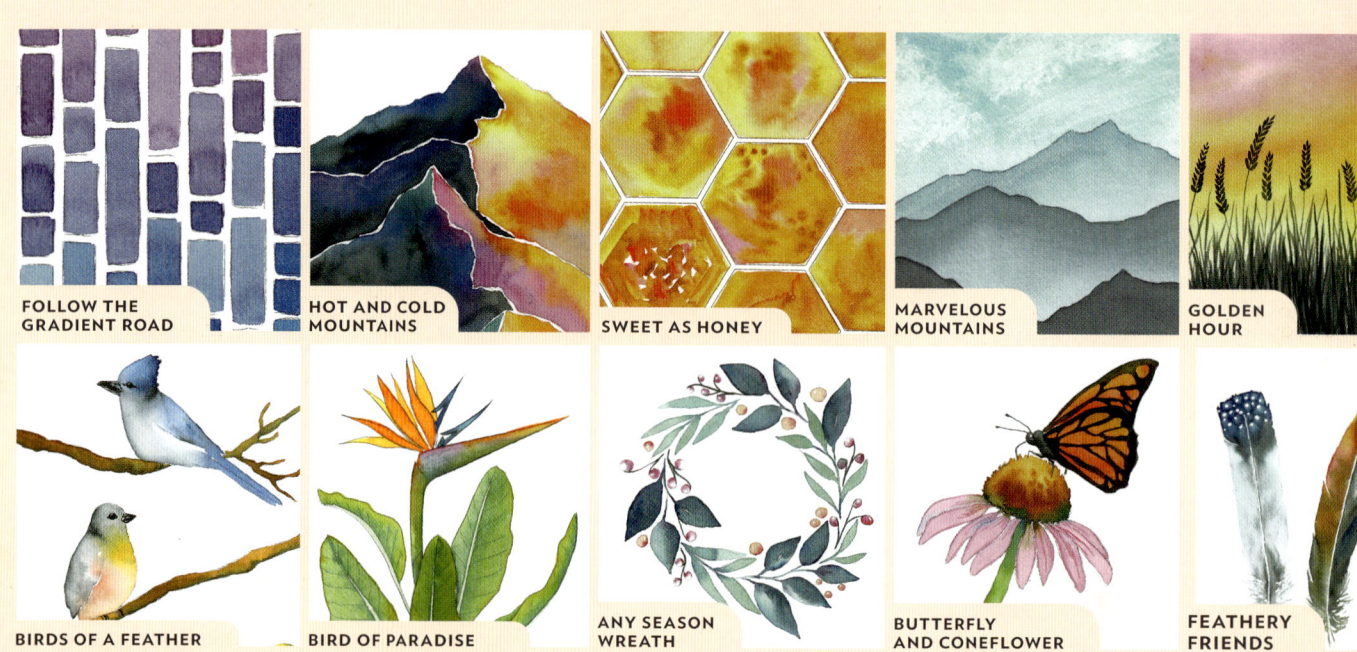

FOLLOW THE GRADIENT ROAD

HOT AND COLD MOUNTAINS

SWEET AS HONEY

MARVELOUS MOUNTAINS

GOLDEN HOUR

BIRDS OF A FEATHER

BIRD OF PARADISE

ANY SEASON WREATH

BUTTERFLY AND CONEFLOWER

FEATHERY FRIENDS

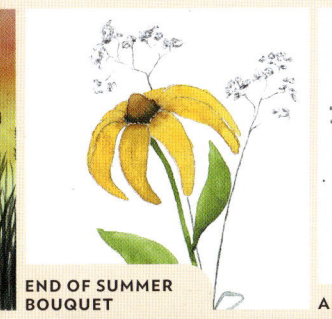

END OF SUMMER BOUQUET

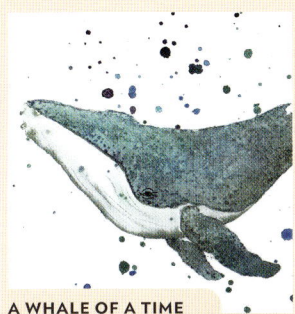

A WHALE OF A TIME

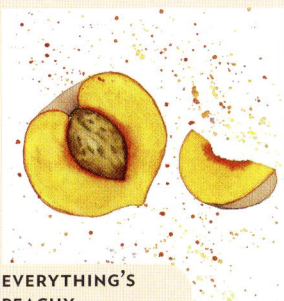

EVERYTHING'S PEACHY

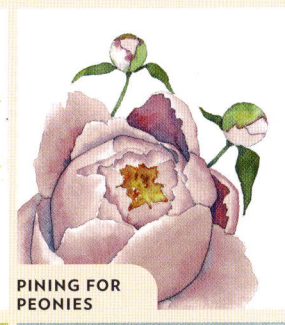

PINING FOR PEONIES

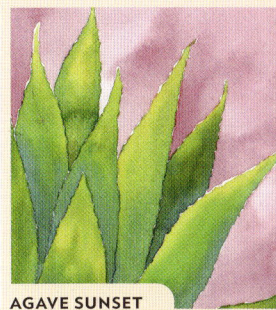

AGAVE SUNSET

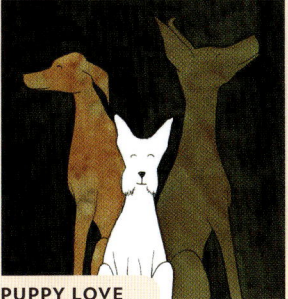

PUPPY LOVE

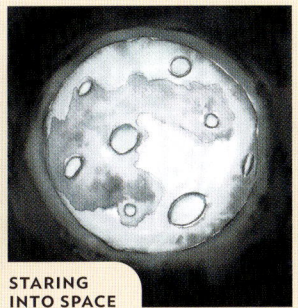

STARING INTO SPACE

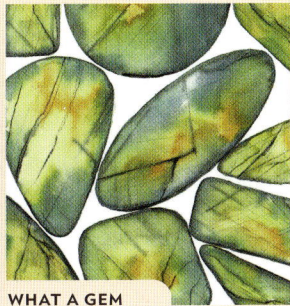

WHAT A GEM

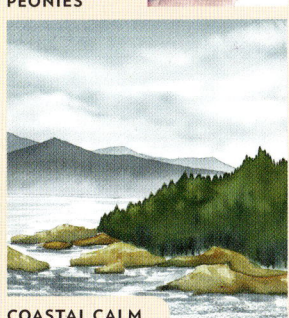

COASTAL CALM

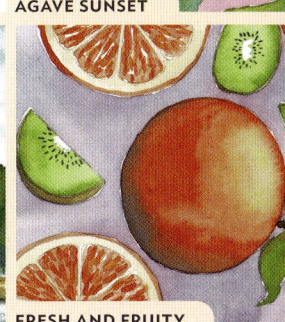

FRESH AND FRUITY

Introduction

HI! I'M LACEY, the Chief Teaching Unicorn at Rebel Unicorn Crafts. You may have met me through my social media accounts @RebelUnicornCrafts, where I share all kinds of art tutorial content, from testing out art supplies to sketchbook exercises, crafting with different mediums to watercolor painting tutorials. I have an unstoppable need to create, and I love sharing my creations with the world and connecting with my creative community!

As a kid I loved creating, drawing, painting, and building things. I was constantly praised for being artistic and creative, but at the same time I was told art was impractical. So, I didn't go to a traditional art school because my family didn't think it would lead to a safe or reliable future for me. Instead I went to business school and got a Bachelor's of Science in Marketing as well as a Master's degree while studying in Sydney, Australia. I jumped feet first into my career. I'd go to work and try to make it fun, but by the end of the day I was too tired to do anything that filled my own cup. We all know how that goes, and so my cup got smaller and smaller.

Eventually, this led to at least five years where I didn't create much of anything. I missed the feeling of working with my hands and being able to hold a physical object that I had produced. I started to feel more overwhelmed, more tired, and less and less like myself as these years went by. Finally I got to the point where I decided something had to change, so I made myself a creative bootcamp. It didn't take

long until all I could think about was creating, and I started to feel more energized, excited, optimistic, and like myself.

After a lot of planning and saving, I decided to pursue my dream of making accessible art content to help others get curious about their own creativity and help them gain the courage to make their own art. It took me a few tries to figure out the best ways to do this, but I am so glad I did.

I have been painting with watercolor for about seven years now, and it's by far my favorite subject to teach. I believe that art and creativity are essential for achieving happiness, escaping from troubles, and improving mental health. Along with that, I believe that spreading knowledge and creativity is key. I genuinely don't know which I love more, creating art or encouraging others to create it.

In this book, you'll find 20 painting projects that will help you unlock your creativity. Even if you have never picked up a paintbrush, you'll be able to create something you are proud of. I've included a watercolor pad with the sketches already drawn on them, so all you have to do is follow along on the painting journey with me. I also included the outline templates here (scan the QR code) so you can print these out or

 trace them onto your own watercolor paper if you'd prefer to make them again after you've practiced on the pad in this book. Don't know what wet-on-wet means or the first thing

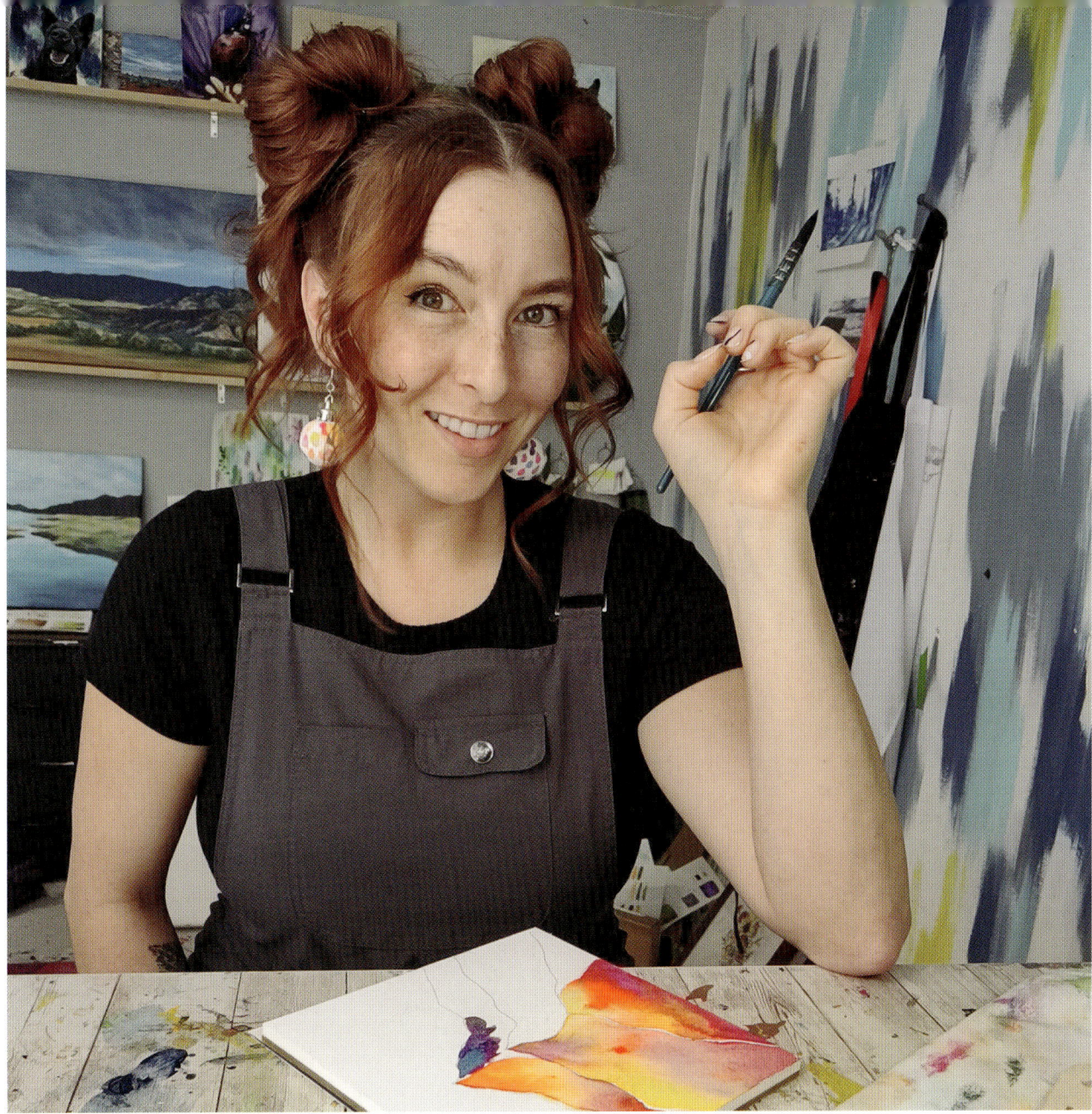

about color mixing? Don't worry. My goal is to help you understand why watercolor does what it does and how you can harness it. Not only that, but I love teaching through practical examples, so the paintings will help to illustrate these techniques so you can learn as you go. I've also included videos to explain some concepts and show how to paint some of the paintings, so look out for the QR codes in this book.

For those who already know a thing or two about watercolor, I love this format because it removes a couple of the biggest barriers to making art—the need to sketch and the question of what to paint. Having the watercolor pad also means this book is infinitely portable. Just bring your brushes and paints along with you and you can paint from nearly anywhere.

I'm so excited to have you along with me on this journey. Let's get creative together!

TOOLS & MATERIALS

I GET ASKED ABOUT WATERCOLOR painting supplies all the time and I understand why. I still get overwhelmed standing in a specialty art store staring at the watercolor options—not to mention the world of supplies available online. So, I get it. However, I am always hesitant to answer these questions because of a few factors:

1 Your budget may be different than mine and I don't want you to think that means you can't explore watercolor. If you already have supplies, I encourage you to try them first. It might take a little adapting with some of the paintings, but try yours first and make changes as needed.

2 Your preferences may be different from mine. You might prefer working with paint tubes, or maybe paint pans. You might work bigger, or brighter, so different supplies might work better for you.

3 I often use the supplies that I love and sell on my website, and frankly that makes me biased towards them. But my goal is for you to learn watercolor, not to have you purchase my supplies.

4 Nothing will help improve the quality of your paintings like taking the time to explore and practice. I often see students stopping themselves from painting because their supplies are not professional grade. I started by playing with discount paints, student grade, and even just basic Crayola-type colors and I learned a lot. You may eventually want to upgrade, but you don't need to do so to start painting!

That being said, I know you still want to learn about the supplies I used to create these paintings. I picked my favorite colors from my stash, which happen to be from different brands, but these colors are widely available across manufacturers, so you can use your preferred brands. I am primarily going to be using tube paints for this book because I think it's easier to show the color mixing, but at times I am also using the equivalent colors and brands in pan form.

Watercolor
PAINT

I limited the number of colors I used throughout the paintings in this book, so if you are just starting out, you need only purchase these nine watercolor paints.

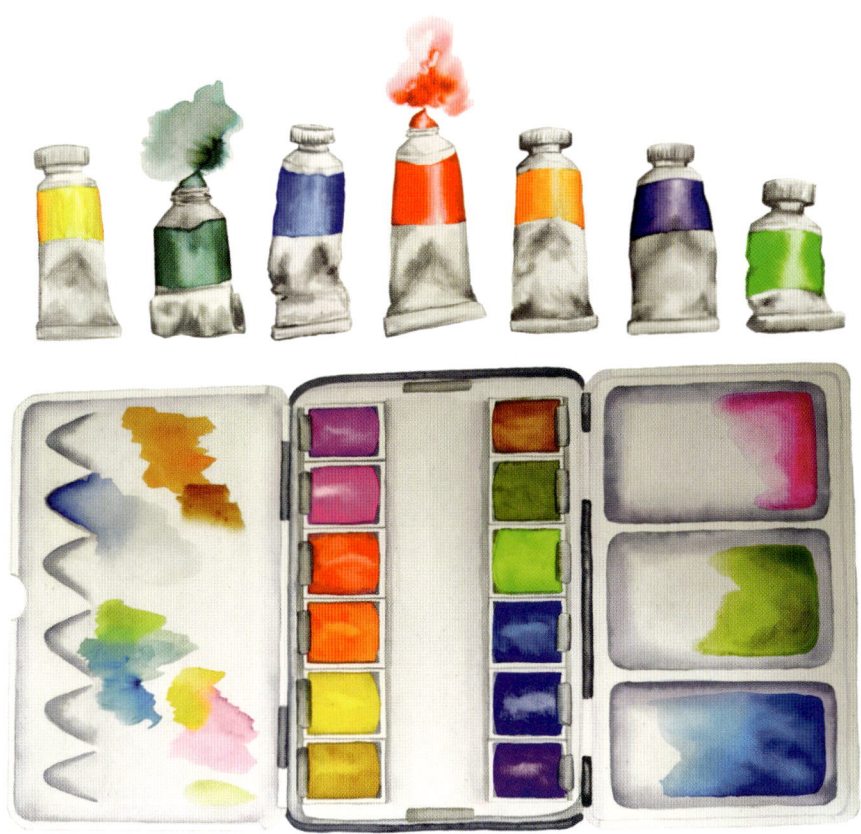

In my opinion, the colors I chose will make the widest range of possible color mixes.

Technically, if you needed to cut that number down, you could and still get pretty far with just Permanent Yellow Deep, Phthalo Blue, and Quinacridone Magenta. This would require you to have a better understanding of color mixing, but that's not a bad thing. The color mixes I will be using take advantage of all nine colors. If you don't have a color, use one that is similar, and even though it may not be exact, it will be close. Below are the paints I am working with along with the brands, but again, please use what you have.

1 Burnt Sienna (Mission Gold)
2 Payne's Gray (QoR)
3 Permanent Yellow Deep (ShinHan)
4 Phthalo Blue (Winsor & Newton Cotman)
5 Prussian Blue (Mission Gold)
6 Quinacridone Magenta (Winsor & Newton)
7 Sap Green (Winsor & Newton)
8 Vermilion (Mission Gold)
9 Yellow Ochre No. 1 (Mission Gold)

Watercolor BRUSHES

For watercolor, especially if you're a beginner, you only need one good brush. Something like a size 10 or 12 round brush with synthetic bristles is perfect. Personally, I find myself primarily switching between using a size 3 quill brush and a size 12 round brush. They are similar sizes and serve similar purposes. The size 12 round brush is my recommendation for novices, because the bristles allow for a little more control than the quill brush. I use quill brushes because I like the fluidity they provide. While I am partial to my own brand of brushes, Winsor & Newton and Princeton both have comparable options in a similar price range.

In this book I do switch between a couple of brushes, but technically I could do everything with a size 12 round brush. It's merely personal preference. If you'd like to invest in a few brushes, this is what I recommend:

- **SIZE 12 SYNTHETIC ROUND BRUSH:** This is great for holding a decent amount of water and creating detail work because it comes to a nice point.

- **SIZE 3 SYNTHETIC QUILL BRUSH:** This does everything the size 12 round brush does, but it holds a bit more water, and the bristles move a little more freely.

- **SIZE 4 SYNTHETIC QUILL BRUSH:** It's similar to the size 12 round and size 3 quill brushes above, but it is a bit bigger and holds more water.

- **⅜ INCH (10 MM) ANGLE BRUSH AND ½ INCH (13 MM) ANGLE BRUSH:** These are good for straight lines and lifting dried watercolor in a precise manner.

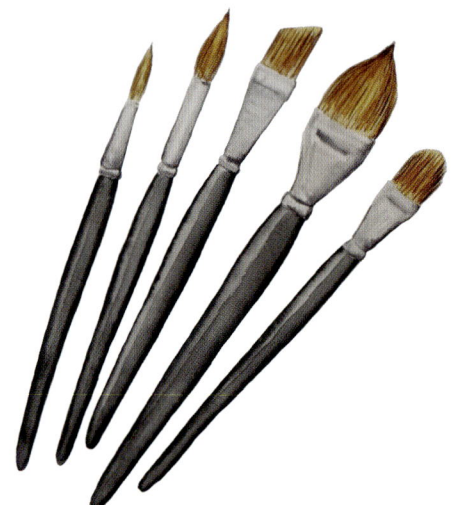

- **2-INCH (5 CM) FLAT WASH BRUSH:** This is great for creating big washes quickly.

Watercolor PAPER

This book includes a practice pad of watercolor paper with the outlines for the paintings pre-printed so you don't have to sketch or trace anything. The pad contains student grade paper; however, I am painting on Stonehenge 140 lb (300 gsm) cold press cotton paper, so some of the effects I can achieve on the Stonehenge paper will not be exactly the same on this paper. It will still give you a good idea of how the exercises work and getting a practice run is a good idea!

When thinking about what watercolor paper to buy, the key is to purchase paper you can afford and will actually use. It's taken me years to feel like my paintings are worthy of the good stuff—paper like Arches and Stonehenge. So, for a long time I bought these and other fancy papers and just let them collect dust on my shelves. The thought of potentially "wasting" good paper kept me from painting. Therefore, I recommend having two types of paper on hand: good paper like Arches or Stonehenge that are cotton, and some practice paper like Canson XL. Something like Canson won't work as nicely for certain effects, but it is cost efficient enough that you won't feel bad about trying new ideas and, if you mess up, you won't feel bad about tossing it. Also, if it's in your budget and you just want to work on cotton paper even with practice and experiments, go for it. The best paper

 solution is one that you'll use and is sustainable for your budget. Scan the QR code to see some of my paintings on Stonehenge vs. the included watercolor practice pad.

Choosing Watercolor Paper

When it comes to watercolor paper, there are three main considerations—paper material, weight, and finish—and understanding what each means will help you choose the right paper.

PAPER MATERIAL: Watercolor paper is typically made of cotton or cellulose fibers. Cotton paper is typically the gold standard. It has a longer dry time, allowing you to work on an area for a longer period of time. It creates less backruns (hard-edged shapes caused by uneven drying), it can hold more color, and it has more gentle bleeding. All the pros of cotton paper come with a price tag to match, so it's not within everyone's budget. Typically, if a paper does not say it's cotton, it's made from cellulose fibers. Cellulose papers can work well, but they do dry faster, and are a little less forgiving in most areas. However, they are by far the most economical choice.

PAPER FINISH: The two main finishes are hot press and cold press, but there are others, like rough, to be aware of as well. Hot press paper has a very smooth finish similar to printer paper. It gets this finish from the way it's manufactured: when the paper is pressed, heat is applied to the surface like an iron. This process compresses the fibers and smooths the surface. Many artists love hot press, but I personally find it the least forgiving of the papers and rarely use it.

Cold press paper, on the other hand, has a textured surface. It gets this finish from the manufacturing process which uses a cold process where a heavy press is used to flatten the paper. Because there isn't any heat applied, the surface used to press it down imprints itself on the paper and each brand has a slightly different print. This process results in a less compressed paper that seems to be a bit more forgiving, plus I personally love the look of the texture.

Rough paper is similar to cold press, but has even more texture to the surface. Some of these papers can create unique effects, especially with granulating watercolors.

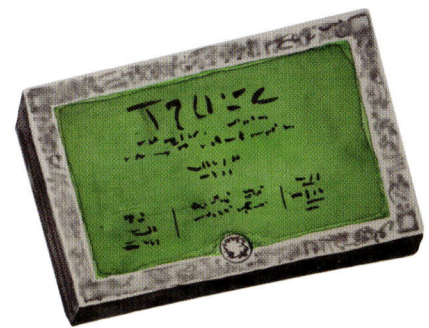

PAPER WEIGHT: The numbers you'll see on watercolor paper pads refer to how much the paper weighs—lb (meaning pounds) and gsm (meaning grams per square meter). The most common paper weight is 140 lb or 300 gsm. This is also my favorite weight because it's thick enough that it can withstand lots of water, but not as pricey as thicker papers. Paper weight can go higher, into the 300 lb or 640 gsm realm. This weight is super thick and nearly unbendable. It can handle the most water and color and is great for special projects, but it's pricey. You can absolutely paint on papers with lower weights, but the smaller the number, the thinner the paper, and that means it can handle less water and color. These papers are also more likely to warp. Typically these are reserved for student-grade watercolor pads or in sketchbooks used for ideas.

TAPE

I tape down most of my paintings before I begin to prevent warping and to keep them in place. I juggle between a few different types of tapes that I think work well.

- **MASKING TAPE:** I look for the cheapest option of masking tape. I find less expensive tape has less adhesive, making it less likely to tear my paper and more economical.

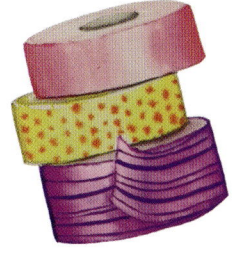

Tips for removing tape without damaging the paper

 Taping your painting has many benefits, but it can be stressful to remove the tape because there's a risk of tearing your paper. Scan the QR code to see how I remove tape without damaging the paper, and follow these easy tips.

GENTLY HEAT THE TAPE. Heating it a bit can release the adhesive, but beware: if you get it way too hot it will transfer the adhesive onto your paper.

GO SLOW. When peeling off the tape, go slow so you can stop before disaster strikes and you rip off a huge chunk of paper.

PULL AT AN ANGLE. Go at an angle away from the center of the paper to achieve less ripping.

- **WASHI TAPE:** Washi tape won't hold as well as masking tape, but the edges stay more crisp. Bonus: They come in fun patterns.

- **NICHIBAN 241 TAPE:** This is my ultimate watercolor tape. It's got great hold, yet it's gentle, and the edges stay super crisp. Plus, when I "make it dry" using my craft heat gun, the tape smells a bit like cedar. It's the priciest option, so I don't use it all the time.

Other SUPPLIES

In addition to the big four supplies, there are a few more necessary and nice supplies to have for watercoloring.

- **PAPER TOWELS OR A RAG:** To dry your brush and for lifting.

- **A BACKING BOARD OR A PIECE OF CARDBOARD:** To tape your painting to. This allows you to move it around to get a better angle.

- **TWO CUPS OF WATER:** One cup to wash your brush, and one clean cup for adding water to your paper.

- **MIXING WELLS:** There are three types of mixing wells I like to use to mix together paint: cute ceramic ones, muffin tin mixing pans that have deep wells for mixing up lots of color, and more traditional long mixing wells that allow you to keep your colors separate. Most watercolor pan tins also have built-in mixing wells.

- **MASKING FLUID:** I'll use masking fluid in a few of the projects in this book to keep certain areas white. If you don't have it, you can just paint carefully around these areas or use a white crayon that will repel paint.

- **SPRAY BOTTLE:** To wet pan paints efficiently.

- **HAIR DRYER OR CRAFT HEAT GUN:** To "make it dry"—my speedy way of making each layer dry.

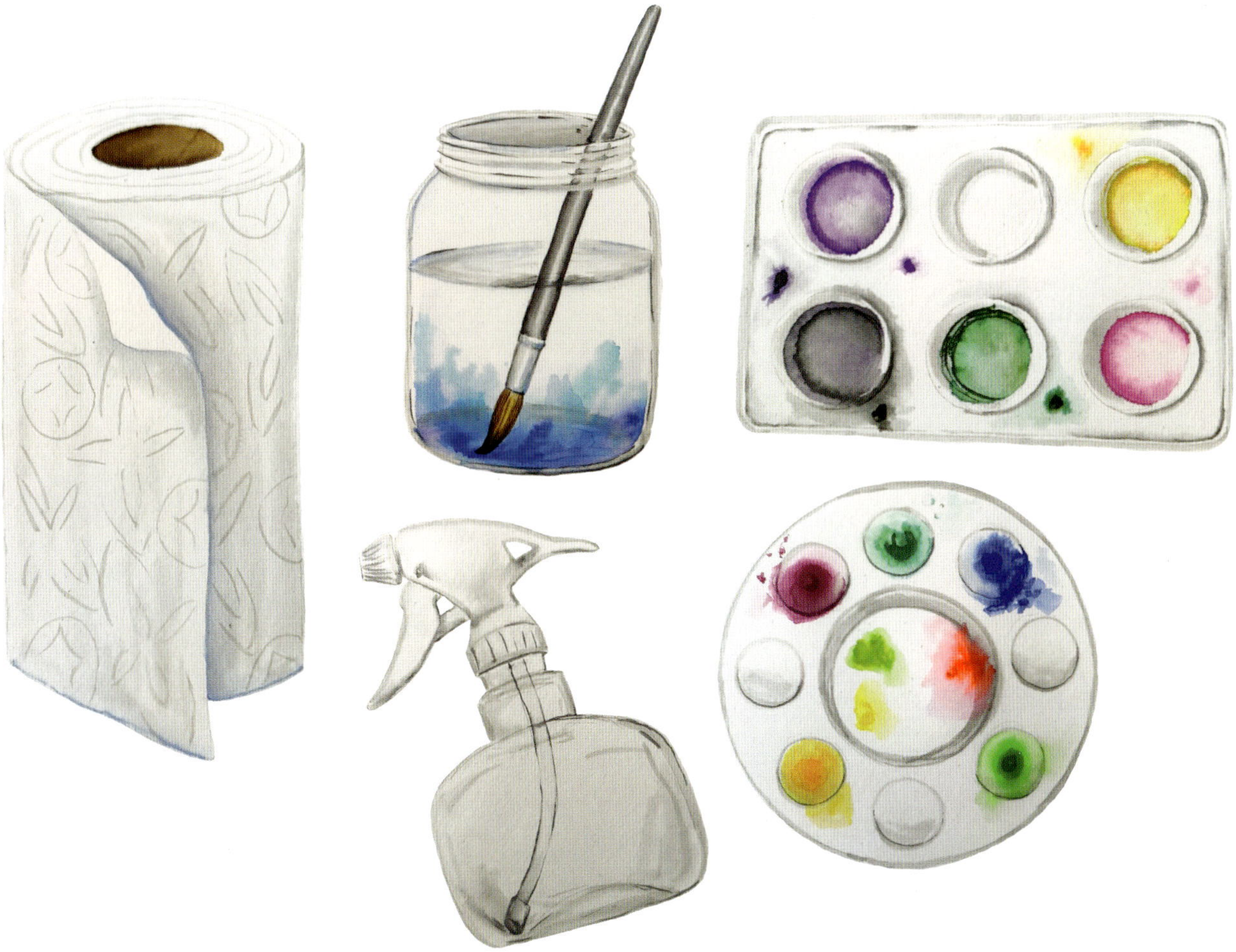

Make it dry!

I am a pretty impatient artist and rarely wait for things to dry on their own. In my social media videos, I make my paintings dry using a craft heat gun, and while I am doing the drying I often bob my head since I am so excited for the next layer. So, if you want to be part of the "make it dry" team, you can dance along as you make your layers dry.

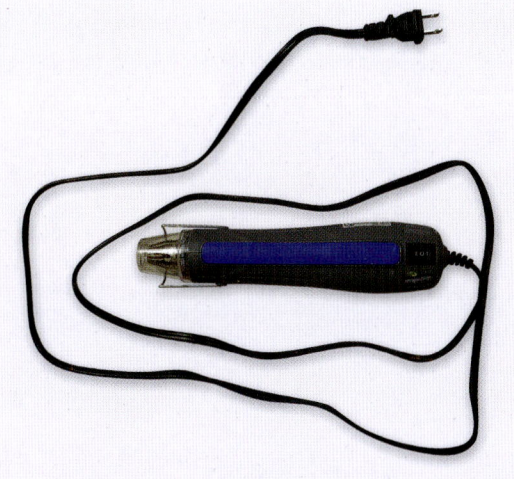

Setting up your workspace

If you already have a painting space set up, that's great! If you're just getting started, here's my suggestion for setting up your workspace.

1 First, identify your dominant hand—mine is my right hand. Anything that is wet or interacts with the water, aside from your watercolor paper, will go on your dominant hand side. This will help reduce the amount of drips you get on your watercolor paper, because you will not be constantly reaching across your work to grab water or color.

2 Much like a place setting, I put my cups of water on the upper right hand side, above my rags and paper towel.

3 I put a rag down first and then a paper towel. I find that paper towels are more predictable and better than rags at drying and cleaning brushes, however,

they can get your space messy, and you end up going through lots of them. So as a compromise, I put a rag down first to soak up any excess water to keep things drier. This means I don't have to replace my paper towel as often.

4 When not in use, my brushes rest on the paper towel. It's a good practice to keep brushes laying flat and not sitting in water so their beautiful tips don't get bent. You can either place your paint palette just to the left of the water cups, to the right of the paper towel, or on the paper towel itself, depending on the size of it.

5 For the paintings in this book, you can either paint directly on the pad with the book open and to the side of your wet setup, or you can remove the watercolor paper and tape it down to a board so you can adjust the angle of your painting easily.

WATERCOLOR PAINTING TECHNIQUES

IF YOU ARE NEW TO WATERCOLOR painting, seemingly simple tasks can feel daunting at first, but they will become second nature. For example, what does it mean to "fill your brush," how do you mix colors together, what's wet-on-wet and why does it matter? If you're a newbie, I've got you. Read on to learn all the basics of watercolor—questions I am asked all the time on social media—or feel free to skip ahead and return here if you want an explanation of any of the terms or techniques you come across. If you have watercolored before, this is a great refresher.

Fill Your BRUSH

"Fill your brush." This is a simple start to most watercolor tutorials, but this can actually mean a lot of things. I can't speak for every watercolor teacher when they say this, but if you watch us carefully, when we dip our brush into the color or water, we decide how much our brush is filled. Most of the time when this instruction is given, the bristles are fully submerged and the paint and water mixture gathers in the bristles. If you do this and then go straight to the page, there is a risk of a big drip. Most of the time I will fill my brush and then lightly touch the bristles to the side of the container, just enough to where it releases the large drip. This keeps the majority of the liquid on the brush, but reduces the risk of drips. For more details on filling your brush for various effects, scan the QR code to the video.

Understanding the Brush, Paint, Water RELATIONSHIP

We talked about filling your brush with paint or water, but that's really only half of the scenario. The wetness of your brush will affect how your paint works. Part of the magic of round watercolor brushes (traditional rounds, quills, or mops) is that they hold a lot of water. Water wants to stay together. You may have seen this illustrated by adding drops of water on a penny repeatedly, until finally that little droplet just can't take any more while staying together. It will fall over the side, and most of the water along with it. This is very similar to how a watercolor brush acts. The water wants to stay together in the brush, until it hits the paper and starts to flow out, then the rest of the water wants to go with it. This can create puddles of watercolor paint if your brush is too full for the application you're using. But in addition to that, even if you put less water in your brush and then touch it to a wet surface, the water will suck down towards the paper. So depending on what you want the watercolor to do, consider how wet the brush is, how wet the paint is that you're picking up with your brush, and how wet the paper is you're applying it to.

One way to think about this relationship between how wet or dry the paint and brushes are is to think about shampooing your hair. Imagine putting a big sticky dollop of shampoo in the palm of your hand and then putting it in your dry hair. It's not really going to spread around. Most of the time you want to have at least damp hair so that the shampoo can be evenly distributed. If your hair is wetter, you can

pick up stickier shampoo. Bringing it back to watercolor, let's say your goal is to get a really concentrated amount of color onto a small area. You may grab some paint straight from the tube, and if your brush is super wet, it's going to turn the paint into a creamier or more liquid format in the brush.

Don't worry about remembering all this; it comes with time and practice. But if you're struggling to get the intended effect and ending up with way too much paint or not enough, there's probably something off with the ratio of how wet your brush is to how wet the paint you're trying to use is.

Paint Wetness STAGES

How wet your paint is will affect how it acts when you grab it with your brush. Different levels of consistency will help you with different effects.

DRY: This is only really possible in dried pans, or tube paints that were squeezed out and left to dry. It would only be useful in a brush that is at least a little damp. Also, you won't get much color this way, so this is for when you just want a little bit.

STICKY: This descriptor best describes the texture of the paint straight from a tube of watercolor. You can also get a sticky consistency with pan paints by putting a small drop of water on the pan and then letting it sit until it dissolves into the paint. If you tried to paint with this level of texture using a dry or damp brush, it would smear on the page. It is good for thick dry brushing or for placing a small amount in a specific area.

CREAMY: Keep the paint thick so that it still has a bit of resistance, but use enough water to allow it to be spread evenly across the page. This is great for covering a medium area with a really concentrated amount of color.

WATERY: When paint is watery, it glides around the page like a liquid. It can have more or less color in it, depending on what you're trying to achieve.

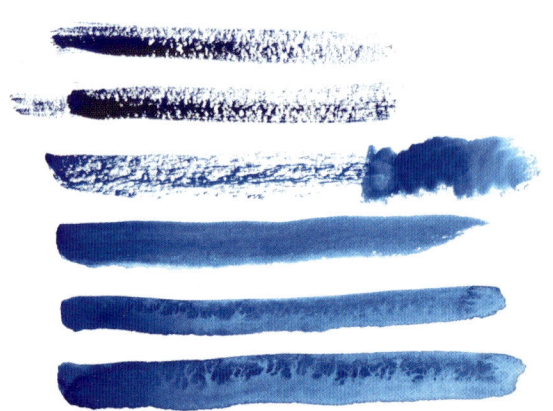

IN THIS IMAGE OF STROKES using tubes of watercolor paint, notice how the first brushstroke streaks across the page and appears "dry." I added some water to my brush before the second stroke and more at each increment before grabbing the paint. In other words, the more water you have in your brush, the more paint you're going to be able to grab and move across the page.

Wet-on-Wet vs.
WET-ON-DRY

Two of the first watercolor terms or techniques you might hear when you begin to paint are wet-on-wet and wet-on-dry. If you've been painting with watercolor for a while, this concept will be as familiar as an old friend, so you can skip ahead. But, if you're brand new to watercolor, you're in the right place, because there are no silly or basic questions here. So, let's discuss it:

WET-ON-WET: Wet-on-wet refers to when you pre-wet the paper and then place wet paint on the wet paper. This typically results in a flowy appearance where the edges are soft, brushstrokes won't be defined and may run to different areas, and the colors bleed together.

WET-ON-DRY: Wet-on-dry refers to keeping the paper dry and then placing your wet paint onto the dry paper. Because the paper is dry, the water might flow around within the brushstrokes you place, but the edges of the strokes you make will remain crisp and they will stay where you put them.

Wet-on-Wet: How Wet Matters

The story of wet-on-wet unfortunately isn't quite as simple as just it's wet or it's not wet before you start painting. Exactly how wet you make the paper first

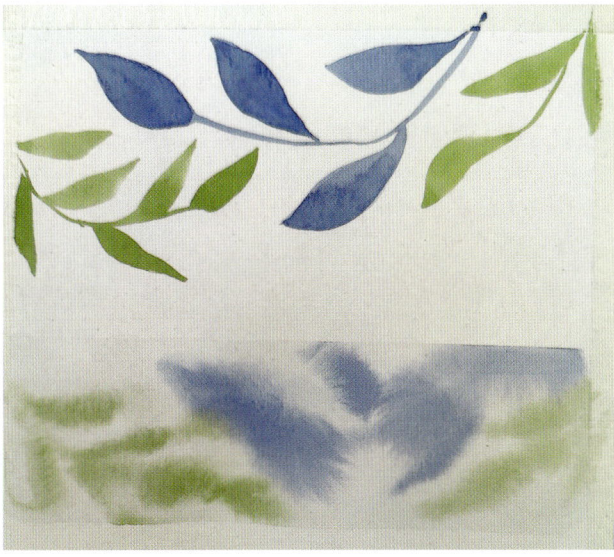

IN THIS IMAGE, the wet-on-dry leaves have crisper edges, the wet-on-wet have less defined edges and are very flowy. You'll use both techniques in this book to create different effects.

changes the types of effects that happen, and getting to know how wet to make the paper for your desired effect will help you in the long run. In general, the more water you add, the less control you will have. The less water, the less all your brushstrokes and colors are going to run together.

But, how do you know how wet the paper is? The best way to tell is to hold the paper up to a light and observe the appearance of the reflection. I personally think understanding it as five different stages is helpful.

1 **FLOOD:** The water is standing on the page, it's raised above the paper, and can flow around. The reflection is shiny and smooth but moves around if you move the paper. *One way to think about this is imaging yourself shrunken down to a miniature size, small enough so you could walk on the paper as if it were the ground. Now that you're teeny tiny, what kind of shoes are you going to put on for each stage of wetness? I like to think of the flood stage as one where I'd want to wear my rain boots.*

Learn by doing

If you learn better through exploring, we will be directly addressing this topic in Sweet as Honey (page 41), which has been designed to show the different stages of wet-on-wet.

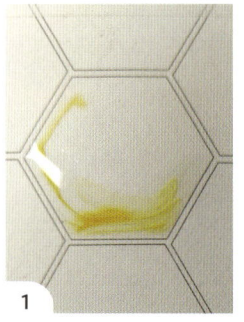 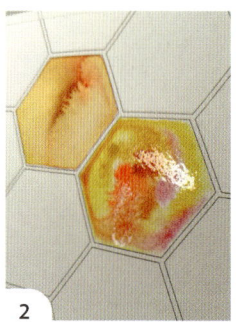 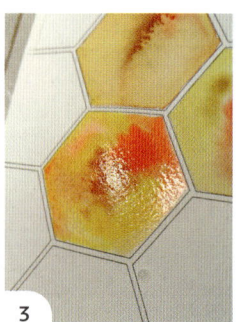 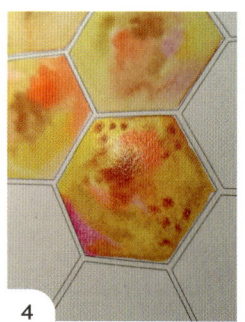 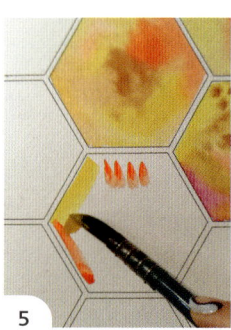

Wetness stages in action

 Need to see the wetness stages in action to really understand? Scan the QR code for a short video that shows what each stage looks like and the type of effects it can achieve.

FLOOD + PAINT: When you add paint to paper at the flood stage, you won't have control over where the colors will end up—they will flow together and mix up. You will not see any brushstrokes. This can result in surprising and beautiful results, but it can also be frustrating to control.

2 GLOSS: The reflection is shiny and smooth, but the water doesn't flow as freely across the page. The water more or less covers all the high points of the paper, but not any more than that. *For this stage, I'd still want something waterproof, like hiking boots.*

GLOSS + PAINT: The colors are going to flow together a lot, any brushstrokes are going to be really softened, and you still don't have a ton of control over what is happening, but where you put the colors is more or less where they'll end up.

3 SATIN: The reflection still has quite a bit of shine, but it's lessened by the texture of the paper showing through. *It's a little damp, but tennis shoes would probably be just fine.*

SATIN + PAINT: The colors will flow softly together, they may even stay separate when painted next to each other, but there won't be any super defined brushstrokes left once it's dry.

4 DAMP: There is a more matte quality to the reflection on the paper and the texture is fully visible. *If the weather is warm, I'm considering sandals.*

DAMP + PAINT: The paint will stay pretty well where you place it, but the colors will all be softened and there will be no harsh edges.

5 DRY: There is no reflection coming from the page. It's dry, just like when you open the pad. *Anything goes, from suede to stilettos.*

DRY + PAINT: The colors will stay exactly where you put them; the brushstrokes will be sharp and have hard edges. This is also known as wet-on-dry.

Wet-on-Wet: How to Fix Too Much Water

Sometimes when you're adding water and paint, you just get too much liquid on your paper and it pools and threatens to run. Even if you're happy leaving a pool, it can have unexpected results when it dries,

How to fix too much water in action

Need to see how to remove excess water in action to really understand? Scan the QR code to watch a short video on removing water.

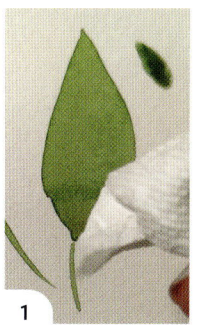 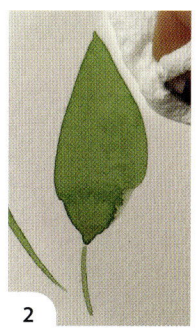 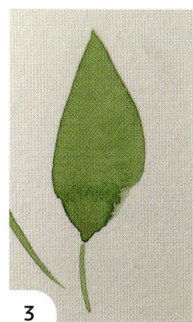

In **IMAGE 1** you can see a leaf painted with an accidental drop of paint near it. Lifting can save the day. Acting fast, I can take a paper towel and remove the paint by dabbing it, as I did in **IMAGE 2**. You can see in **IMAGE 3** there is still a bit of color that remains, but you'd have to look very closely to see it.

which I'll touch on in the section about backruns.

So, what do you do when you have added too much water? The good news is that there are two simple ways to pick up excess water:

1 **DRY YOUR BRUSH.** The first way to grab excess water is to take your brush and dry it really well on a dry paper towel. Once your brush is dry, you can touch the tip of the brush to the wet area and it will help to suck up the extra water. You might need to dry the brush a couple times and touch it to the wet spot to get most of the water up. This works especially well with round brushes. They are almost like little syringes.

2 **BLOT WITH A PAPER TOWEL.** The second way is to take the edge of a paper towel and lightly touch it to the wet spot; this will suck up the extra water. You really only want to remove water until it's no longer moving around. You don't want to dry it more than the paper around it, or again you can get those unintended backruns.

LIFTING

Lifting is a powerful technique in watercolor. Not only can it be used to remove unwanted color and potential mistakes, but it can also be used to create interesting effects and elements. Lifting is removing color that was previously placed on the paper. It can be done when the paint is wet or dry to varying degrees of success. If you want to explore the practical side of lifting, head over to Marvelous Mountains on page 44, where I use lifting to form distant clouds.

When lifting, there are a couple factors to consider; namely, is the paint wet or dry, and how likely is it that the color you want to lift will stain?

Is the Paint Wet or Dry?

If the paint is still wet, all you need is a dry or dampish brush or paper towel to simply press on the area to lift out the color. If the paint is dry, you'll have to do a bit more work, but it's still possible. You will need to lightly re-wet the area you want to remove. You can either re-wet and then push down with a paper towel to remove a little color. Or for more precision, wash your brush and dry it until it is just damp. Then use the brush to swipe or gently scrub until the paint starts to lift from the paper. This might push some of the color around; when this happens, wash and dry your brush with clean water until it's just damp and continue lifting out more of the color.

WASHES

A wash of watercolor is a smooth, even color or colors across a larger area of paper. The wash doesn't have to be just one color, but it often is; it's also sometimes a gradient or smooth transitions between many colors. Sunsets or skies are some of the best examples of where you might want to paint a wash. Washes are also often used as backgrounds, or even as the main color on an object before or after creating shadowing. In my opinion, washes are one of the most difficult things to get a handle of in watercolor.

For the **flat wash** and **gradient**, I use a technique called a drip line, and for the **variegated** wash, I loosely follow that as well. I personally like working on washes as wet-on-dry. They can be a little harder to control that way, but I find the colors are more predictable. When you work wet-on-wet, the colors are desaturated by the water on the page so you're more likely to have to paint a second layer, and if you're impatient like me, you probably don't want to have to do that. Here are a few tips to remember when you are painting washes in watercolor:

CAUTION: You do need to be careful of how much you "scrub" the paper. I recommend getting to know how much scrubbing your paper can take when wet on a scrap piece of paper. You'll know you've scrubbed too much when the paper starts to ball up. This has damaged the top layer of the paper, and you'll see it in the final result. If you plan to paint another layer on top of this, damaged paper will act differently, so scrubbing too much can impact further painting.

How Staining Is the Color?

Different colors of watercolor paint have different properties. There isn't a hard and fast rule for which colors are staining and which aren't. As a loose general rule, reds and pinks are the most staining of colors, and blues, especially ultramarine, are non-staining. This doesn't hold true for every brand, but in general you can expect this. Notice in image 1 I lifted in the same manner across all the colors I am using in this book, and some have stained the paper more than others.

1 **GRAVITY IS YOUR FRIEND.** If you work at an angle (about 45 degrees), the water will flow in a predictable manner so you can better control how the color is applied to the page.

2 **MIX A LOT OF COLOR.** It's better to have too much color mixed than to run out halfway through a wash, so mix up more color than you think you'll need.

3 **WORK WET.** Any time you run out of color in your brush it will invite striping or uneven drying, so don't shy away from water.

4 **WORK QUICKLY.** This goes hand in hand with working wet. You want to make sure that you are working

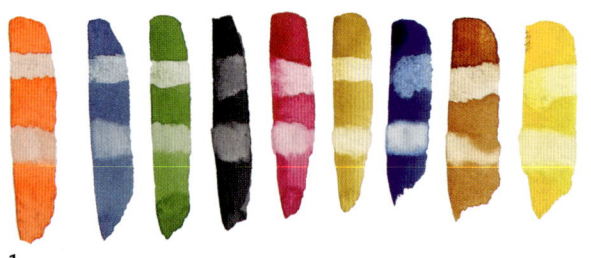

1

in a quick manner so that the paint doesn't dry before you make it back to an area you were previously painting. Sometimes this is called a **wet edge**. You can even go back and drop a little extra water or color in an area that has been sitting for a bit to make sure it doesn't start drying.

FLAT WASH

GRADIENT

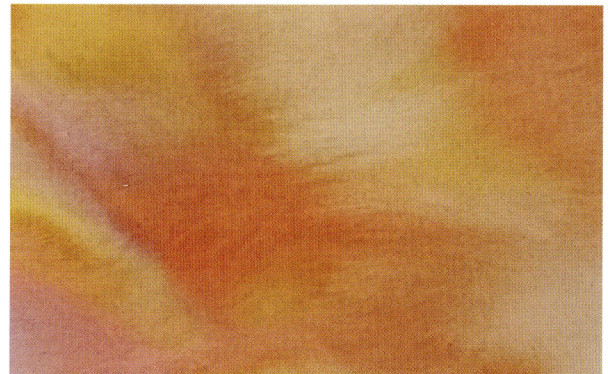

VARIEGATED

How to Create a Flat Wash

1 Mix up a large amount of color, enough to allow you to easily repeatedly refill your brush.

2 Hold your piece or rest it at a 45-degree angle.

3 Fill your brush until it's sopping wet and make a stroke across the top of the page. Notice that there's so much that at the bottom of the stroke it looks as if it's going to drip, hence the name *drip line*.

4 Refill your brush, even if you think you have enough in that drip line, and make a stroke directly under the first one, letting the tip of your brush catch the drip from the previous stroke.

(continued)

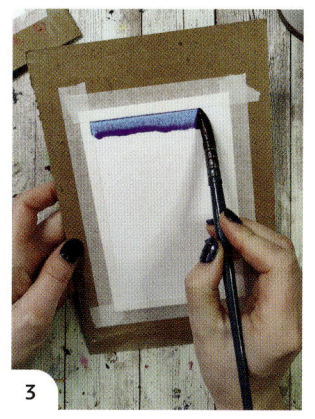

3

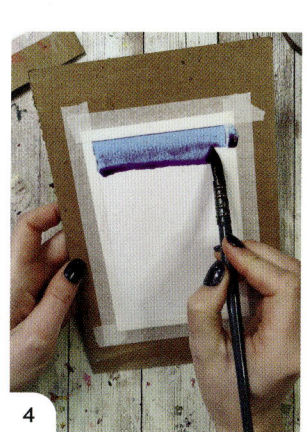

4

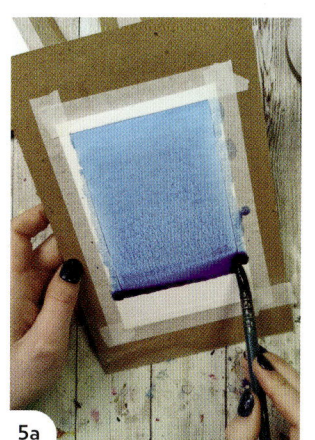

5a

5b

5 Continue this to the very bottom of the page. Keep refilling your brush to avoid running out of water halfway down. You will probably have a bunch of water at the bottom when you're done. That's fine. Just dry your brush and soak up the excess water.

How to Create a Gradient Wash

The same technique used to create a flat wash applies to the gradient wash, but you'll change the color you're dipping into.

1 Mix up large amounts of the colors you will need to create the gradient, using enough paint to easily refill your brush.

2 Hold your piece or rest it at a 45-degree angle.

3 Fill the brush until it's sopping wet and make a stroke across the top of the page. Repeat until you'd like the color transition to start.

4 To transition colors, simply refill the brush by dipping it lightly into the water or second color. Avoid completely replacing the pigment in the brush on the first transition stroke. Instead slowly change it over, so the first few times you dip into the second color or the water, do it lightly. You can get a little more aggressive the further into the transition you go.

How to Create a Variegated Wash

1 Mix up large amounts of the colors you will need to create the variegated wash, enough to allow you to refill your brush repeatedly.

2 Hold your piece or rest it at a 45-degree angle.

3 Fill the brush until it's sopping wet and make a stroke in sections or beginning in the corner. Wash your brush and change colors at any point, just make sure you're using gravity and keeping a wet edge so it doesn't dry on you.

Gradient wash in action

A gradient wash is used in the Marvelous Mountains painting on page 44, and there is a video demonstration if you want to see this in action.

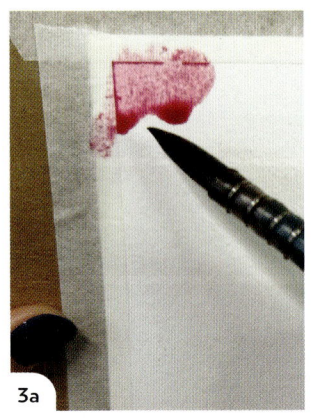

3a

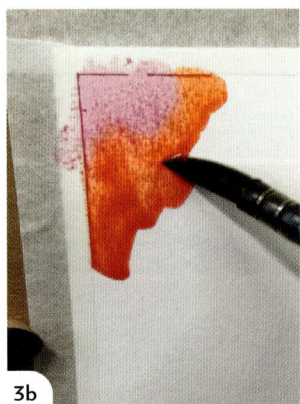

3b

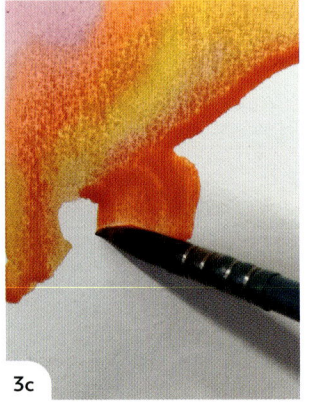

3c

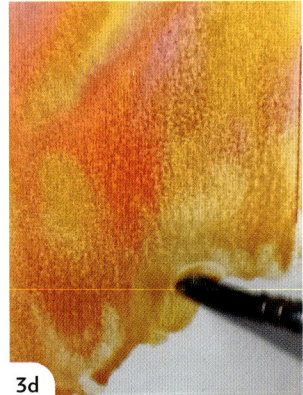

3d

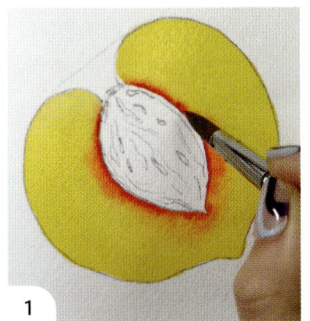

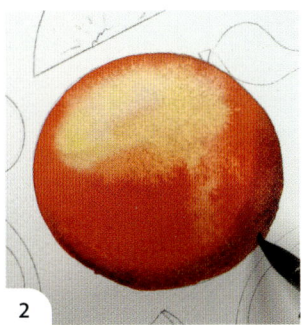

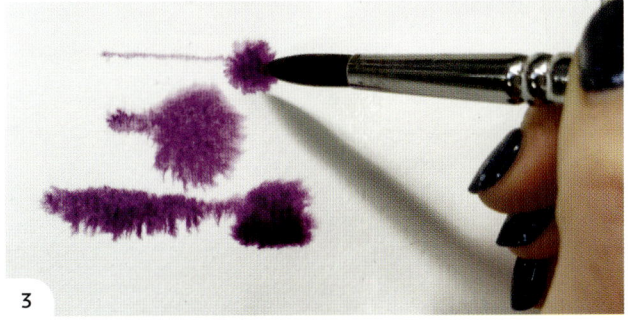

pick it up will have the most color dropped in. The swipe between these points will have a lighter amount of color, and typically the spot you pick up your brush will have the most. Conversely if you charge or drop in with a ton of water pre-loaded on your brush, the first point of contact may have the most color deposited. For example, in image 3, you can see how the most water and pigment is distributed at the release point of the brush.

This means you need to be aware of how much water and paint you have in your brush when you start charging. For softer, more controlled effects, I like to fill my brush with the color and then lightly tap it on a paper towel to remove the majority of the color and water from my brush, but not all.

CHARGING

This technique is when you paint an area and add a second color while the first is still wet, painting it gently and allowing the colors to bleed together. The technique of charging is often referred to as "dropping in." You'll use charging throughout the paintings in this book, but it's especially effective in creating the reddish interior flesh of a peach in Everything's Peachy (see image 1 and page 54) and some shading in Fresh and Fruity (see image 2 and page 91).

You can use this technique with abandon if you want random effects or just fun color changes, but you can also use it in a more controlled manner to carefully add colors that can be used to mimic the appearance of objects or to add shading. This requires a little more control over the amount of paint in your brush, the consistency of the paint you pick up, and how wet the area you plan to charge into is.

One of the key things to note when charging is that wherever you first place your brush and then

Dry BRUSHING

Most of the time with watercolor, water is essential to getting the colors to flow around the page. However, occasionally you want to create a choppy texture that leaves some white space on the page. To do this, you can utilize a technique called dry brushing. Fill your brush with your color and then tap it until it's mostly dry. The interior of the brush will still be a little damp with paint and water, but not enough to deposit a steady flow on the page. Dry brushing

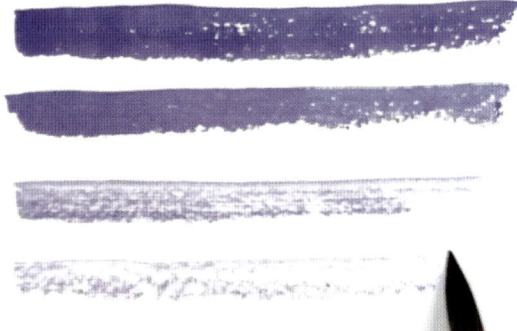

HERE ARE FOUR STROKES using the dry brushing technique. They are done with different amounts of water and color in the brush to create different effects.

is most effective with a light touch on the paper. Gently brush the bristles on the page in the direction that you want the texture to move. Experiment with this to see what brush works best and how dry it needs to be.

Letting Things Dry vs.
MAKING THEM DRY

Paint needs to dry at the end of a project or between layers, but if you're like me, you're impatient. Sometimes it's best to let things dry naturally. My best example of this is if you're painting something with masking fluid—it stinks when heated and it can bubble up. But most of the time, it's okay to speed up the process with a hair dryer or a craft heat gun. There are a few considerations, though, before you "make it dry":

1 You shouldn't "make it dry" when there are still big puddles of water on the painting; this is going to cause paint to fly around. It's best to remove the puddles or wait until it settles into the paper.

2 If you're using a hair dryer, it puts out a lot of air and items can go flying. So make sure everything is secured before you turn it on.

3 Don't stay on one spot too long. When drying, especially with a craft heat gun, it's best to work on a low speed and keep the air moving evenly across the painting. If you let it set in one area only, it can cause it to dry unevenly or even potentially burn the paper. So keep it moving!

Blooms and
BACKRUNS

Blooms and backruns are closely related, but with a few key differences. They can add character and texture to your pieces, but they are often something you want to actively avoid in certain situations. Understanding what they are and why they happen can help you to prevent them when you don't want them or encourage them to develop when you do want them.

Blooms

Blooms look like little bursts, snowflakes, or flowers and can create interesting textural effects. I often like to use them in the foregrounds of landscapes to add texture to a field without having to paint in the details. They are achieved by dropping water or a desaturated color onto a previously painted but still wet surface. For example, paint a wash over an area and then let it settle into the page until it's at about the Gloss or Satin stage. Then wash your brush and tap it so it's not going to drip but there's still water in it, and then dot the clean wet brush onto the paper, depositing little drops of water. The water drops will push away the pigment particles. These blooms spread and grow as the watercolor dries, so you often need less of them than you initially think.

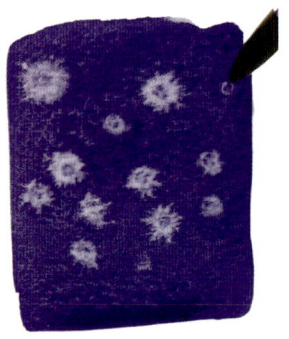 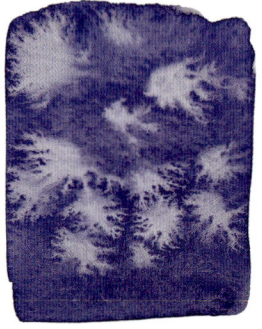

BLOOMS WHEN WET   **BLOOMS WHEN DRY**

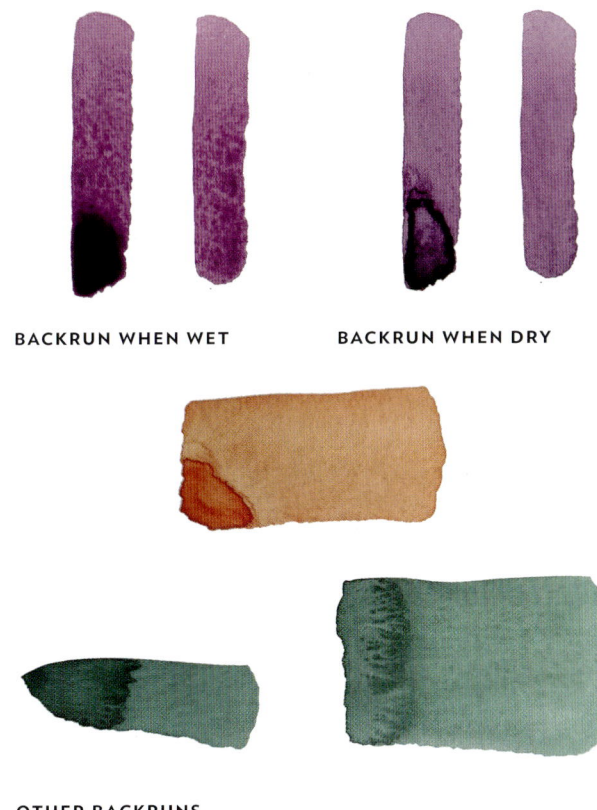

BACKRUN WHEN WET

BACKRUN WHEN DRY

OTHER BACKRUNS

Backruns

Similarly, backruns happen when water settles and pushes pigment particles around it, but in a different way. Typically backruns happen when you're painting and you leave one area with a puddle of paint. As the paint around the puddle dries, the puddle pushes the pigment to the dry edges and creates a texture. This can either add character or ruin the look and feel of the painting if you're trying to keep everything smooth and soft. The best way to avoid backruns is to prevent puddles from forming. So, if you're working super wet and a puddle forms, take a second to dry the brush and lightly touch the tip into the puddle to suck it up. Try to only touch the puddle instead of the paper with the brush, as it can create a different type of texture.

Taping Your PAPER DOWN

There are a lot of advantages to taping your paper:

- It looks good. First, and least practical, is that it looks nice. The clean, crisp edges create a border, adding a finishing touch to some paintings.

- It prevents warping. Taping the paper down will help to prevent warping. Warping will still occur to some degree, depending on how thick your paper is. However, taping makes the warping more predictable and will help to reduce it.

- It holds the paper in place. I often work at an angle, and taping my paper down to a board helps it stay in place while I'm moving it around.

Keeping WHITE SPACE

White space is where you keep some of the paper exposed, with no color. This can be important in helping to create highlights, or sometimes it simply creates some breathing room, allowing your mind to imagine what is going on. Often the spaces between our brushstrokes are just as important as the strokes themselves. This is one of those tricky skills to get the hang of, so if you're not great at it right away, that's okay, you're in good company. Also, this is a judgment-free zone, so if you couldn't leave any white space and it needs it, there will be no judgment on adding it. Once your painting is dry, you can do this with a variety of mediums, including white gel pens, white gouache, or even acrylic paint.

That said, if you can get the hang of it, leaving a little white space will save you time in the end. You can either achieve this through careful brush placement or by using masking fluid. Masking fluid comes in all sorts of forms; I prefer to find the ones that have a fine tip applicator so that I don't have to apply it with a brush, because that's dangerous business. If you don't have the type with a built-in applicator, you can protect your brush by dipping it in dish soap before dipping it into the masking fluid. I still wouldn't use a good brush for this; I'd dedicate a brush for masking fluid. Masking fluid goes on as a liquid, and wherever you put it, it protects the paper. You apply it, let it dry completely, and then paint on top of it. Once you're done painting and everything is dry, you can remove the masking fluid to reveal the fresh white paper underneath. See Feathery Friends (page 75) to try out masking fluid.

Removing masking fluid can be done once the paint is completely dry. There are a few ways this can be achieved:

- With freshly washed and dried hands, you can use your finger to roll the masking fluid gently off the paper.

- Use a clean, soft rag to gently rub the masking fluid off. I recommend using small circular motions.

- Use a rubber eraser similar to a pencil eraser, and rub it over the masking fluid. The fluid will collect and release from the paper.

A few additional considerations for masking fluid and its removal are:

1 Masking fluid is similar to liquid latex—don't use it if you have a latex allergy.

2 Your paper must be completely dry before you try to remove it. Any remaining moisture makes the paper more prone to ripping.

3 Don't peel it off. I know it's tempting and can be fun, but grabbing an end and peeling it can easily rip a section of your painting. The best approach is to use small gentle motions.

If you're still not convinced about the importance of white space, take a look at these two examples. Notice that even though these are simple paintings, the flower and orange on top, which have white space, have a bit more life and convey more depth.

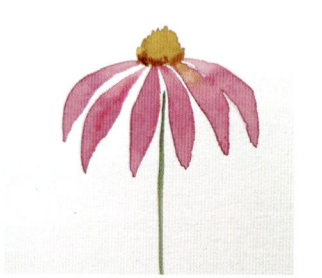 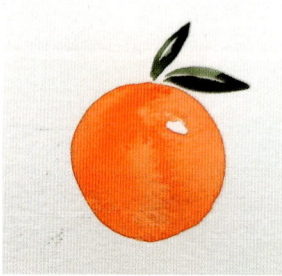

WITH WHITE SPACE

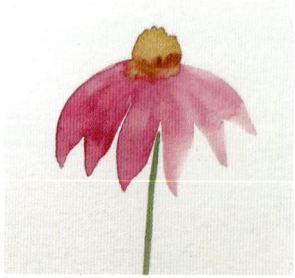 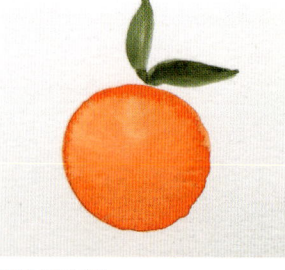

WITHOUT WHITE SPACE

LAYERING

Layering is one of my favorite techniques in watercolor because it's a great way to get distinct shapes, as well as build depth of color. When I talk about layering, I mean layering paint on dry layers. Make sure the previous layer is completely dry before painting the next one. If you misjudge this, it will spread into the next layer and not give you crisp lines. Take a look at images 1 and 2, as an example of layering mountains on a nearly dry, but not quite dry layer versus a dry layer.

Layering is a great way to build in new elements you don't want to bleed in together, but it also greatly improves your depth of color. Notice that by painting

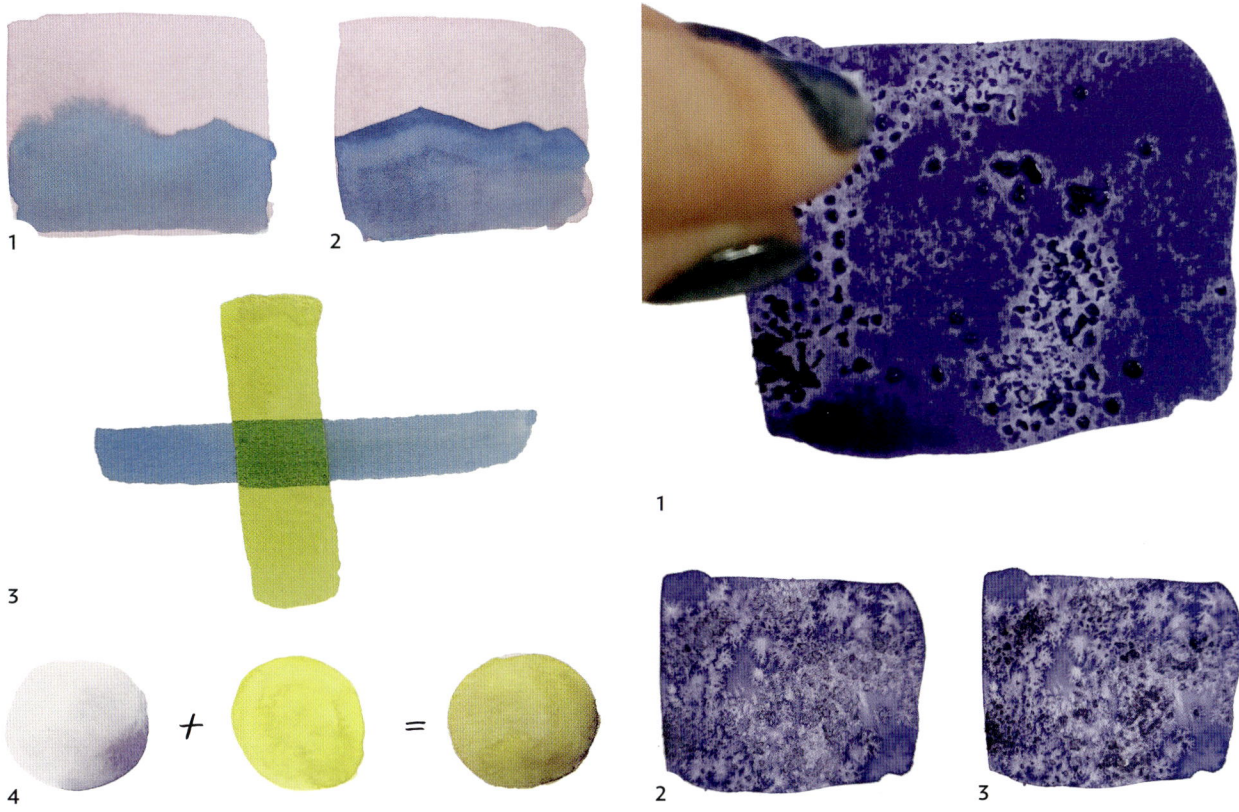

the yellow and blue lines in image 3, the first of which dried before I placed the second on, the area where they cross is a vibrant green. You can brighten up areas, or this can be used to darken or add shadows, working with dry distinct layers on top of each other to build up layers of colors. In image 4 I first put down the circle with purple and allowed it to dry, then I added the bright yellow on top. Just like that I have a built in shadow and depth to my object.

SALT

For one of the paintings in this book, A Whale of a Time (see page 52), we'll be taking a trip to the kitchen for salt. Using salt on wet watercolor can create interesting textural effects. The key to using salt is to sprinkle it while things are still wet, at the Flood or Gloss stage. The pigment is going to clump around the salt, and then once it's dry you can either leave it on for true texture or brush it off to reveal the areas where the salt was sitting. To remove it, gently rub it with your fingers or a clean rag. This can smear the paint if you do it before the paint has fully dried or apply too much pressure. It's nearly impossible to remove 100 percent of the salt, so expect a little texture to remain on the page. In images 1, 2, and 3, you can see me applying the salt to the wet paint, the painting with dry salt, and the salt mostly removed after the paint has dried.

COLOR THEORY AND COLOR MIXING

THIS WILL BE FAR FROM a full explanation on color theory, but we'll hit a few of the basics that I think are important to know as well as explain why I chose the colors I chose to use in this book. As with the techniques, if you've never mixed custom colors before, never fear. You'll be mixing up colors and understanding concepts of value and saturation in no time.

Primary Colors

The primary colors I use are Quinacridone Magenta, Permanent Yellow Deep, and Phthalo Blue—these are colors that cannot be mixed up by combining other colors on the wheel. That's what makes them "primary"; they are necessary for mixing up other colors. I have labeled these with a "P" on the color wheel.

Color WHEEL

If you've been painting for a while, you've probably seen a color wheel, but let's explore it as well as touch on what I have found to be the three most useful parts of using the color wheel. If you've never made a color wheel with your paints, I highly recommend it; it will teach you more about your paints than you'd expect. There is a lot you can understand about color from the color wheel, however, the main points we'll be considering are: primary, secondary, and tertiary colors; warm and cool colors; and complementary colors.

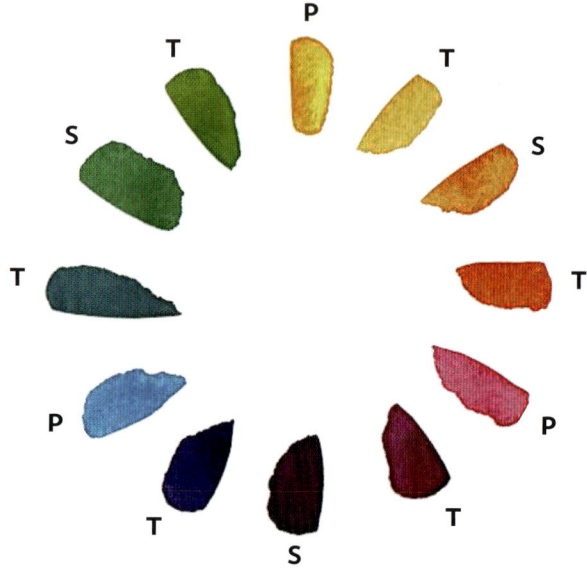

Secondary Colors

Secondary colors are the points in between the primary colors—these are green, orange, and purple. They require a mix of approximately equal parts of two primary colors to make. For example, equal parts Quinacridone Magenta and Permanent Yellow Deep will create orange. I have labeled these with an "S."

Tertiary Colors

Tertiary colors are the points between the primary and secondary colors. For example, colors like yellow green, teal, or fuchsia. These are formed by mixing either primary colors at more of a 25/75 ratio, or a secondary color with a primary.

Warm vs. Cool Colors

Warm colors have undertones of yellows or reds, and cooler colors have undertones of greens and blues. A line drawn through the color wheel divides the warm from cool colors. A good way to think of warm colors is that they are like the sun or fire, and cool colors are like ice or water. Understanding a color's undertones will help you to mix up more pure colors. For example, if you want to mix a nice vibrant orange color, mix a yellow that has a warmer undertone with a red that has a warmer undertone. If you were to use a yellow and red with cool undertones, it's going to make a muddier color because you'll effectively be mixing in blues and greens into your orange as well as the yellow and red.

Complementary Colors

Complementary colors are colors located directly across from each other on the color wheel. When painting, it's useful to know complementary colors for two main reasons. First, they typically look nice together, you might notice that they are the colors you often see used for sports teams or holidays. Secondly, they help mute colors when you want a color that is more subtle instead of super bright. We'll explore this more in the color mixing section.

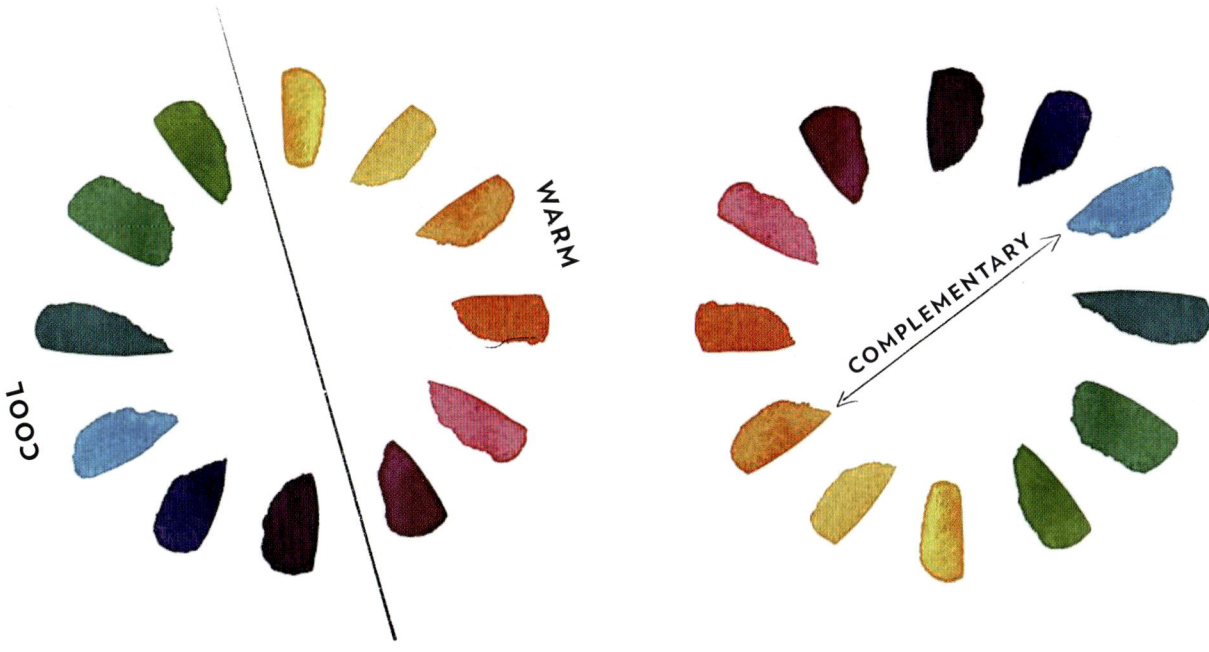

What about Red?

If you're like me, in school you learned the primary colors as blue, red, and yellow. So...why does the color wheel in this book use a magenta color instead? You can use red as your primary color, however,

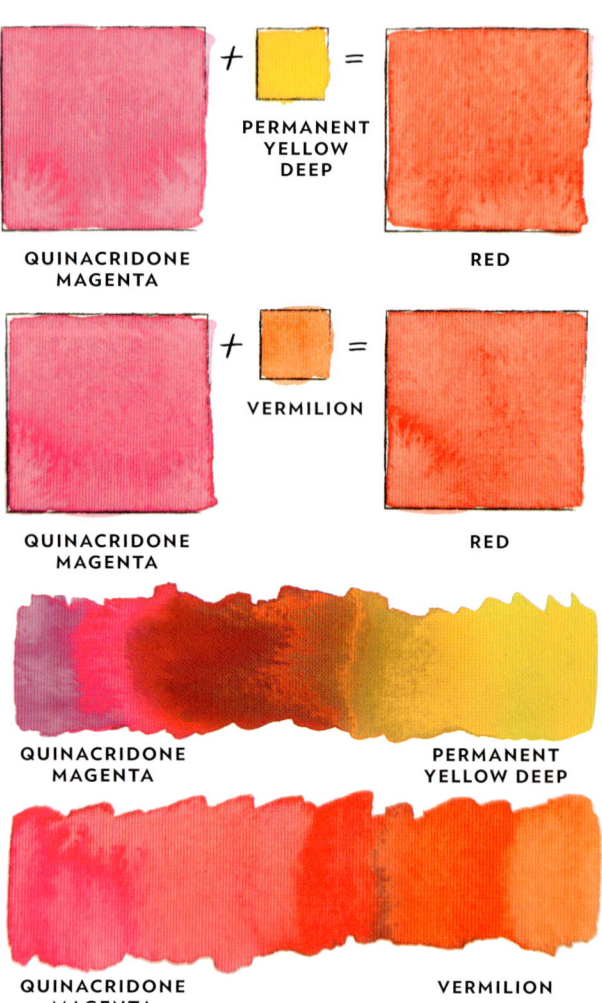

QUINACRIDONE MAGENTA + PERMANENT YELLOW DEEP = RED

QUINACRIDONE MAGENTA + VERMILION = RED

QUINACRIDONE MAGENTA — PERMANENT YELLOW DEEP

QUINACRIDONE MAGENTA — VERMILION

I find that most reds have an undertone to them that impacts the brightness of colors you're able to make, and I find that pinks or magentas make more vibrant mixtures when used in the set of primaries. It's a lot like a printer: if you've ever loaded the ink cartridges, you've probably noticed that the colors are cyan, magenta, and yellow, and yet printers can make any color. The primaries I use are more closely related to these colors, and I personally believe they are better at making a wider range of vibrant colors.

Another reason I went with magenta is that with the colors I have, we can mix up a range of reds, but there isn't a way to work the other way and use a red to make a super vibrant pink. This means that we're able to get the best of both worlds with fewer colors. Notice in the images to the left that using a combination of the Permanent Yellow Deep and Quinacridone Magenta, or even the Magenta and Vermilion, I can get a variety of vibrant red colors. We could add a little blue to red to make it a little more magenta colored, but it won't have the same intensity as using the magenta color straight from the pan or tube.

VALUE

While the color wheel is important, it doesn't tell the whole story. Value is how light or dark a color is. For example, a dark blue is going to have a higher value than a yellow. It can also mean how much white or water you have mixed into your color. A concentrated blue color is going to have a higher value than a blue with lots of water mixed in.

Having a variety of values in your painting adds interest. If everything's the same value a painting can feel flat. This can be tricky to understand when you're just learning, but there are two ways to explore this: the squint method, and viewing your painting as black and white.

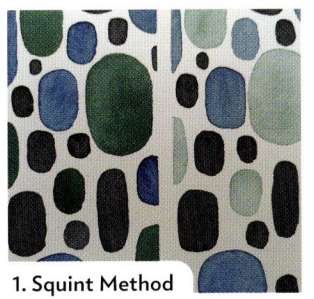

1. Squint Method

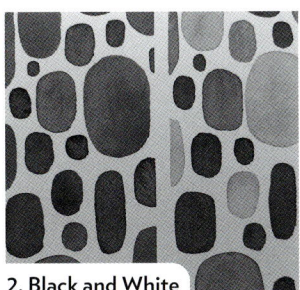

2. Black and White

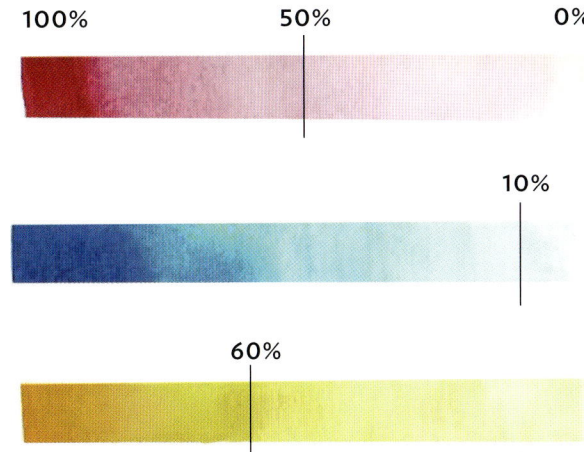

Squint Method

Have you ever noticed an artist looking at their piece and intentionally squinting their eyes to make their vision blurry? They are often checking for value. In image 1 I have divided the page in half. On the left side of the page I painted green, grey, and blue bubbles, all of a similar value. When you squint at that side the colors all kind of look the same. On the right side of image 1 I used the same colors, but varied the saturation to create different values. When you squint at the right side of image you may notice that some of the bubbles seem to pop out more than others.

Black and White

The other option is to take a photo of your piece and then turn it black and white. A black and white image can only really pick up the values. Image 2 is the same image as image 1 but in black and white. In the left side of image 2 all the colors appear to be the same value. On the right side of image 2 you can clearly tell the colors were different even in black and white. Contrast and varying values direct the eye to the important things. Without these things, the eye can get overwhelmed.

SATURATION

Value and saturation go hand in hand. Saturation is how strong or close to its full value a color can be. A color can be desaturated with either water, a grey,

black, or even a complementary color. In general, less saturated colors have a more pale or dull appearance. You can see three color strips above. They are at their full saturation on the left (100%) but as they move towards the right, I have added more and more water, which desaturates the color. When I talk about mixing colors to a certain saturation, imagine 100% saturation and then adjust with more or less water to achieve the desired percentage.

Mixing
COMPLEMENTARY COLORS

Understanding complementary colors is one of the best things I did to better understand mixing colors. It helped me learn to mute colors to create more lifelike paintings. Complementary colors are located directly across the wheel from each other. They complement each other in an aesthetically pleasing way, which is why these combos are seen often. However, in the same way that they look nice together, they are kind of the law of opposites attract. The bright points of the colors on either side of the wheel cancel each other out when mixed. When they are mixed in approximately equal parts, complementary colors

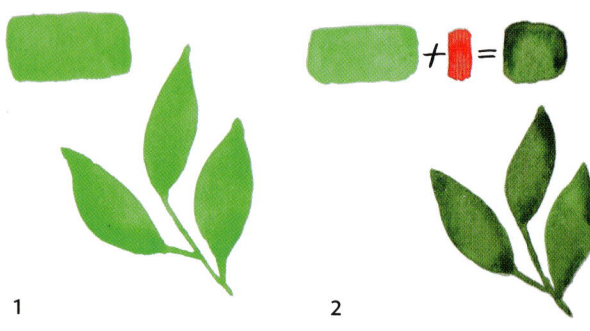

1   2

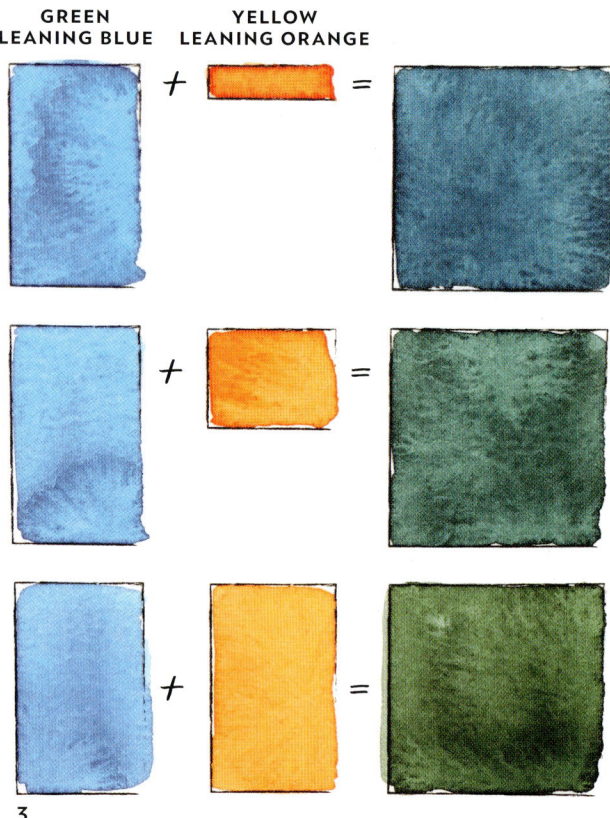

GREEN LEANING BLUE   **YELLOW LEANING ORANGE**

3

make browns and greys. This can come in handy if you don't have brown or grey and only want to use a couple colors to mix it up. But also, if you play with adding just a bit of the complementary color to the main color, you can get a lovely, muted shade.

Often when you're painting things in nature, the colors are more muted than what you might get straight off a pan of watercolor. Not all leaves are going to be a super bright green, many will have a warmer or more olive undertone. For example, the leaves in image 1 are a full saturation super bright green that could work if you're trying to push the boundaries for color. But for more realistic looking leaves, mixing a tiny bit of red into the green, as in image 2, will deepen the color and create a more natural muted quality to the green.

Undertones

To correctly cancel each other out, complementary colors must have the correct undertones. For example, looking across the color wheel from Phthalo Blue, we know we need an orange, but that's not the end of the story. Phthalo Blue has a slightly green leaning undertone, which means it moves more towards yellow on the color wheel. So if we choose an orange that leans more towards yellow, we're effectively adding in one part blue, one part orange, one part yellow. In image 3, we have Phthalo Blue that has a slightly green leaning undertone and an orange with a yellow undertone. As you can see, when I combine equal parts blue and

orange, we get a muted green rather than a muted orange, blue, or grey—that's because of the yellow and green undertones. With less of the orange added, the color begins to approach a teal. Experimenting with complementary colors will help you better understand the undertones of the colors.

How to MIX COLORS

I've described some of the properties of colors to keep in mind to mix a pleasing variety of hues. Here's how to mix them.

Mixing Pan Paints

Pan paints often come in a dried format that is typically found in a little square of plastic and stored in a

Color mixing in action

Mixing colors or mixing up enough of one color can often feel tricky. To see how it's done, scan the QR code to watch the video.

tin. Start by pre-wetting your paints by dropping some water on them or spritzing them with a spray bottle filled with clean water. Add some water to a mixing well. Swipe or swirl your brush on the color you want to mix up a larger quantity of, and once some of the paint is on the brush, swirl it into the water in the mixing well. Continue going back and forth between the mixing well and pan of paint until you've reached your desired saturation. To mix a custom color using multiple colors, swipe the brush onto the first color, mix it in the well, then swipe the brush over the other color and mix it into the well with the first color. Revisit each of the pans as necessary until you reach the desired color. If you're concerned about transferring colors between pans, wash your brush between colors and make sure to dry it off thoroughly. If you use a wet brush between each color switch, you'll be constantly desaturating the mixture with water, making it difficult to achieve your desired saturation.

Mixing Tube Paints

Watercolors that come in a tube are in gel or paste form. Open your tube paints and squeeze out a little dot—you don't need much, maybe the size of a pencil eraser or less. I like to place these little dots of watercolor in between my paint wells. Wash a brush and tap it on the side of the well so it's not sopping wet. For a really concentrated color, you can tap that damp brush on your little dot of paint and paint right from there. However, if you're looking to mix up more of

a single color to use in something like a wash or a custom mixture, you'll start by adding some water to a mixing well and then alternating between tapping a damp brush on the dot of color and then mixing it into the well with the water. Keep adding more color until your desired mixture is achieved.

Color Strength

With watercolors, each color has different strengths as well as abilities to impact and balance other colors. This means that when I or other watercolor teachers tell you to mix up 50% of one color with 50% of another color, it might not literally mean to take a dollop of each, at equal sizes and mix them together. Instead, work from one end to the other, adding more of the second color in increments, until

The magic of pre-wetting pan paints

In my social media videos, you will usually see me spraying my pan paints before I start painting. This isn't just a weird attention grabber, it's one of the best pieces of advice I can give. Pre-wetting your pan paints is key to unlocking more of the color. By either spraying them or putting a few drops on them and letting them absorb into the paint for 30–60 seconds before using them, you will unlock the color. If you've been struggling with getting saturated or vibrant colors, this might be the tip that helps the most.

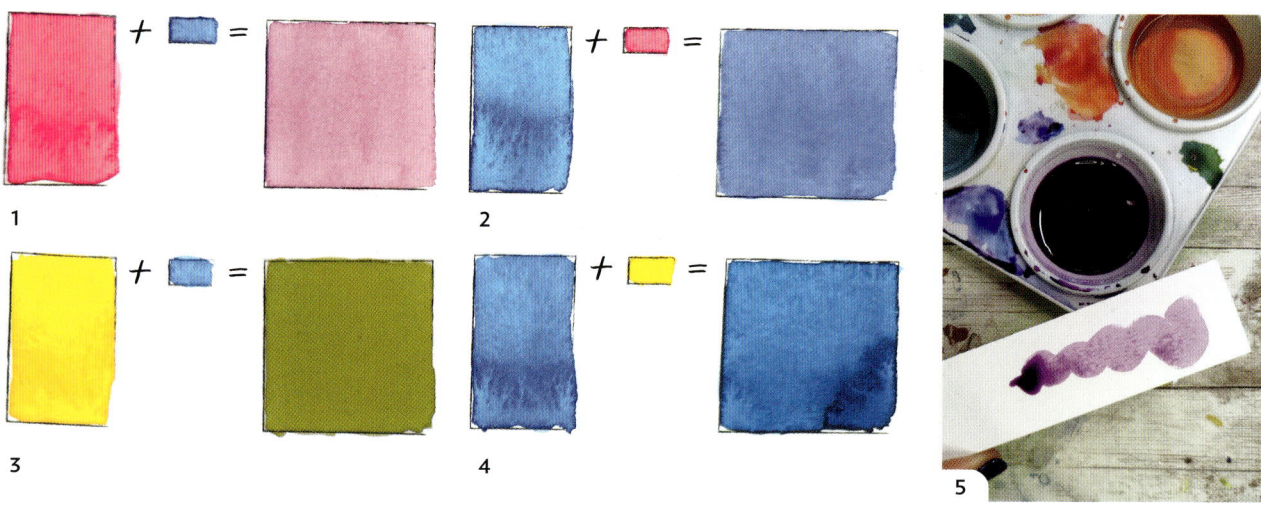

1

2

3

4

5

you can no longer detect the beginning color, and asking yourself visually where would 50% be? Some colors, such as yellow, are not that strong. But different brands of paint also have different strengths. In image 1, you can see how a tiny bit of blue mixed into magenta creates a purple. However, in image 2, a tiny bit of magenta mixed into blue has very little effect. This helps to illustrate the strength of the blue color. Likewise, in image 3, a tiny amount of blue mixed into yellow really changes the color to a greenish yellow. However, in image 4, a tiny amount of yellow mixed into blue creates a less noticeable change. So even if you are mixing what logically should be 50/50 as suggested by the instructions, you may have to adapt this to your color strength. I recommend following your eyes and your gut over the instructions. The color mixing instructions are there to help, but if you're using different supplies you will have to adjust as you see fit.

Tester Strips

Be sure to save your scrap pieces of watercolor paper. When you're mixing colors, the mixing wells can deceive you. The colors appear a lot darker in the well than they will on paper. I always cut up little pieces of my scrap paper to test out the colors as I'm mixing before I place them on my actual painting. In image 5, the dark purple in the well is the color I have painted on the strip—there's quite a big difference.

A Few Important
REMINDERS

You may have bought this book because you're a beginner and just getting started. If that's the case, here are a few tips to get the most out of it.

1 Be kind to yourself. You're learning a new skill, and it takes time. Grant yourself the gift of compassion and the space to learn.

2 Don't immediately throw away all your "failures." Sometimes, something I paint will look dreadful to me right when I finish painting it. However, after leaving and coming back the next day I often feel differently about it. Sometimes, with the gift of time, you might like it. Another reason to save your paintings is for progress tracking. When you're in the middle of the struggle, it's easy to think, "I will always be this 'bad' and I have always

been this 'bad.'" But in reality being able to look back on some of your first pieces will give you perspective about how far you've come and how much you've learned.

3 Your paintings don't need to look like my paintings and your paintings don't need to look like your friend's paintings. This is your practice and you're exactly where you should be at this time.

4 Be brave with water. Experiment with using more water than you're comfortable with. Most often when I see beginner watercolorists complaining about how their paintings don't look how they want, they're just not using enough water. I get it, all that flowing water can be scary, but give it a go.

5 Take time to play. If you're painting and you start to think "oooh, look how this color moves, that's fun," go with it, play, embrace it. Having some time for play will keep things light, keep you motivated, and it will teach you more than you can imagine about your supplies.

Tips for More Experienced Watercolorists

You may have bought this book because you love watercolor and have some experience, but you're either stuck, or it's been a long time since you painted. If so, read on.

1 Remember there isn't a single right way to do things. The best way to do them is the way that works for you. I recommend trying out my suggestions, but if you know a better way, that's great. More than likely it can be used in combination with the rest of the directions.

2 Use these exercises as a jumping-off point. I encourage you to challenge yourself with the colors; make a couple changes to what I have done to see how you can personalize the paintings by modifying them just using colors. Add additional touches or modify the compositions. Sometimes what you need to get out of a rut is an initial idea that you can stray from.

3 If you're not as good as you used to be, that's okay. You've changed, your perspective has changed, you might find yourself gravitating toward a new style, and change is okay.

No matter who you are, I want you to know, you've got this!

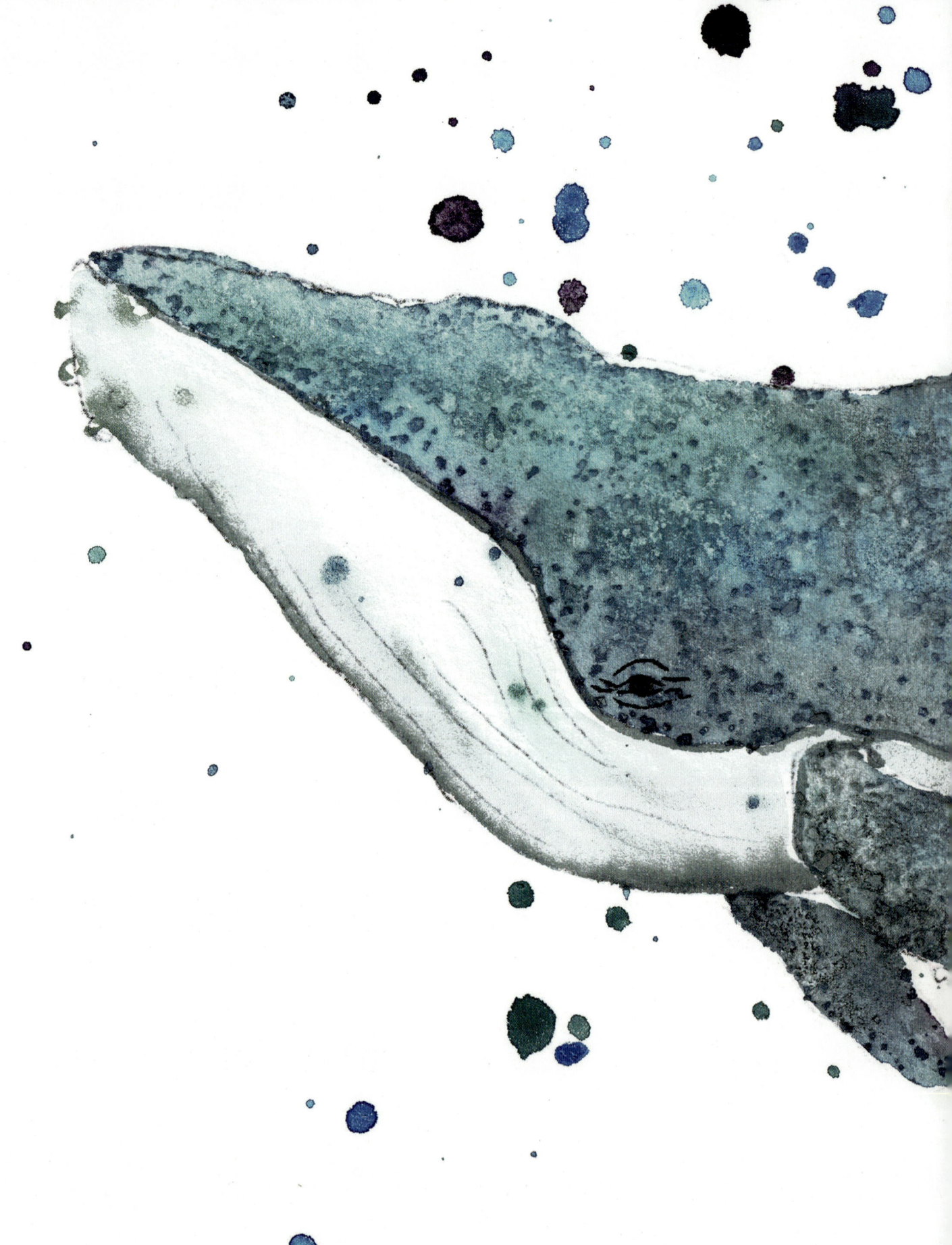

PAINTINGS

FOLLOW THE GRADIENT ROAD

Forget the yellow brick road, the gradient road will lead you to far friendlier places. This simple but super satisfying painting will help illustrate how many different colors you can make by just moving between two colors. Even though this whole exercise is about color mixing, there aren't any specific formulas you have to follow here. You can use whatever two colors you like for your gradient road; you don't have to use the two I chose. The mixes between two different colors can be really surprising, and you'll notice things about color mixing that you might have a hard time learning just by reading about color theory. Plus at the end you'll be left with a super cute abstract piece that's absolutely hangable.

Supplies

Size ½ inch (1.5 cm) angle brush

Color Palette

■ Phthalo Blue

■ Quinacridone Magenta

Techniques

How to Mix Colors, p. 30

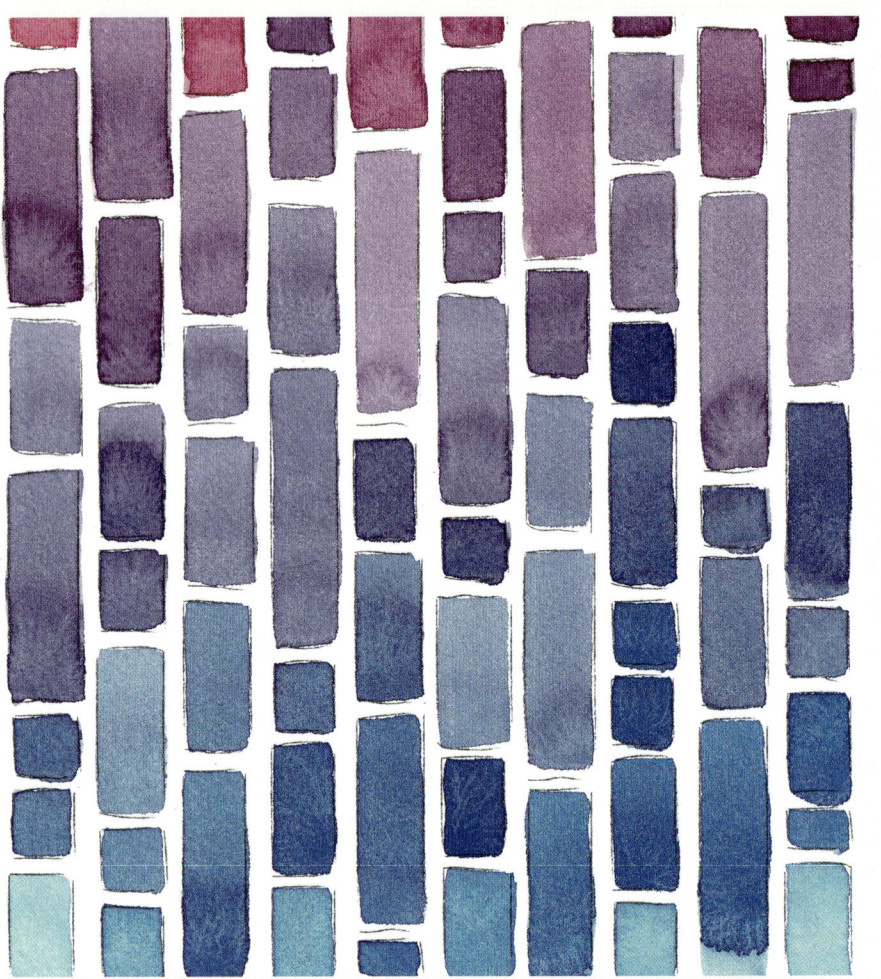

Struggling with mixing colors?

If you're struggling with how to gradually mix between colors or making sure you have enough color to fill the page, scan the QR code to watch this video, where I show you the process and give you tips and tricks.

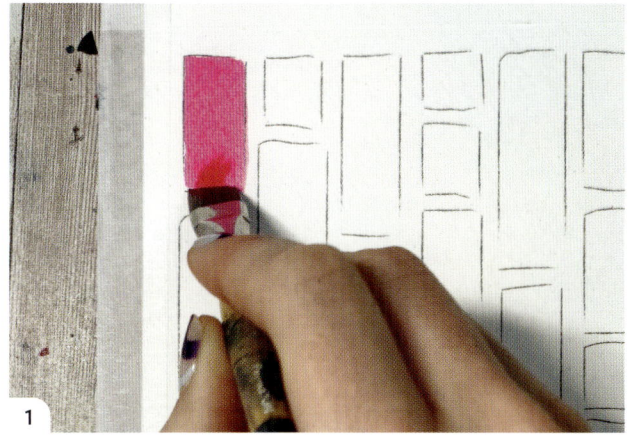

STEP 1

Start with a concentrated mixture of your first color. I recommend starting with your lighter hue, in this case Quinacridone Magenta. Make sure you mix up a decent amount so you'll be able to refill your brush over and over again. Begin by filling in the top left brick with that pure color.

STEP 2

Add a little Phthalo Blue (or your darker second color) to a separate well of your palette, and dip just a tiny edge of the paintbrush into the blue. You don't want too much because you want the colors to be a slow gradual change from magenta to blue. Once you've grabbed the tiniest amount of your second color, mix it into your first color. Make sure you thoroughly mix. Place a stroke of this newly but slightly changed color in the second brick cell. Repeat this process, moving across the row and adding the tiniest amount of your second color each time. Notice that even though each stroke individually doesn't appear to be much different, from one end of the row to the other there's a huge change.

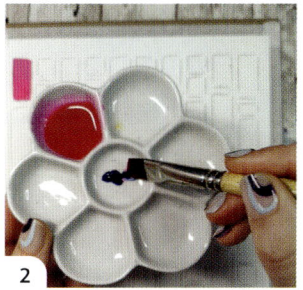

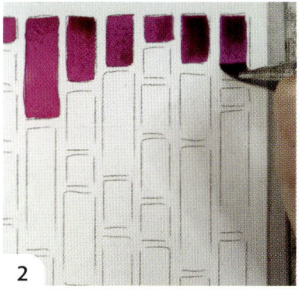

STEP 3

Work your way down the page, adding tiny amounts of your second color to your mixed color. I suggest working your way down the page left to right, then right to left, then left to right and so on. If you are concerned about running out of your color mixture at the end of a row, fill up your brush with water and add it to the mixture before starting the new row so you can keep enough water in your mixing well to continue moving. Keep going until you've filled the entire page.

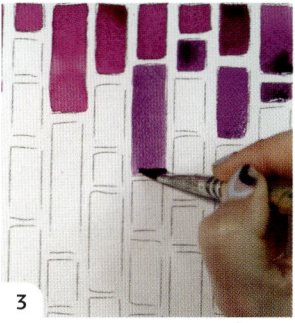

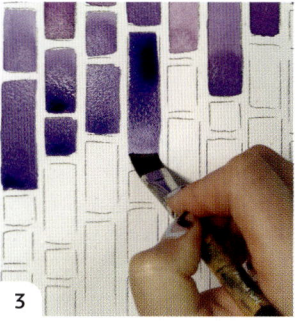

STEP 4

When you finish, take a moment to really observe how many different color shifts there are between the two colors. Each of my strokes makes up about a 5% change in the total color composition ratio.

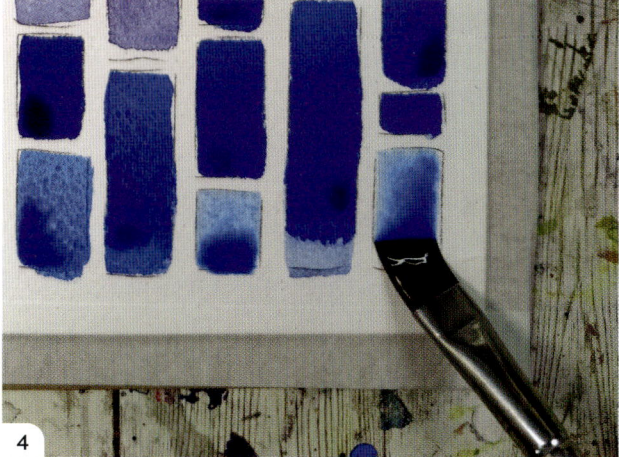

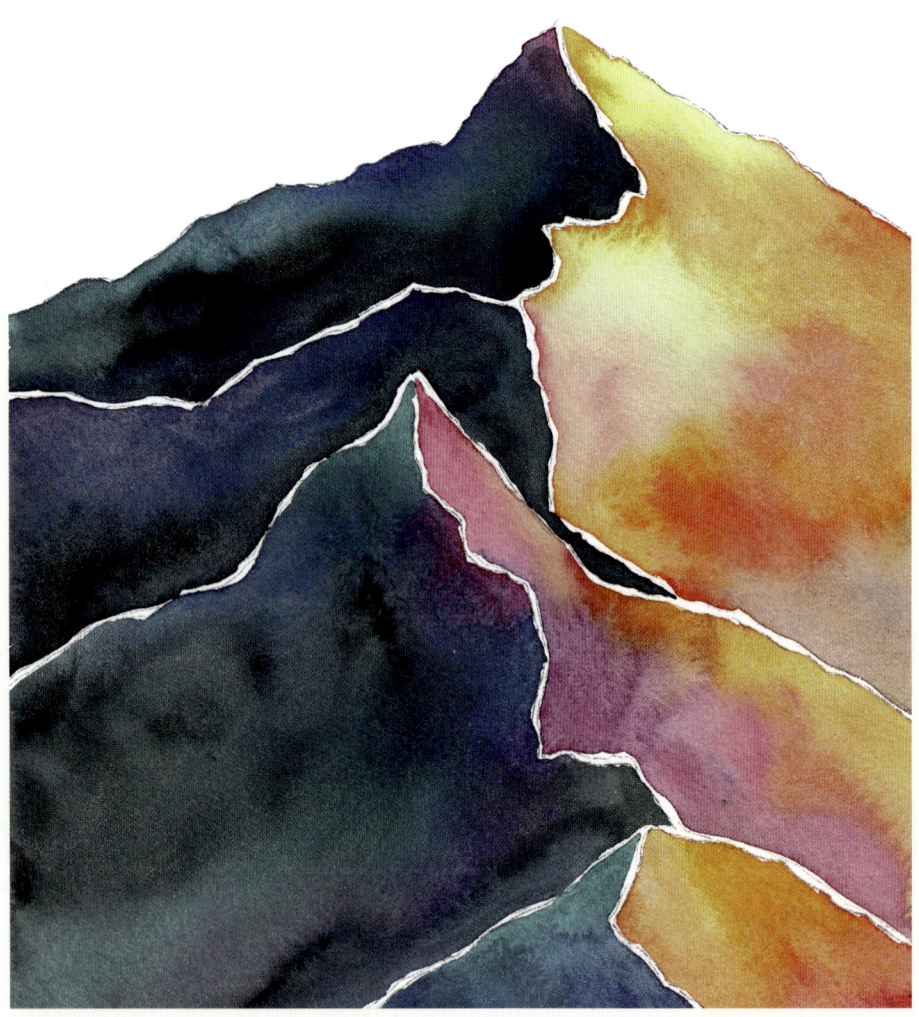

HOT AND COLD MOUNTAINS

Mountains are a common theme in my paintings due to my Colorado roots and how much I missed seeing them during the years I was away from my home state. Sometimes trying to paint detailed mountains can leave them feeling a little flat. Instead, we'll be using a simple combination of warm and cool colors to capture the feeling of light and shadow on a mountain ridge.

In this painting, the warm colors will all be on the right side and the cool colors will be on the left—this mimics light coming from the right and the left falling into shadow all without painting any details.

Supplies

Size 3 quill brush or size 12 round brush

Color Palette

Payne's Gray

Phthalo Blue

Permanent Yellow Deep

Prussian Blue

Quinacridone Magenta

Sap Green

Vermilion

Color Mixing

YELLOWY ORANGE: 50% Permanent Yellow Deep and 50% Vermilion at 60% saturation

PURPLE MOUNTAIN: 50% Quinacridone Magenta and 50% Prussian Blue at 75% saturation

COOL TEAL: 25% Sap Green and 75% Phthalo Blue at 75% saturation

Techniques

Warm vs. Cool Colors, p. 27

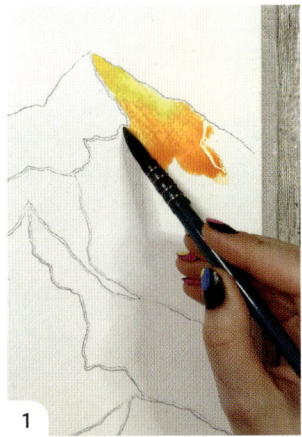

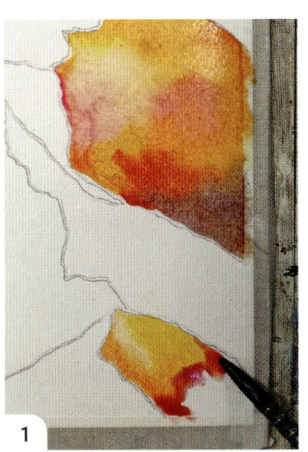

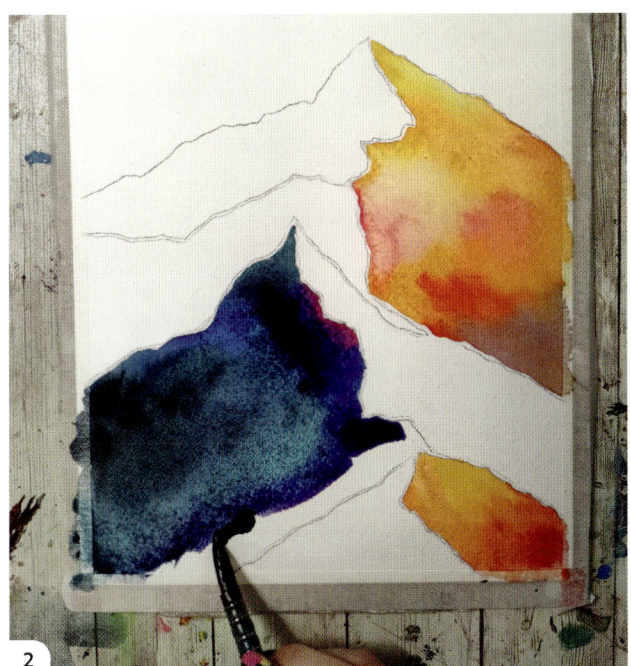

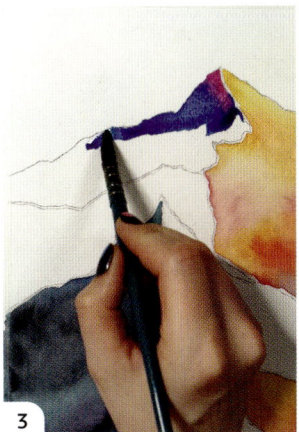

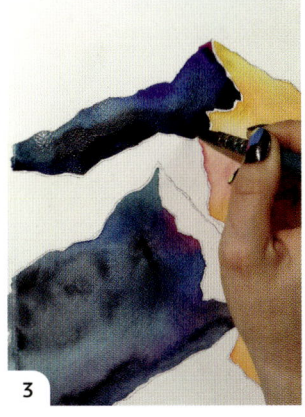

STEP 1

Start by mixing the custom colors. On the upper right-hand side, begin painting the lightest and brightest of the warm colors: Permanent Yellow Deep and custom Yellowy Orange. The color placement should be loose and organic, so switch between refilling your brush with water and painting in Quinacridone Magenta or even the custom Purple Mountain as you make your way towards the bottom of the segment. Use lots of water and lots of color and just let the magic happen. Repeat in a similar fashion on the bottom right-hand segment. We're skipping over the middle segment for now to keep the segments separated so we don't have to dry after every single segment.

STEP 2

On the left-hand side, paint the largest bottom segment in a similar manner, using cool colors. This means we're dropping in super saturated versions of Prussian Blue, Phthalo Blue, the custom Cool Teal, and Payne's Gray near the bottom. Add a teeny amount of saturated Quinacridone Magenta near the top to make it appear as if a little light is pouring across the ridgeline. Let this dry or make it dry! Everything must be completely dry to prevent the cool colors from running into the warm colors.

STEP 3

Starting on the top left segment, add cool colors in a similar manner to the dark segment in the previous step plus a little saturated Quinacridone Magenta at the top. Try to make the colors saturated but a little lighter or brighter near the top of the segment. For the warm side, that means placing the yellow and oranges near the top and adding a bit more water. For the cool side, I tended to use a little pink or add water to my brush before picking up any of the blues to give them a lighter value. By making the colors lighter near the tops and edges and darker as you go down, you will be able to mimic how the light is often caught on the top of the mountain, and the shadow will give this a bit of depth while helping to separate the segments.

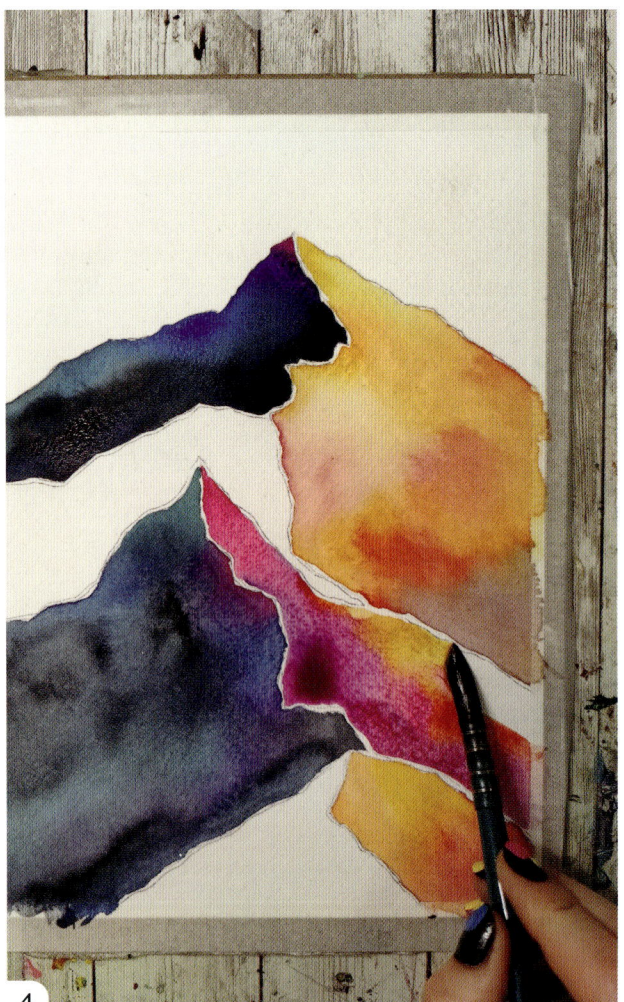

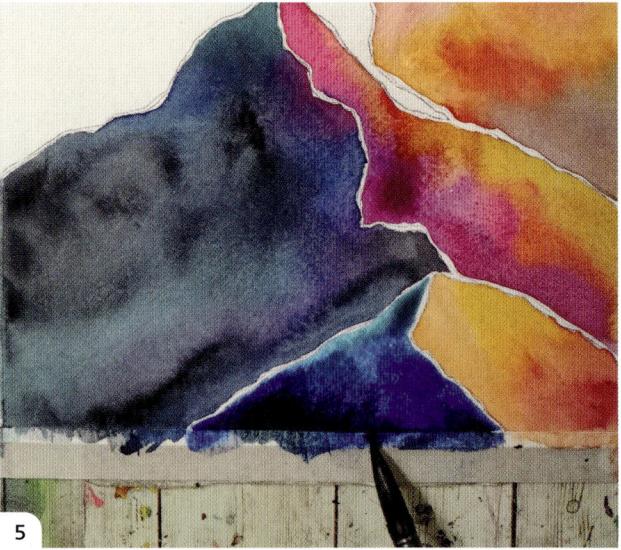

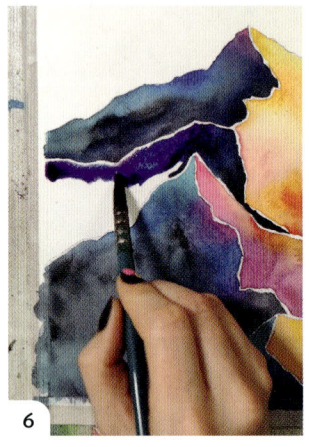

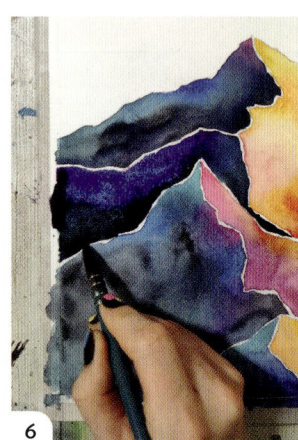

STEP 4

In the right-hand side middle segment, pack lots of warm colors, starting with Quinacridone Magenta on the top, to help give us the illusion of the light flowing over to the other side. Finish this segment with Permanent Yellow Deep on the top of the right-hand side.

STEP 5

Paint the bottom left segment in a similar manner as the rest of the left-hand segments. Let this dry or make it dry!

STEP 6

The final segment is painted in a similar way, but the crevice is extra dark to really throw it into shadow. You can do this by using more Payne's Gray here than in other areas, or by using either of the Blues at their most intense value right from the tube or pan.

Supplies

Size 3 quill brush or size 12 round brush

Color Palette

Burnt Sienna

Permanent Yellow Deep

Quinacridone Magenta

Vermilion

Yellow Ochre

Techniques

Paint Wetness Stages, p. 14
Wet-on-Wet, p. 15
Wet-on-Dry, p. 15

SWEET AS HONEY

This is one of my favorite paintings because it's so low pressure, and even if you're not happy with one or two of the hexagons in this honeycomb, once it's completed it all comes together. The other reason I love it is because it's segmented, which encourages us to play with different variables.

For this exercise we're going to focus on exploring the different stages of wet-on-wet. Through each stage, this painting will change a lot. I will show you what it looks like when all the colors have been added but it's still wet, and then once when the colors are completely dry. Remember, watercolor gets lighter in color as it dries.

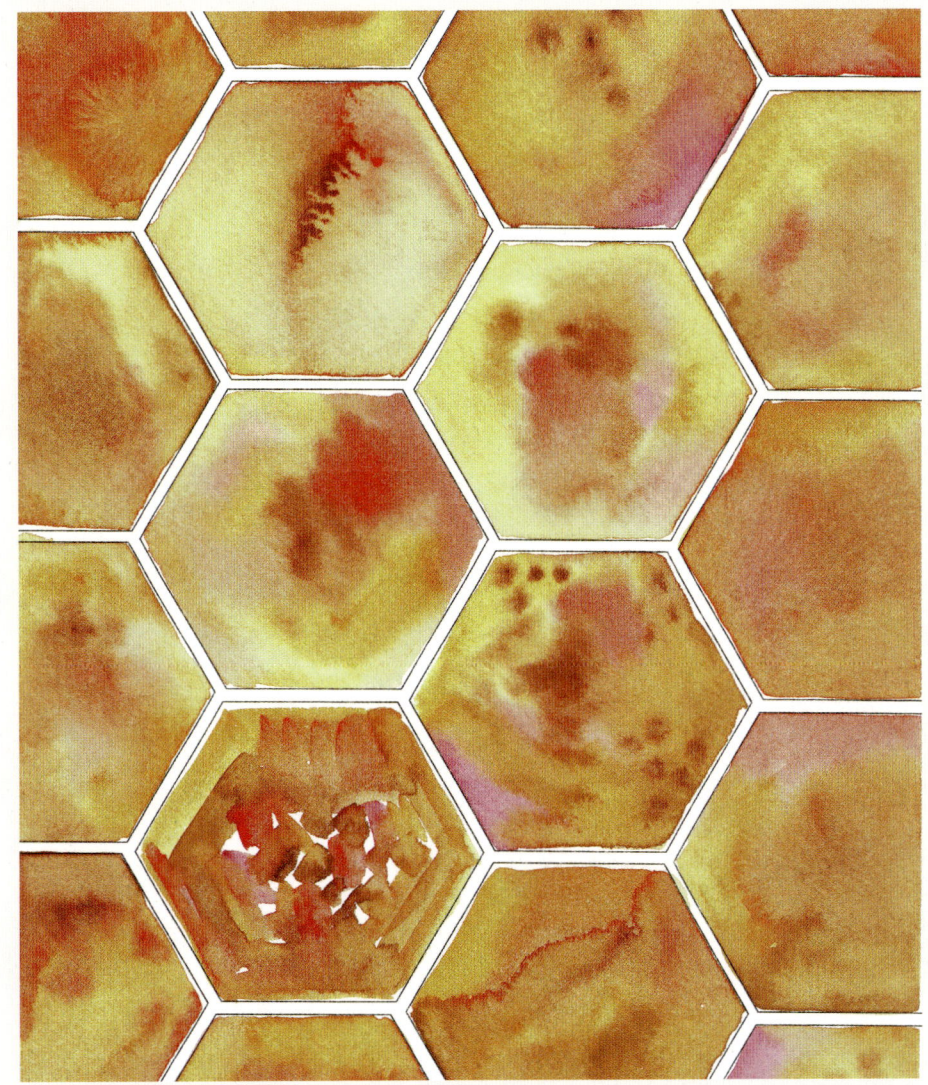

STEP 1

Tape down your paper to a backing board. We're going to be adding a lot of water to this one, so it will buckle less if you do this step. Pick any of the hexagons and fill it up with so much water that if you picked it up and tilted it, you'd be worried about the water running everywhere—this is the Flood stage. Place any of the colors you desire into the cell. In some areas I brushed them on, and other areas I dotted them. Don't over-think this one; it's so wet the colors are going to move unpredictably and may have surprising effects once dry, so don't try to control it.

STEP 2

Pre-wet your next cell to the Gloss stage and drop the colors into this cell wherever your heart desires. I recommend using at least three different colors at this point. The colors will move a lot, but they are going to stay in the general area you place them (unlike in the Flood stage).

STEP 3

Pre-wet the third cell to the Satin stage, and again drop three or four of the colors into the cell wherever your heart desires. There will be a lovely softness to how the colors flow together. This stage is where things start to get more predictable with how the colors are going to dry.

STEP 4

Pre-wet the fourth cell to the Damp stage. This means there should only be a slight light reflection from the water. On this one, drop your colors in as you desire, but play around with dropping some defined drops onto the paper. To do this you'll want to make sure there isn't too much water on your brush, so fill it up with your desired color and then tap it lightly on a paper towel to remove most but not all of the moisture. Since this is the most predictable stage of wetness, the colors should stay where you put them, but they will have a softness along the edges.

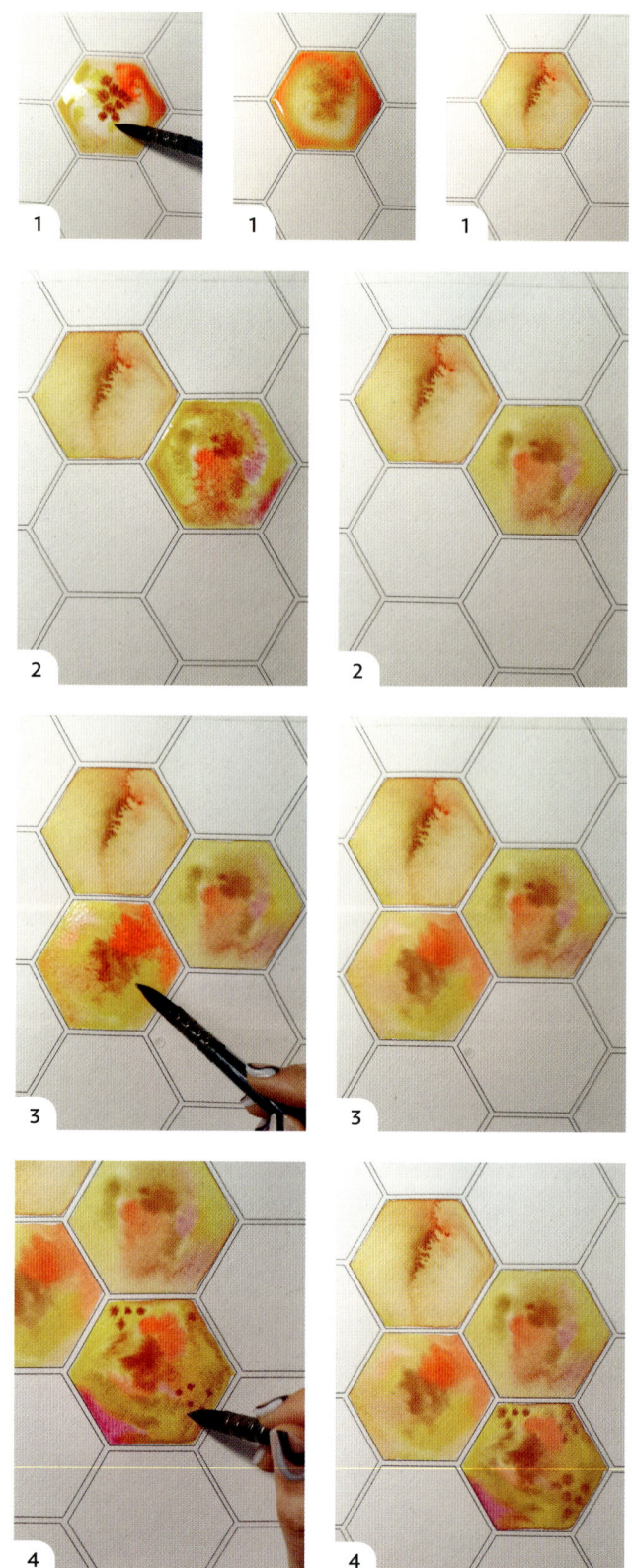

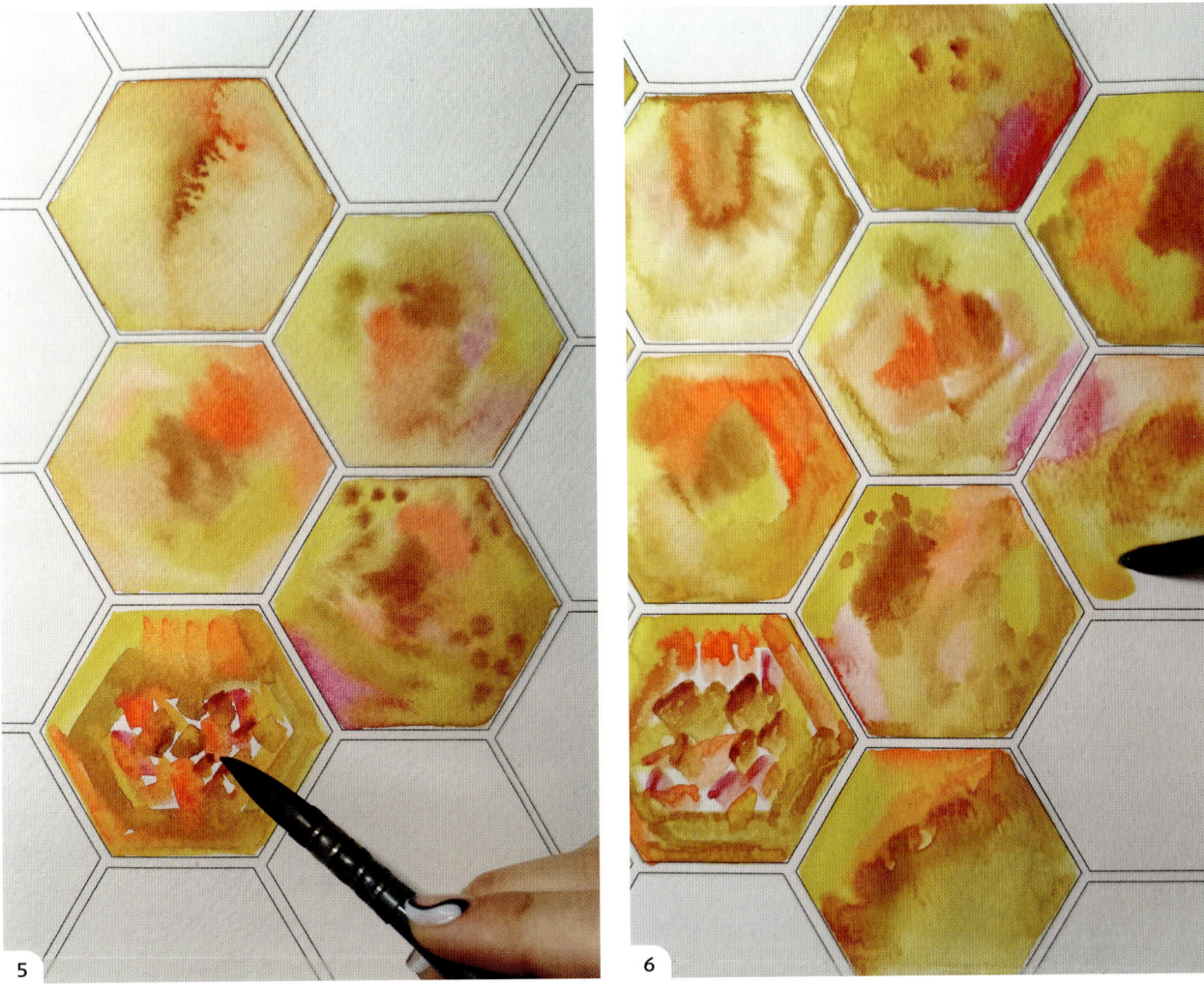

STEP 5

In the fifth cell, we'll explore the Dry stage. Keep the paper dry and start adding brushstrokes to it. Notice how the edges stay sharp, the strokes stay defined. Also, notice that in this stage, you can preserve white space for highlights. This is one of the great parts of painting wet-on-dry.

STEP 6

At this point you can choose your own adventure and continue to explore the Flood, Gloss, Satin, Damp, and Dry stages. Continue filling the remaining cells using a variety of the stages or choose your favorite one. I encourage you to play here, and not overthink it. The more you experiment at this stage, the more you'll understand how your supplies work later in the exercises.

MARVELOUS MOUNTAINS

This is hands down one of my favorite paintings to teach. In part because the view of the mountains just never gets old for me, and in part because this painting teaches so many skills.

In this painting we'll be exploring washes, gradients, lifting, and layering. In addition to that, you'll learn a little about perspective and depth by using the phenomenon of atmospheric perspective—where things that are farther away appear lighter in color and a bit more out of focus. By making the back layer of mountains lighter, we'll be able to help them appear as if they are farther away.

Supplies

Size 4 quill brush or size 12 round brush
Paper towel

Color Palette

- Quinacridone Magenta
- Prussian Blue
- Payne's Gray

Color Mixing

1ST LAYER: 70% Payne's Gray and 30% Prussian Blue at 20% saturation

2ND LAYER: Remainder of 1st layer color and add a little color to increase saturation to about 30–40% using about 70% Payne's Gray and 30% Quinacridone Magenta

3RD LAYER: Remainder of the 2nd layer color and add a little more color to increase saturation to 60–70% using about 60% Payne's Gray and 40% Quinacridone Magenta

Techniques

Washes, p. 18
Lifting, p. 17
Layering, p. 24

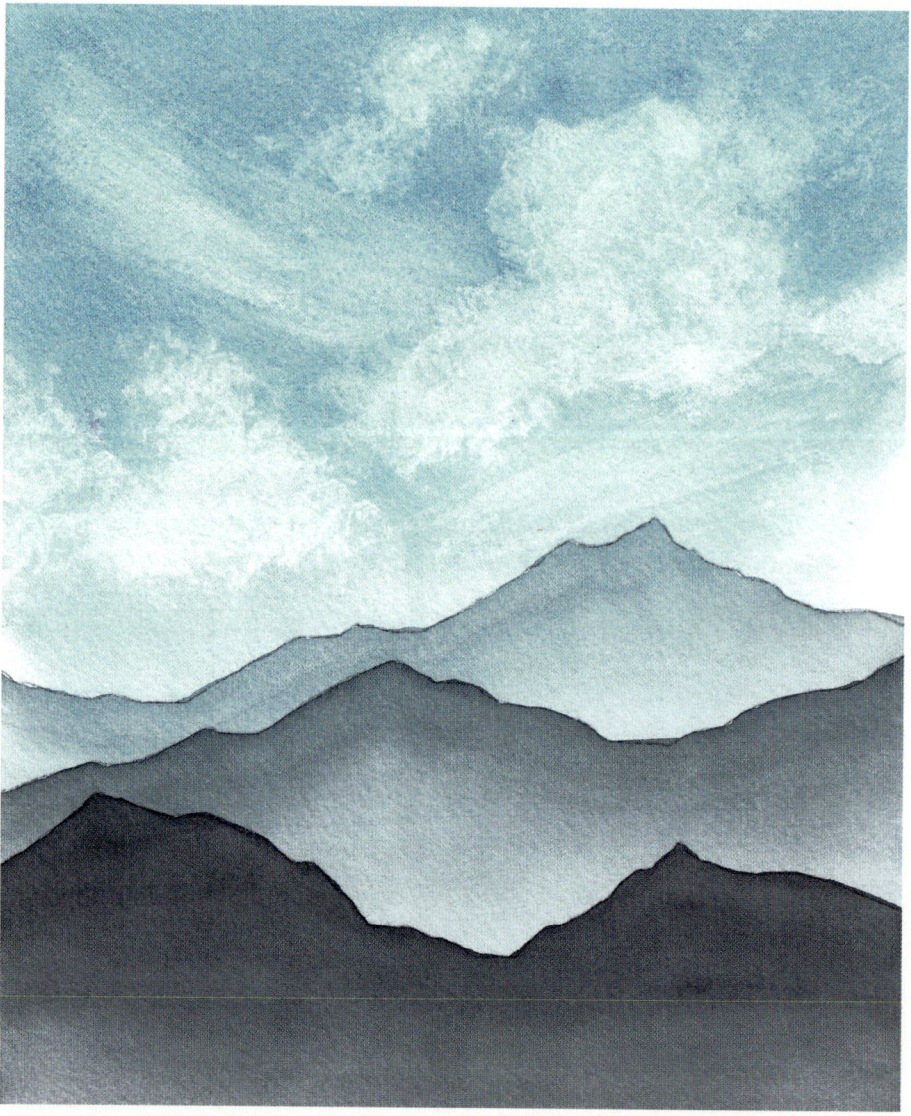

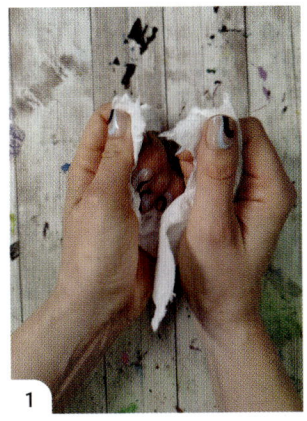
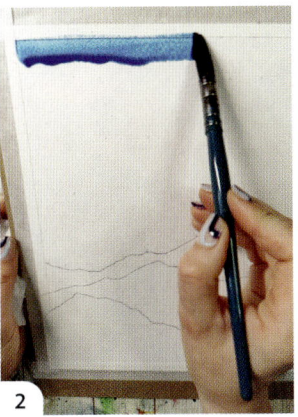
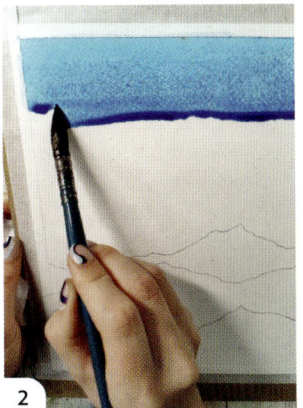
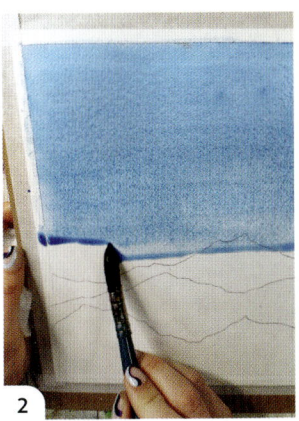

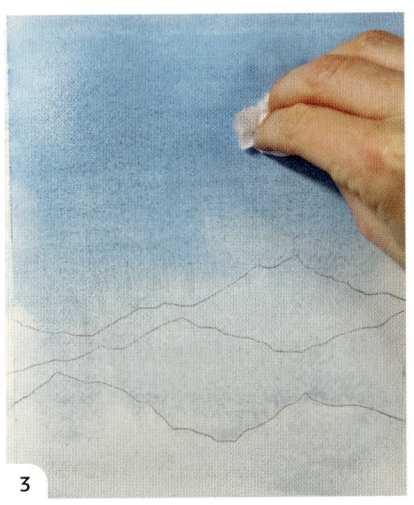
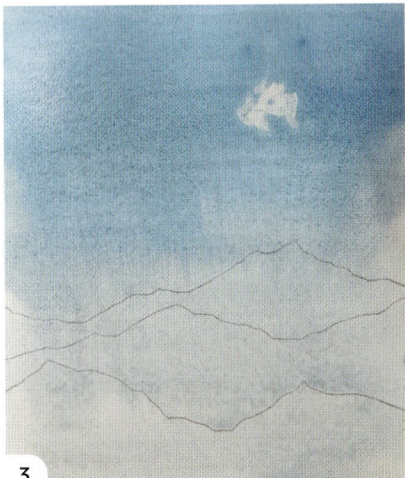
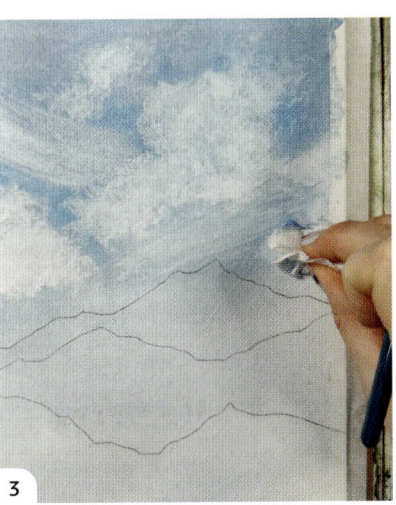

STEP 1

Tape down your paper. We're going to be adding a lot of water to this one, so it will buckle less if you do this step. We're also going to be exploring lifting, so grab a paper towel, scrunch it up, and tear it. The natural texture of the ripped edges will help us get fluffy clouds.

STEP 2

In this step you'll create a gradient wash. Mix Prussian Blue at about 40–50% saturation using clean water. You want to mix a decent amount of this, enough to refill your brush with it multiple times—err on the side of too much mixed color. Once you have the color mixed, use the drip line wash method, reloading your brush four or five times with the blue color until you're about one-third of the way down the page. Then continue the wash to the bottom, dipping your brush into clean water so it slowly replaces the color in the brush with more and more water, creating a gradient over the mountain outline.

STEP 3

Quickly, before the wash dries, grab your ripped paper towel and start lifting out the cloud shapes as they call to you. To get a little variety in the shapes, twist your paper towel as you blot it on the wet color. If you want high wind clouds, swipe it across the page. Every sky you paint like this will look a little different. Let this layer dry or make it dry!

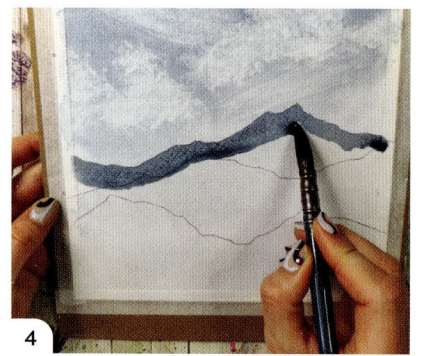 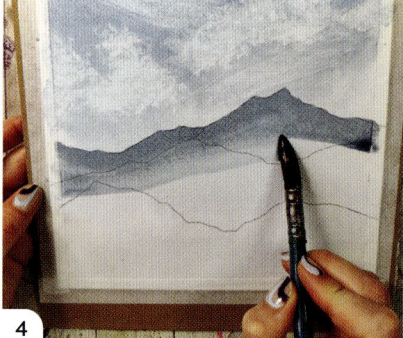 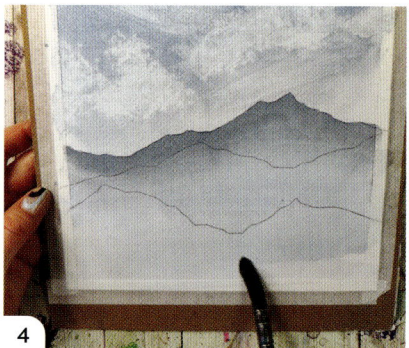

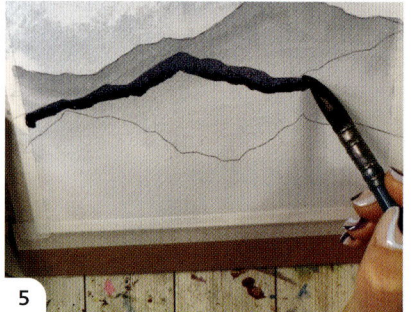 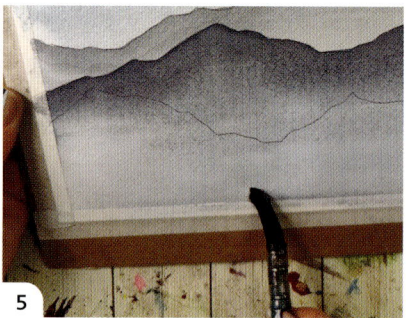 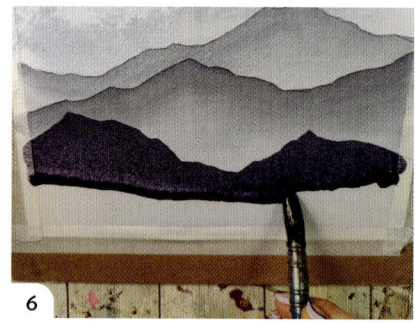

STEP 4

Mix the custom 1st Layer color. Fill your brush and follow along the outline of the back layer of mountains. Add about two lines of this color before rinsing your brush and washing this down to create a pretty drastic gradient. Rather than stopping abruptly, you are bringing each layer all the way to the bottom of the paper. Because watercolor is a transparent medium, you will see the final stroke you make and where it ends. Once you're finished with this layer, let this dry or make it dry!

STEP 5

Make sure that you have dried the previous layer well, which will create a nice, crisp top edge for the layered mountains. For the second and third layers, we'll increase the saturation of the color and make it a bit warmer by adding a larger percentage of the Quinacridone Magenta. The goal is to make sure each layer you add is a little bit darker to mimic the appearance of depth in the mountain range. Mix the custom 2nd

Layer color and repeat the steps from step 4 to wash this color down the middle-distance mountains. Let it dry, or make it dry!

STEP 6

Mix the custom 3rd Layer color and repeat the process from step 4 to wash this color down the mountains. Let it dry, or make it dry and you're done!

Mountains in action

This exercise is sometimes easier to do on a smaller scale. Scan the QR code to watch a video where I demonstrate the basic techniques shown here, but at a smaller scale and without any outlines so you can see how easy it is to create little mountain scenes.

Supplies

Size 4 quill brush or
size 12 round brush
2-inch (5 cm) flat wash
brush

Color Palette

Payne's Gray

Permanent Yellow
Deep

Phthalo Blue

Quinacridone
Magenta

Vermilion

Techniques

Wet-on-Wet, p. 15
Wet-on-Dry, p. 15
Layering, p. 24
Blooms and
Backruns, p. 22

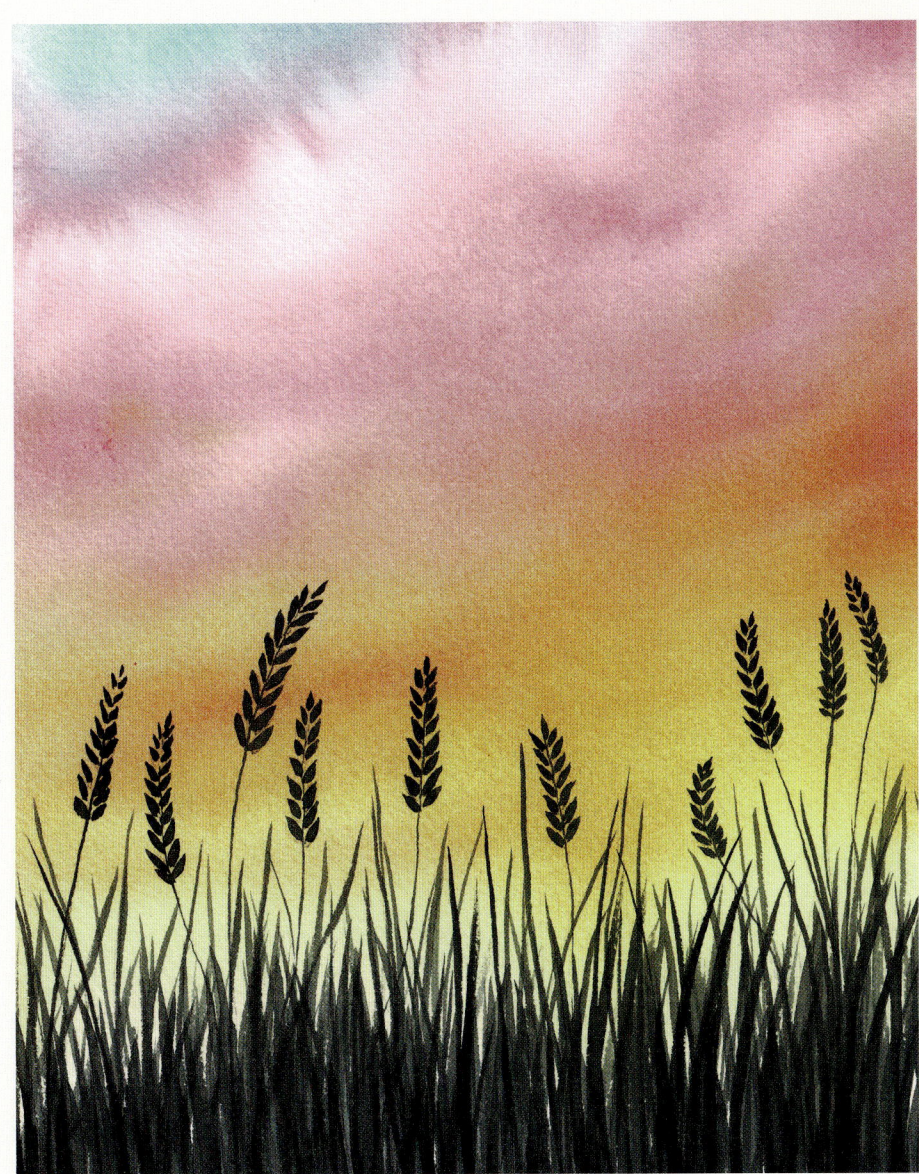

GOLDEN HOUR

Sunsets have always been one of my main inspirations. I love the combination of the soft bleeds of color and the surprising brightness. I have even been known to pull the car over into an open parking lot just to watch the sky give me a show. This painting combines a stunning sunset with a simple foreground shadow technique. The shadows create a big impact but require less work than painting details.

STEP 1

Mix a little of each color except the Payne's Gray to about a 40% saturation so they are easier to grab and add to the page in step 2. Tape down your paper to a hard backing board, as we're using lots of color and water. Using your flat wash brush, wet the entire page to about Gloss stage.

STEP 2

Before you start adding color, remember that all skies look different, so prepare to go with the flow. Fill your brush with Permanent Yellow Deep and make a few strokes around the heads of the wheat. Then, without washing your brush, add Vermilion above the yellow strokes. Wash your brush, then load it with Quinacridone Magenta and add it above the Vermilion. If you don't wash your brush, the pink may be a little muddy. In the upper left corner, I want to hint at the fact that there is blue sky above the sunset. Wash your brush, fill it with Phthalo Blue, and place just a few strokes in the corner and then just let it soften into the wet page.

STEP 3

Continue making random diagonal strokes, leaving some areas of white and concentrating the color more in other areas. Make sure the paper stays wet while you are working—if any area starts to dry, drop more clean water in that area. Add in more bright spots of the Quinacridone Magenta to get some areas of higher concentration of color. I chose these colors in this order because when they bleed together they make the color that would be between them on the color wheel. If I placed the yellow next to the blue, I'd have green skies. Stop working on this layer before the paper starts to dry. Dry your brush on a paper towel and use the dry brush to pick up any excess water collecting around the edges to prevent backruns. Let this layer dry or make it dry!

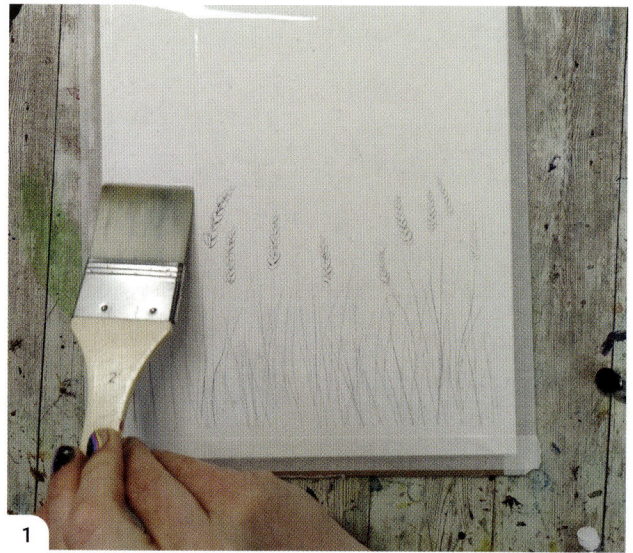

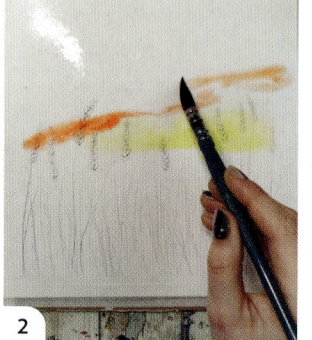

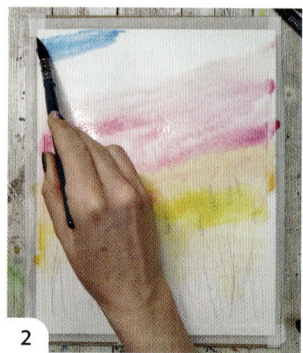

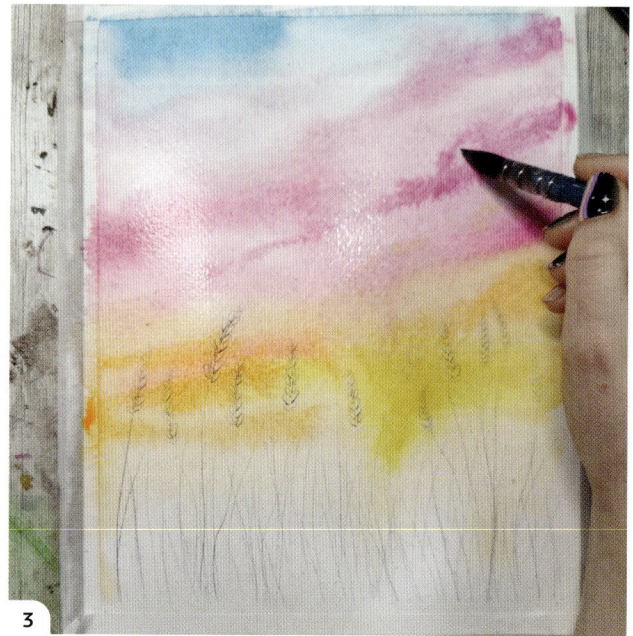

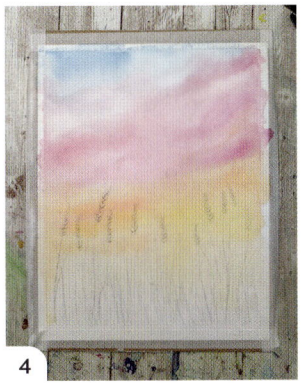
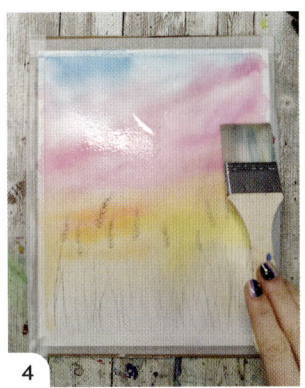
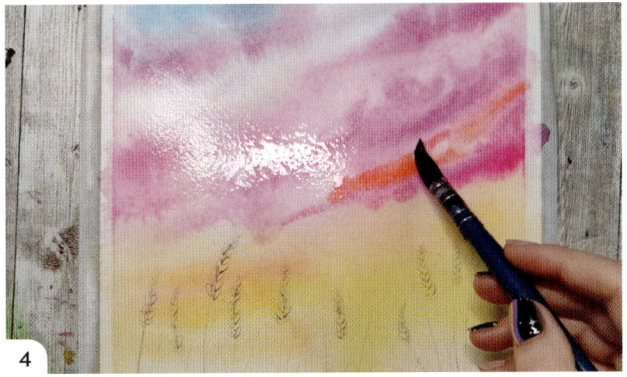
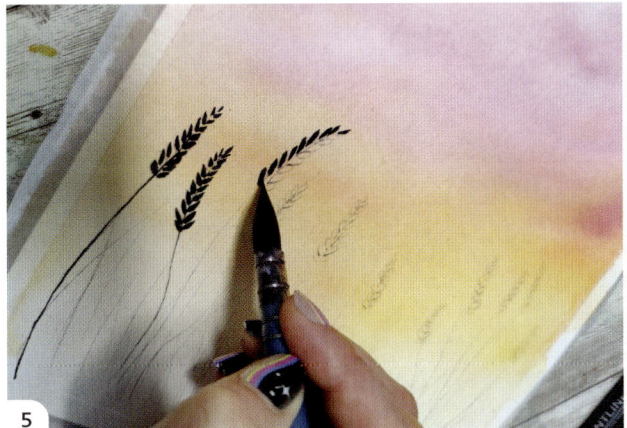
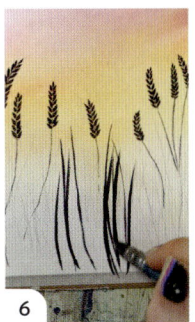
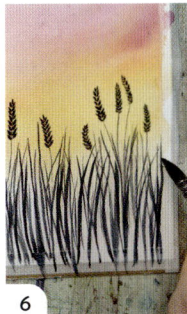
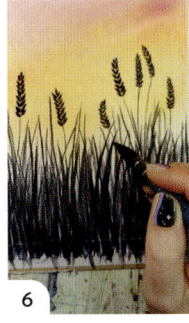

STEP 4

Watercolor really lightens as it dries. You may notice that your stunning vibrant sunset is instead soft and pastel like mine once dry. The wonderful thing about watercolor is you can always add another layer on top of it. If you want to add another layer, wet the entire page to a Gloss or Satin stage and add colors as you wish. Evaluate what your previous layer has given you and embrace what went well and compensate for things you'd prefer to have been brighter or softer. I only added more of the Quinacridone Magenta, Vermilion, and Permanent Yellow Deep and was bolder with my placement. The previous layer will show through and help weave these two layers together. Let this layer dry or make it dry!

STEP 5

Fill your brush with a creamy consistency of Payne's Gray and starting on the wheat heads, turn your paper so that your brush angle lines up nicely with the direction of one side of the wheat kernels. Tap the tip of your brush and push lightly to form each of the kernels. Rotate your page so that the kernels on the opposite side line up with the natural angle you hold your brush and repeat on the other side. Tap off any excess paint in your brush so that just a little remains in the tip and lightly drag down the center and towards the bottom of the page. Do this with all the wheat heads.

STEP 6

To add the grass at the bottom, fill your brush with the creamy consistency of Payne's Gray and lightly flick it up and down in individual strokes to make blades of grass. Continue this along the page. I wanted lots of coverage across the bottom so I took about four separate passes of these flicking strokes , letting it dry between passes so I wasn't picking up excess pigment. Continue until you're happy with your coverage. Let this dry or make it dry!

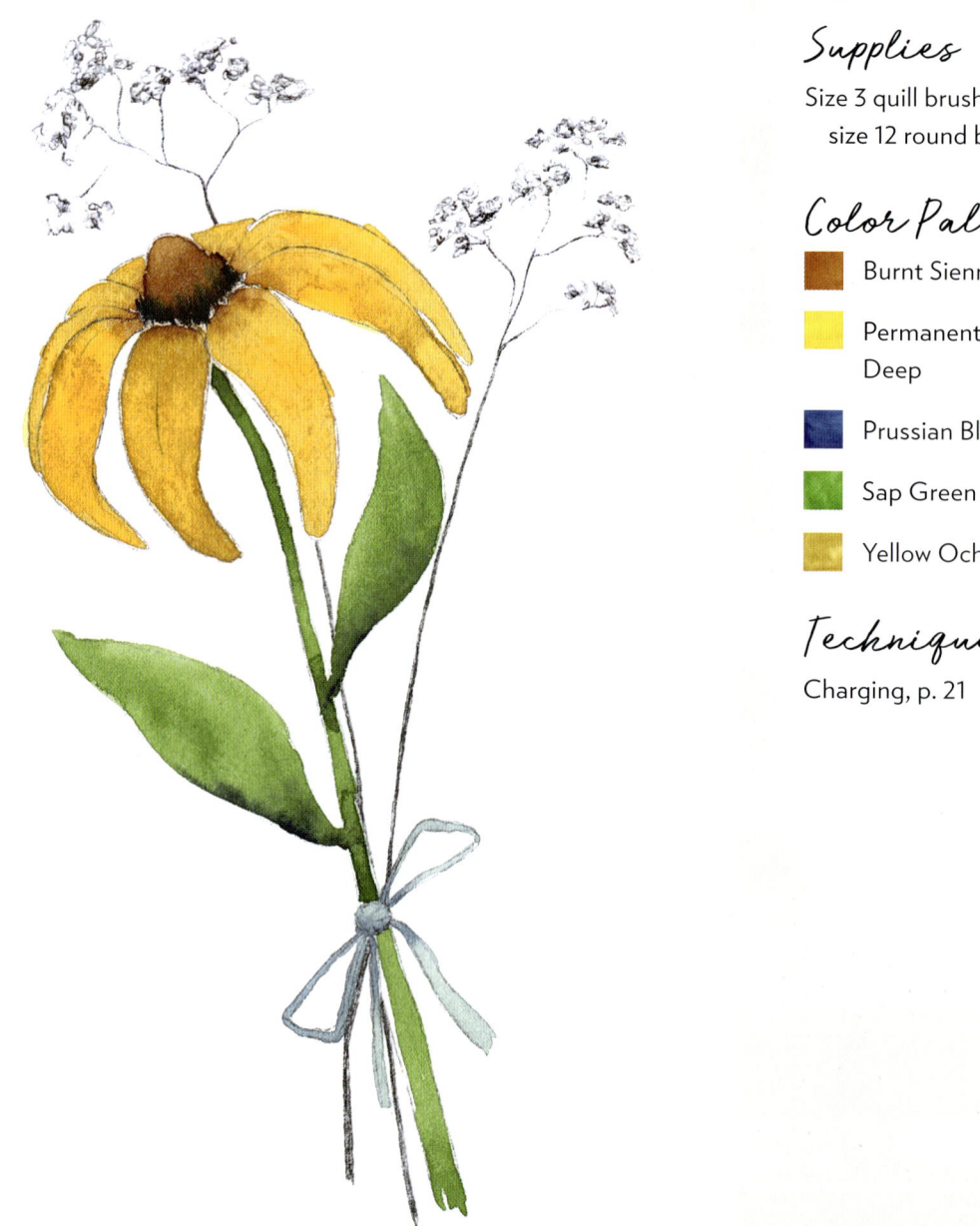

Supplies

Size 3 quill brush or
size 12 round brush

Color Palette

Burnt Sienna

Permanent Yellow
Deep

Prussian Blue

Sap Green

Yellow Ochre

Techniques

Charging, p. 21

END OF SUMMER BOUQUET

The end of summer brings some of my favorite flowers, especially Black-eyed Susans. I love the bright yellow petals, with their interesting centers that really draw the eye. I often pick them for bouquets, to bring a little summer joy inside!

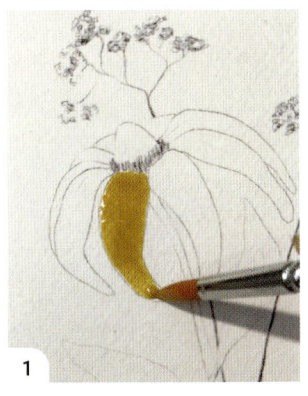

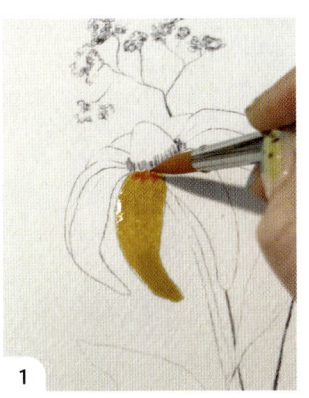

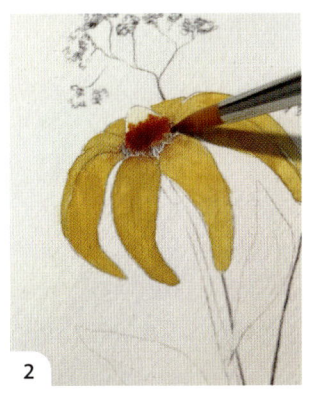

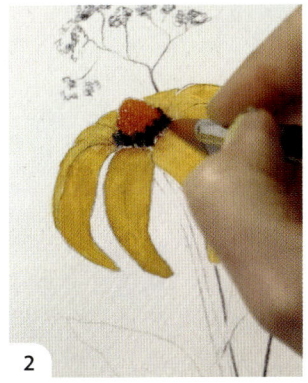

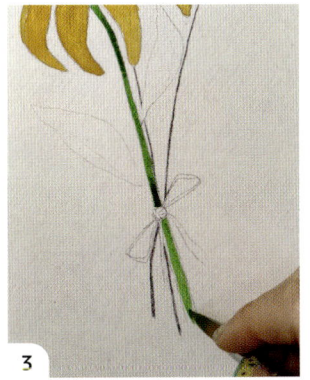

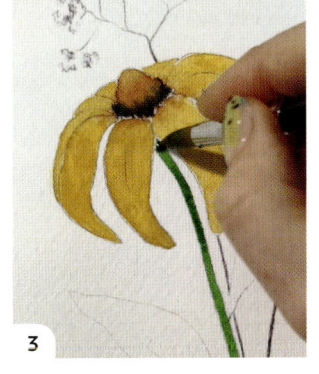

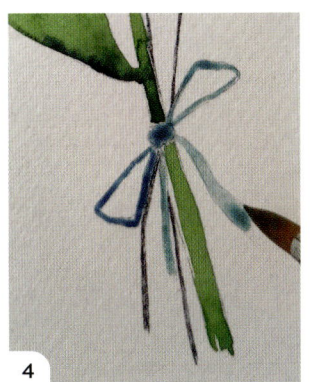

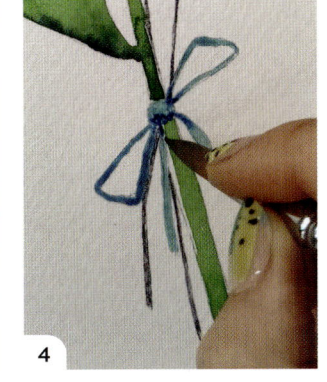

STEP 1

Mix Yellow Ochre to about 50% saturation. Starting with the petals at the front of the flower, paint each of these to about a Gloss wetness. In the middle of the petal drop a concentrated amount of Permanent Yellow Deep. You might not see a big difference while it's wet, but it will add vibrancy once it's dry. Place a little Burnt Sienna in the tip of your brush and dot it where the petal meets the center—you are charging one color into the next. Repeat this step for each of the petals on the front and back of the flower. Let this dry or make it dry!

STEP 2

Once dry, wet just the tip of the center cone. Paint Burnt Sienna across the bottom of the cone, allowing the water and color to bleed together. Wait for this to get to the Satin or Damp stage of wetness and then dip just the very tip of your brush into some creamy textured Prussian Blue. Using up and down strokes, place some of the Prussian Blue across the bottom of the cone to create the additional texture and a bit of shadow.

STEP 3

Mix Sap Green to a 70% saturation and paint the stem and leaves. While it's still wet, at about the Satin or Gloss stage, fill your brush with Prussian Blue at about a 40% saturation and place a drop right at the top of the stem under the petals for a little shading. Drop a little shadow at the bottom of the leaves and where they attach to the stem. Let it dry, or make it dry!

STEP 4

Fill your brush with Prussian Blue at a 20% saturation and paint the bow. Allow this to get to a Satin level of wetness and then fill the tip of your brush with a more concentrated Prussian Blue and drop it in where the parts of the ribbon overlap to create a bit of shadow using charging.

A WHALE OF A TIME

There's something peaceful and yet mysterious about whales. I love the fact that even though we have studied them extensively, they have a bit of a secret life in the ocean depths that we'll never truly understand.

In this painting, we're exploring making fun textures with a kitchen staple, salt. Your results will vary depending on the size of salt grain you use, so this one might be fun to do a few different times with different salts to see what you like best.

Supplies

Size 3 quill brush or
     size 12 round brush
Salt

Color Palette

Payne's Gray

Phthalo Blue

Prussian Blue

Quinacridone Magenta

Sap Green

Color Mixing

TEAL: 50% Phthalo Blue and 50% Sap Green at 70% saturation

DEEP PURPLE: 50% Prussian Blue and 50% Quinacridone Magenta at 50% saturation

Techniques

Charging, p. 21
Salt, p. 25

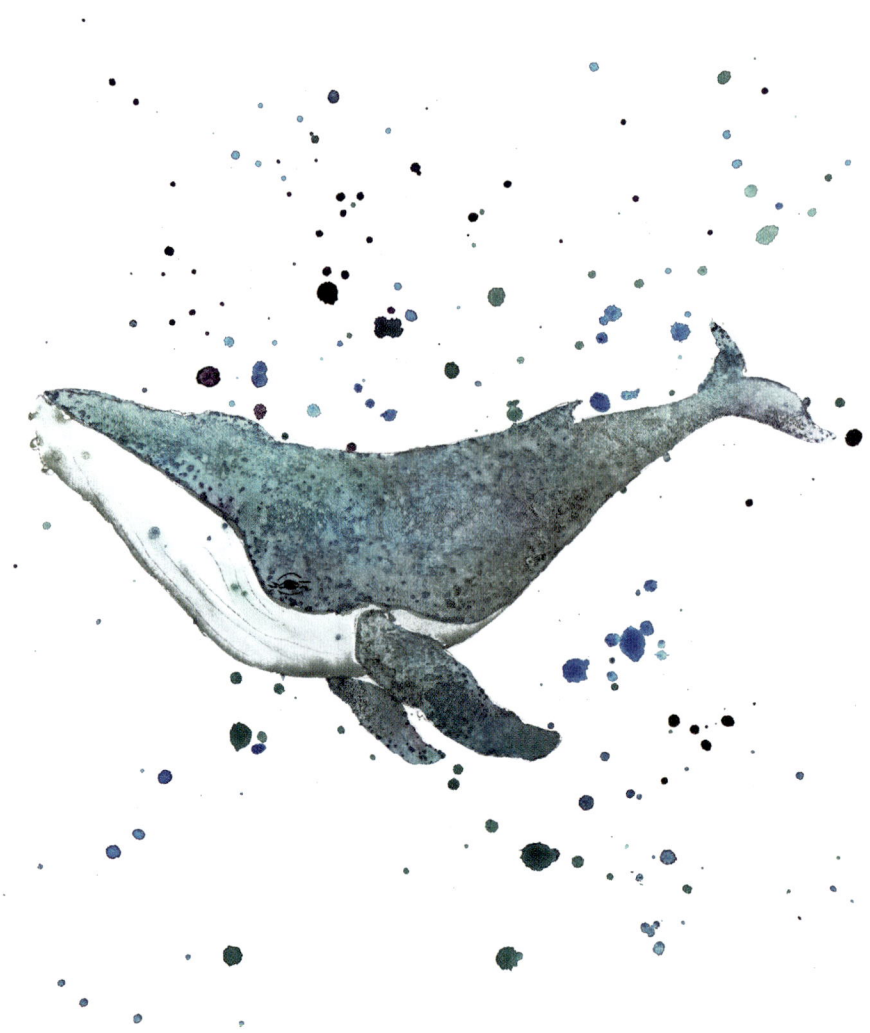

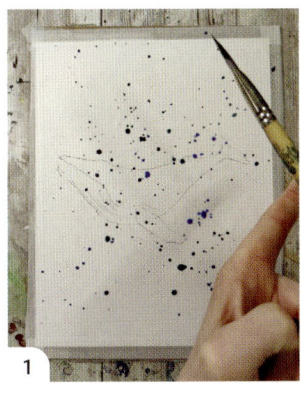

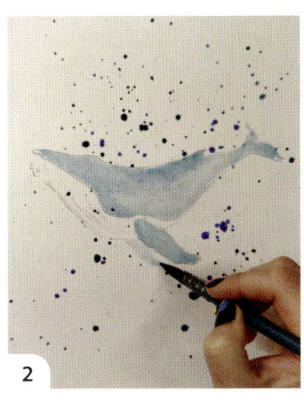

STEP 1

Mix up a watery mixture of the Phthalo Blue, another of the Prussian Blue, and then the two custom colors. Fill your brush with any of the colors and then splatter it on the page by hitting the handle of your brush against your finger.

STEP 2

While the splatters are still wet, fill your brush with clean water and brush it over the top of the whale and the fins, leaving the belly white. The water will combine with the splattered colors and give you a nice base coat.

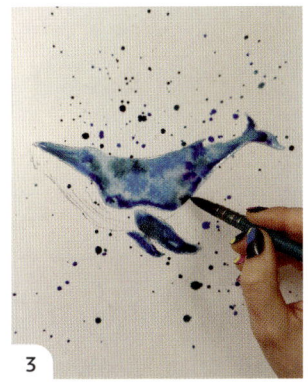

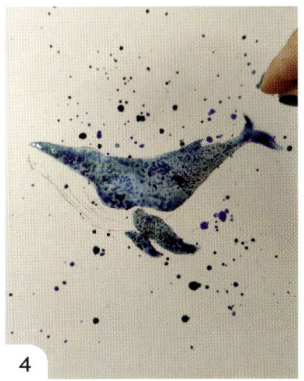

STEP 3

Drop some watery Prussian Blue, Phthalo Blue, and the custom Teal and Deep Purple mixtures into the body and fins. Err on the side of too much water and color.

STEP 4

While the colors are still wet, sprinkle salt generously on the whale where you want the texture. Notice how the pigment clusters around the salt. You can also add a bit of Payne's Gray along the bottom of the whale to add shadow. Let it dry or make it dry!

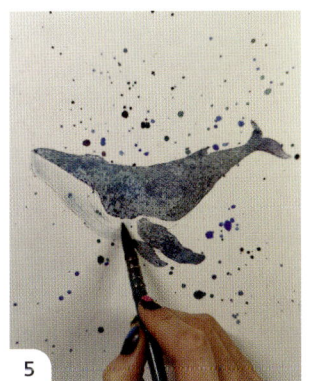

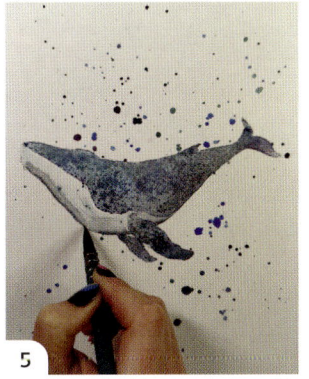

STEP 5

Once the top of the whale is dry, wet the belly with water and paint a light wash of very desaturated Phthalo Blue. Drop some Payne's Gray along the bottom and any of the lines you want to emphasize. Let this dry or make it dry!

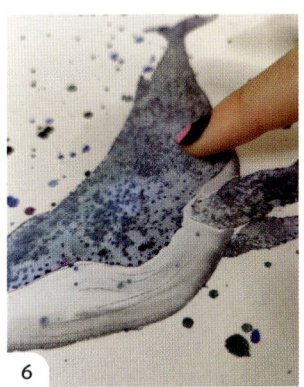

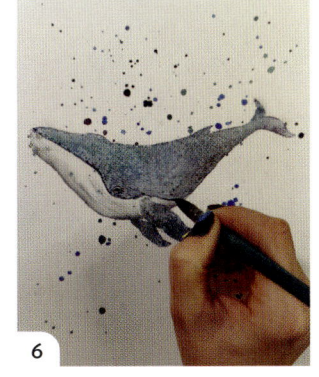

STEP 6

When fully dry, remove the salt using a clean finger or a brush with sturdy bristles. Some salt will remain, so just focus on the big chunks. Then, take a clean damp brush and wipe it off so there's barely any water left in it, and dip the tip in some concentrated Payne's Gray. Then use the tip of your brush to paint in the eye details and add a thin line along the line between the belly and body.

EVERYTHING'S PEACHY

To me, there's nothing better in the late summer than the juicy first bite of a ripe peach. I often get a flat and eat the whole thing by myself in a few days. For this painting we'll be using the charging technique for a burst of color and shading. You may have noticed that the colors I used for this include pink, but there is not really any pink in this painting—by using the charging technique we'll be creating a custom reddish mixture right on the page.

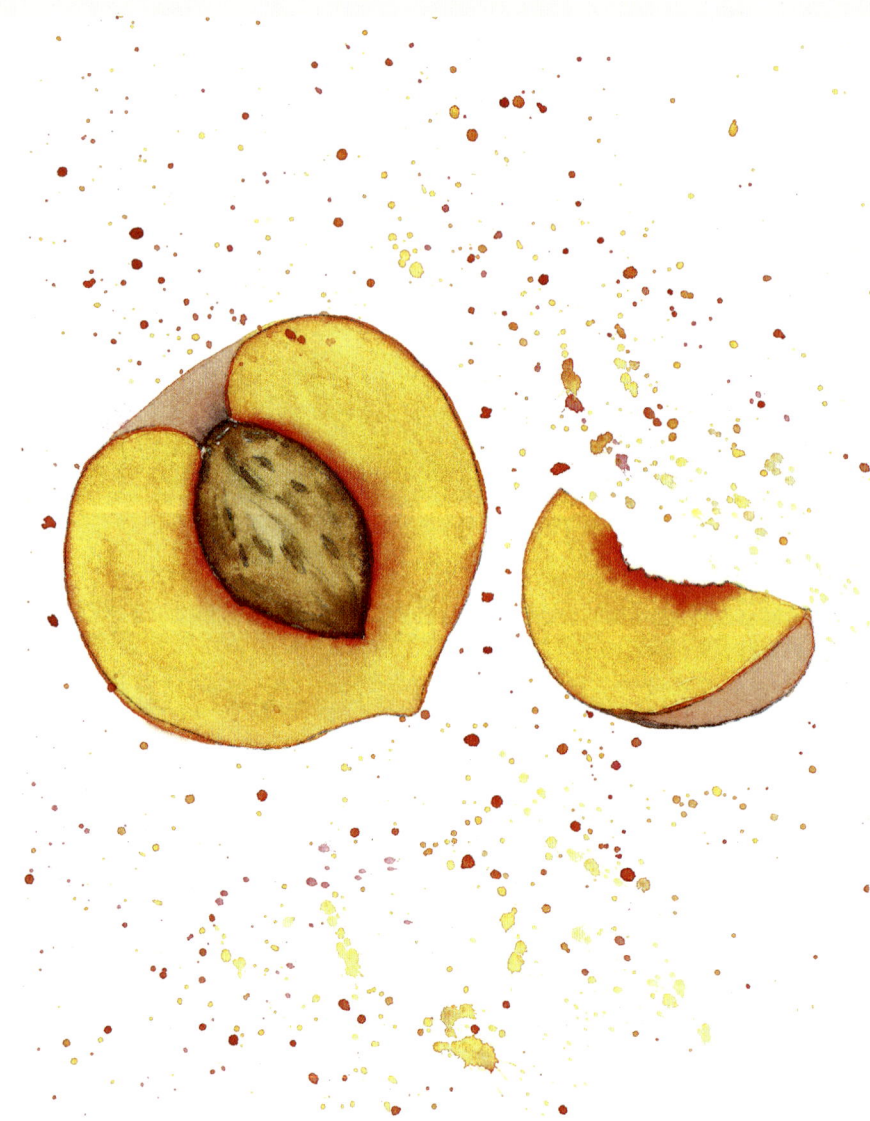

Supplies

Size 12 round brush
Paper towel

Color Palette

Permanent Yellow Deep

Burnt Sienna

Quinacridone Magenta

Prussian Blue

Color Mixing

PEACHY: 50% Permanent Yellow Deep and 50% Quinacridone Magenta at 30% saturation

SHADOW PURPLE: 50% Quinacridone Magenta and Prussian Blue at 50% saturation

DARK BROWN: 75% Burnt Sienna and 25% Prussian Blue at 90% saturation

Techniques

Charging, p. 21
Wet-on-Wet, p. 15

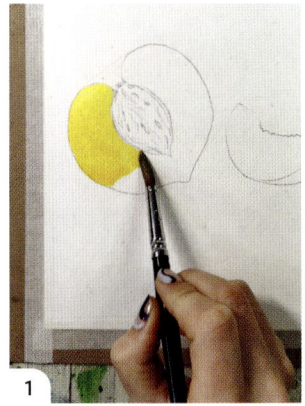
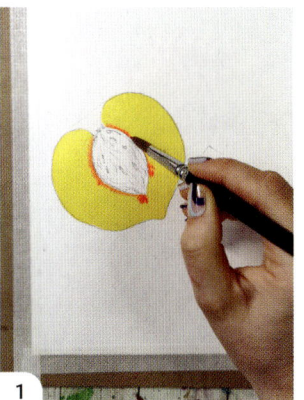
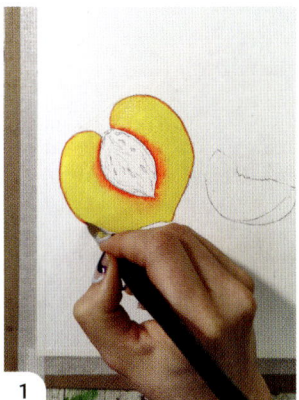
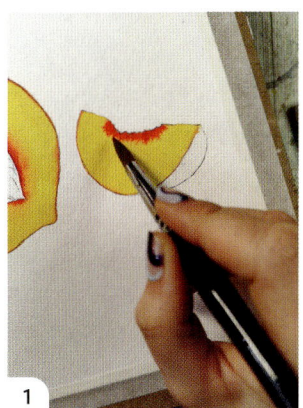

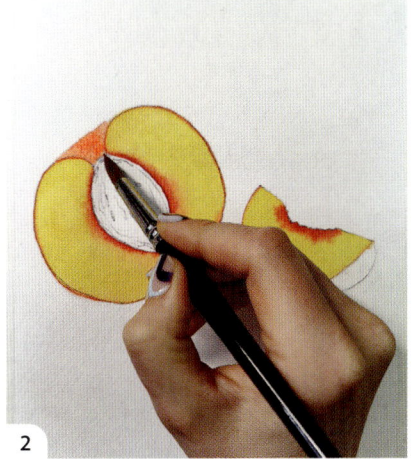
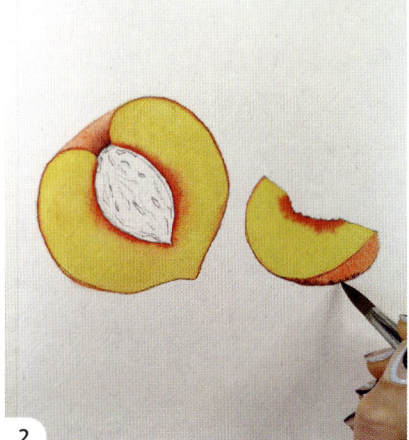
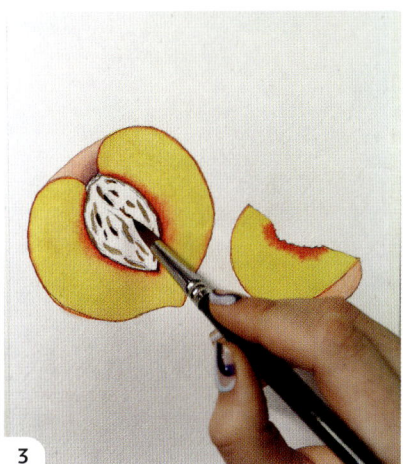

STEP 1

For the interior pulp of the peach, paint an even layer of Permanent Yellow Deep at a Satin wetness level. Grab a tiny bit of Quinacridone Magenta at the creamy texture on the tip of the brush and add it along the pit outline, allowing it to mix and bleed softly out—you are charging the pink into the yellow. It might take a couple layers of pink dropped in lightly to achieve the color and bleed you want. Once the inside is painted, the rest should be applied a little drier, more towards Damp stage with a bit of the creamy consistency Quinacridone Magenta. Lightly swipe along the outer rim of the pulp to create the skin color and let it softly bleed in. Repeat these steps on the little slice. Let sit for a minute or two to blend and then let this layer dry or make it dry!

STEP 2

Paint the custom Peachy color on the middle part of the peach skin that is visible. While it's still wet, add a little of the custom Shadow Purple color, dropping it in right along the top of the pit. This is going to create a little shadowing to show it's sunken in. Repeat these same steps for the skin on the slice and drop the shadow color lightly along the bottom.

STEP 3

Fill in a few of the textured spots on the pit with the custom Dark Brown. You can go over all the lines or fill in only some of them; we're just using this as a layer to give a little texture, so it doesn't have to be perfect. Let this layer dry or make it dry!

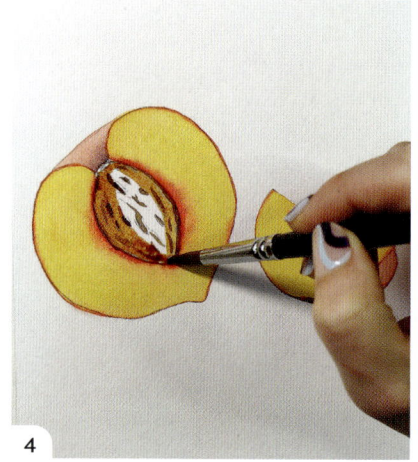 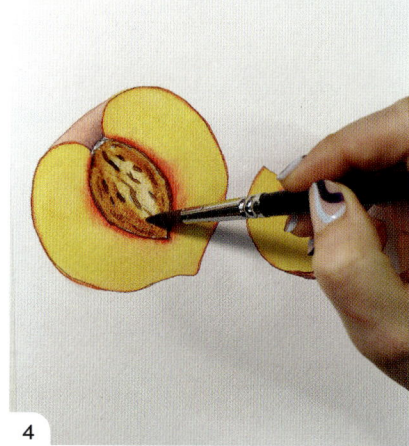 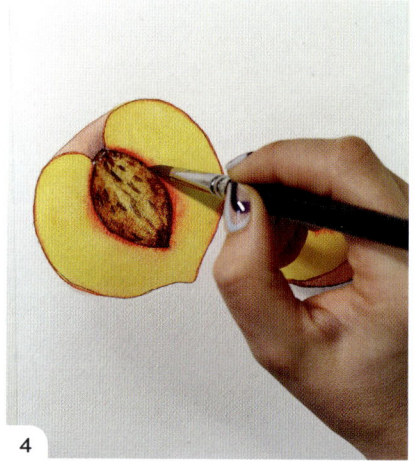

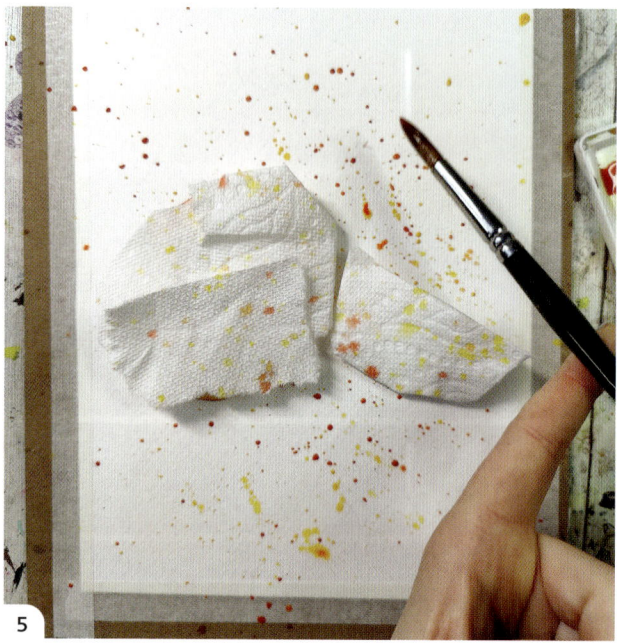 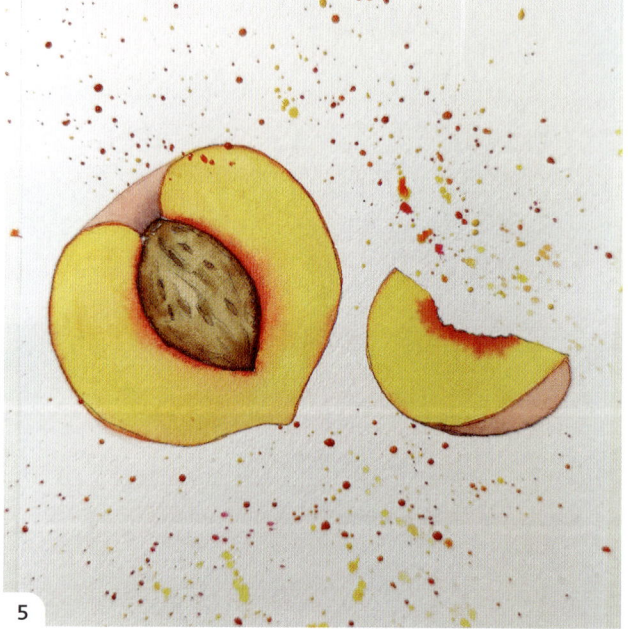

STEP 4

Once the previous layer is dry, pick up some Burnt Sienna at about 50–75% saturation and place this around the outside of the pit. Wash your brush and fill in the middle of the pit. The middle of the pit will be lighter in color, which creates a 3D effect. While it's still wet take some of the very concentrated custom Dark Brown mixture and drop it along the edges. Let this dry or make it dry!

STEP 5

You can stop at step 4, or if you want to add a little more color to this page, you can play with paint splatters. To minimize the splatter on the peach, take some paper towels and fold them on top of the peach shapes. Then fill your brush with one color at a time, washing your brush in between, and tap your brush against your finger to make it splatter.

Supplies

Size 3 quill brush or size 12 round brush

Color Palette

- Burnt Sienna
- Permanent Yellow Deep
- Phthalo Blue
- Quinacridone Magenta

Color Mixing

PEONY PINK:
75% Quinacridone Magenta and 25% Permanent Yellow Deep at 40% saturation

LEAFY GREEN:
50% Phthalo Blue and 50% Burnt Sienna at 70% saturation

Techniques

Wet-on-Wet, p. 15

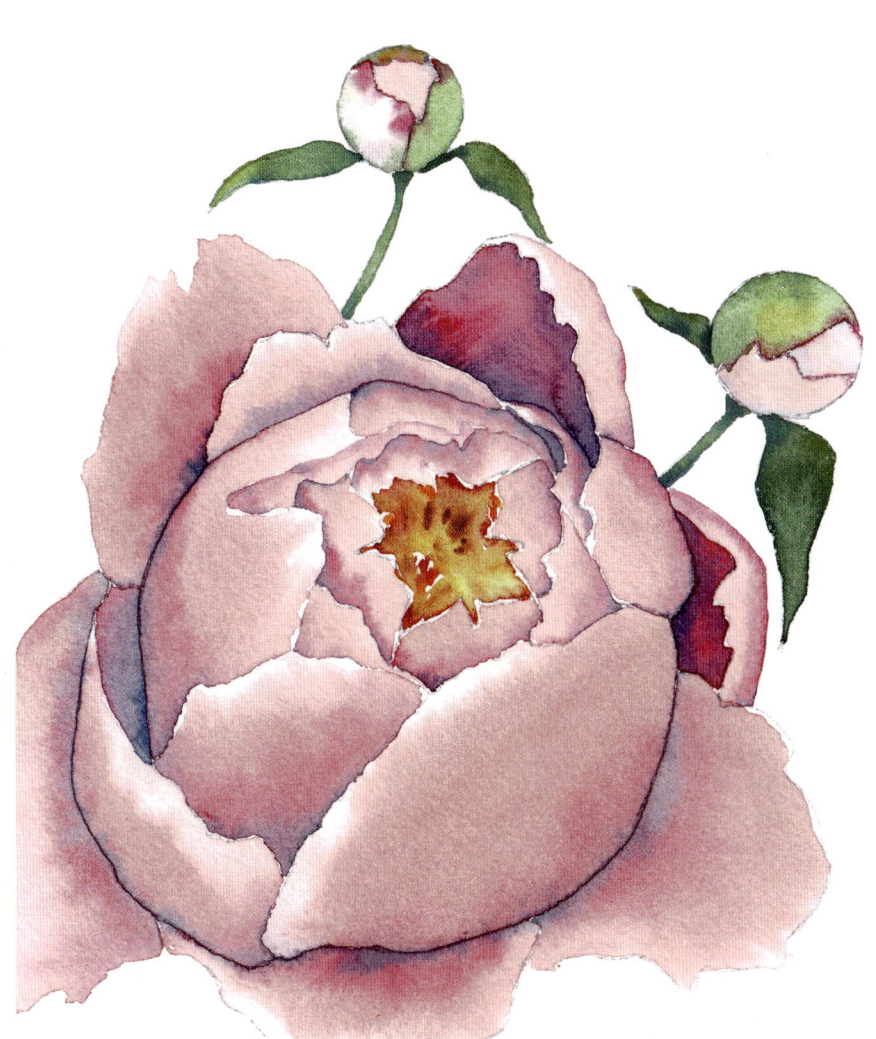

PINING FOR PEONIES

To say that I fell in love with peonies over the past year would be an understatement. There's a flower farm near where I live where you can pick fresh peonies, and I became obsessed. I loved how their scent filled my house and their soft petals just melted my heart. I have now planted so many peony plants and I have high hopes and fingers crossed for spring.

This may look like one of the most complicated paintings in this book, but you might be surprised by how simple it is. It is a bit tedious, however. Don't be discouraged by this, as the methodical painting of each petal results in a big payoff and can give you a real confidence boost.

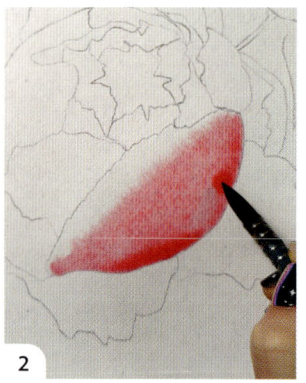

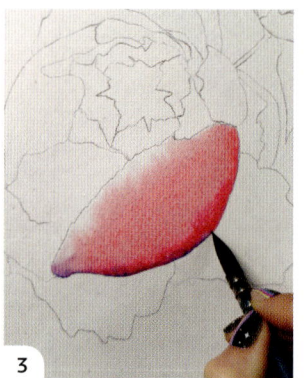

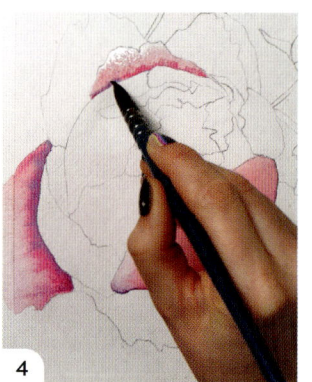

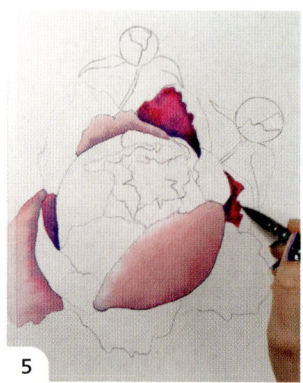

STEP 1

Mix the custom Peony Pink and Leafy Green. I used the muffin tin mixing wells and I mixed enough of the pink to fill the cup about halfway full—you don't want to run out. For the Leafy Green, Phthalo Blue leans towards green and Burnt Sienna has a bit of a yellow undertone, so when you combine them it makes a lovely rich green color.

STEP 2

This is the step you'll be doing over and over again, so get ready. First, some terms to help you follow along: when I refer to the "top" of a petal I mean the outer edge of the petal, the one not connected to the base of the flower. When I refer to the "bottom" I mean the part that connects to the main flower head, or any other overlapping area. Starting with a clean brush filled with water, wet the top of the petal until it's at about the Gloss or Satin stage. Then fill your brush with the custom Peony Pink color and paint in the rest of the petal, touching your brush to the wet area and allowing the paint to soften on its own. This will help to create a shadow. Make sure you fill this with enough paint for it to be at the Gloss or Satin stage of wetness.

STEP 3

Dry your brush, get a creamy consistency of Quinacridone Magenta in the tip of your brush, and drag it along the bottom of the petal, depositing that color

and letting it bleed into the softer pink. It might not look like a lot right now, but this subtle effect really helps once dry. Then before this dries any more, dip the tip of your brush into some saturated Phthalo Blue and tap your brush on a paper towel. Again, run your brush along the bottom edge of the petal, depositing that color.

STEP 4

Repeat that same step for a couple more of the petals that are not touching. Remember that the "top" and "bottom" will be relative to where the petal is located in relation to the center of the flower. Notice that for the petal to the left, the "bottom" where it attaches to the main flower head is actually on the right. After you've filled in a few, let this dry or make it dry!

STEP 5

We're going to be treating the rest of the petals as described in steps 2 and 3, with a couple exceptions. There are a few of these petals that cup over, and we can see both the outer part and the inner part of the petal. We want the inner parts to recess and appear to be more in shadow. Grab some fairly concentrated Quinacridone Magenta in your brush and paint the entire inside of the petal. Then put some concentrated Phthalo Blue in your brush and drop it in along the bottom and along the top where the petal is hanging over. Let this dry or make it dry!

STEP 6

Continue painting the petals as described in steps 2 and 3. I like to work in batches of two or three petals that are not touching each other. In order to keep each petal distinctly separate, you want to make sure you always dry it before starting on one directly next to it. This is the part that gets a bit tedious, but it's exciting to watch the petals come to life.

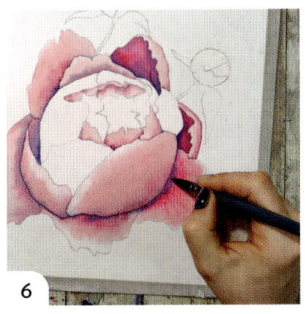
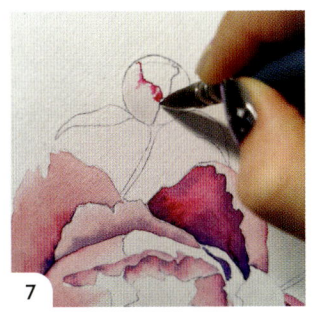
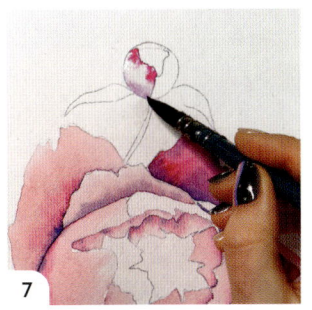
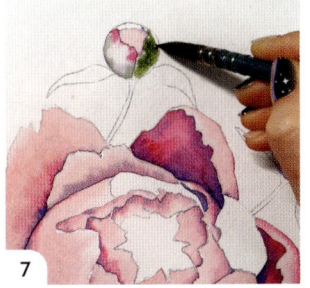
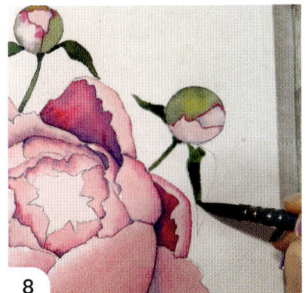
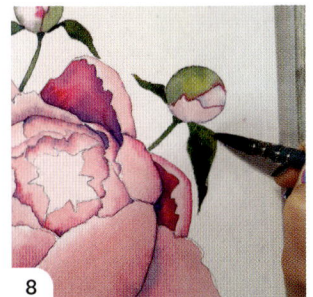
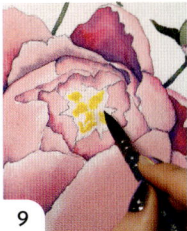
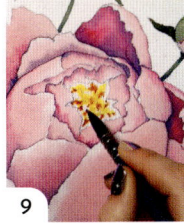
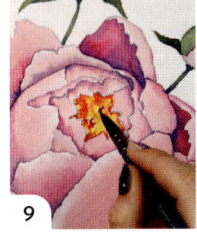

STEP 7

Once you have completed the petals of the main flower, it's time to paint the buds. On real peonies the buds often have soft pinks, vibrant pink, and even greens, so you can go with the flow of those colors or follow along with me. Starting with the first bud section on the left, pre-wet the area with water, then drop really concentrated Quinacridone Magenta along the inner edge. Then drop a little Phthalo Blue on the outer and bottom edges of the bud to give dimension. Fill the center of the bud with Peony Pink. On the next petal add in concentrated Leafy Green, and along the edge drop concentrated Quinacridone Magenta. For each segment on the bud, I dropped a tiny amount of Phthalo Blue near the base to give it a little shadow. Keep working back and forth until you've filled all the bud segments. Let this dry or make it dry!

STEP 8

Fill your brush with the custom Leafy Green and paint both of the leaves on each bud and the stem. While it's still wet, wash your brush and grab some Permanent Yellow Deep and then drop that on the high spots of the leaf. Wash your brush and grab some Phthalo Blue and drop that below the bud, where the stem disappears behind the flower and where each of the leaves meet the bud. Let this dry or make it dry!

STEP 9

For the center of the peony, we're going to allude to those beautiful yellow stamins. Wet the center until it's at Flood or Gloss stage, and then drop in some Permanent Yellow Deep and Burnt Sienna randomly to get some variation. Concentrate more of the Burnt Sienna around the outer rim. Let that flow together a bit. If it's not dark enough, put some Burnt Sienna in your brush and then dip the tip of it into some Phthalo Blue. This will mix as you put it onto the page into a slightly darker color. Add in a couple little lines to allude to the stamens. Let this dry or make it dry and you're done!

AGAVE SUNSET

Over the years keeping succulents has become somewhat of an obsession for me. The moment I realized you could propagate them, my house exploded with a number of plants in each room.

Another thing I love are opposites, and I think this is reflected in this painting in two ways. First there are the opposite colors green and pink, as they are located on opposite sides of the color wheel—in other words, complementary colors. The second opposition is the spikey nature of the plant in contrast to the soft pink background.

Supplies
Size 4 quill brush or size 12 round brush

Color Palette
Permanent Yellow Deep

Prussian Blue

Quinacridone Magenta

Sap Green

Techniques
Color Wheel, p. 26
Wet-on-Wet, p. 15
Washes, p. 18

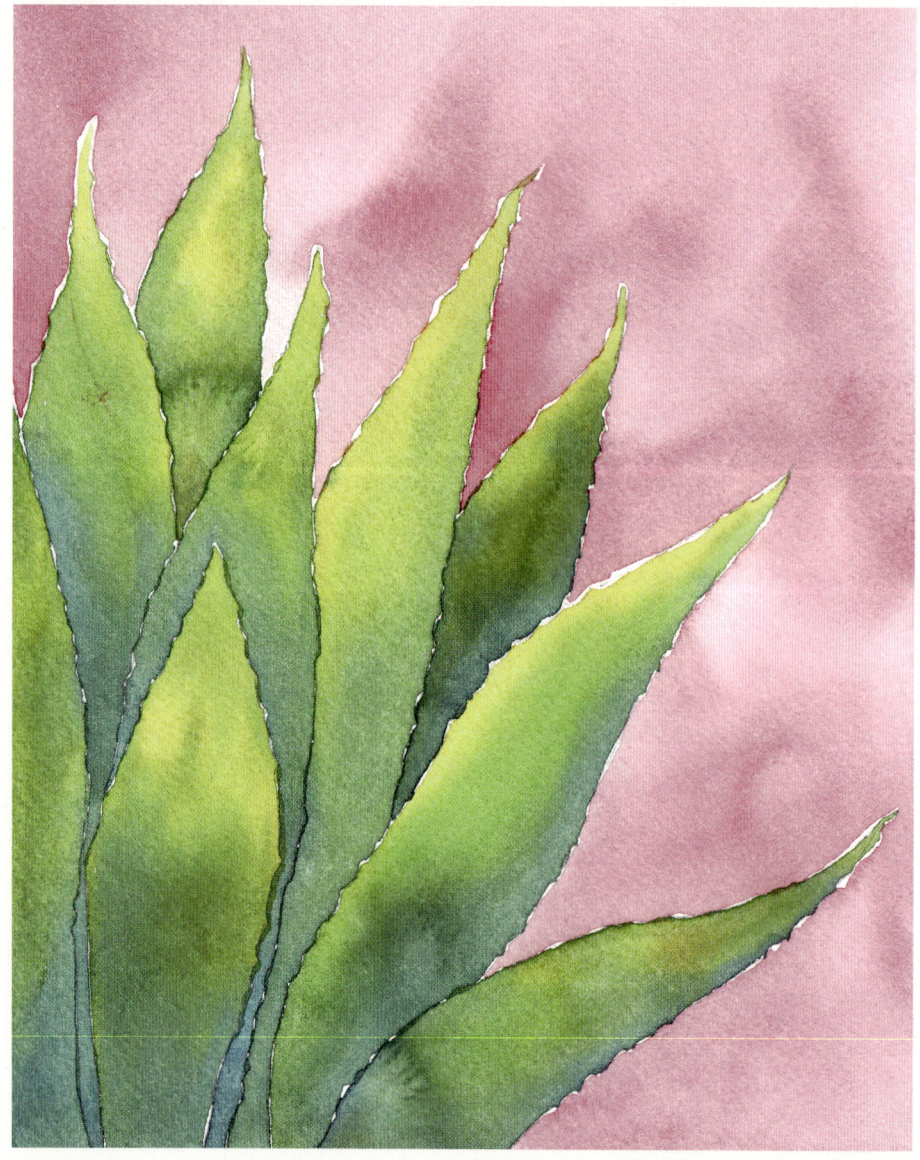

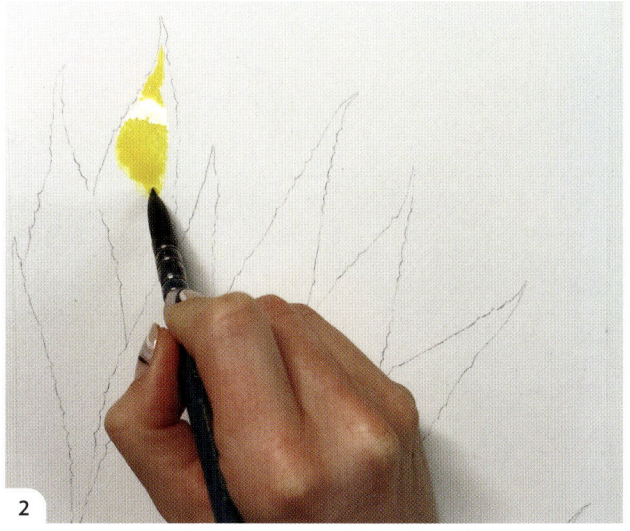

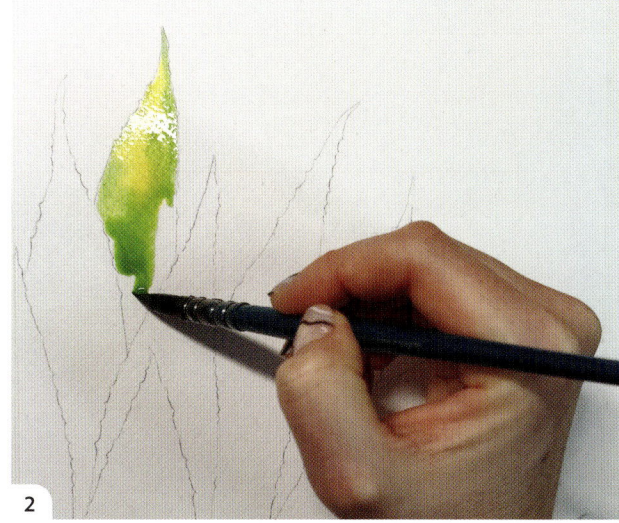

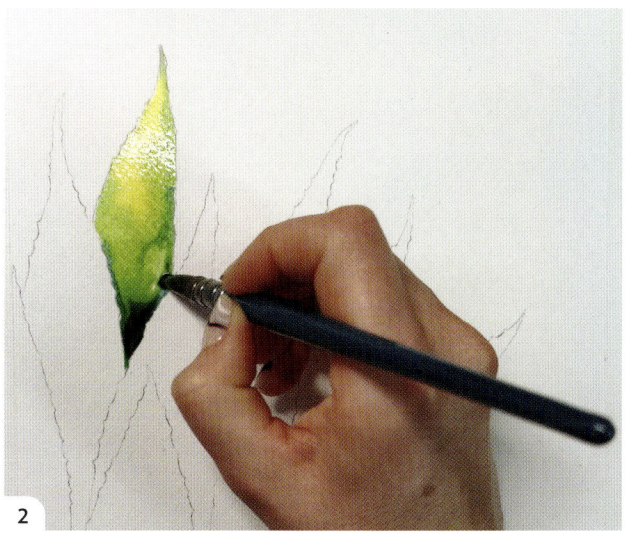

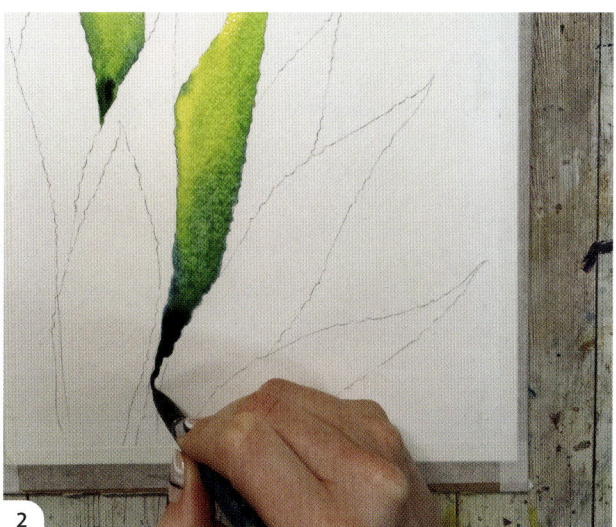

STEP 1

Mix a 40% saturation of Permanent Yellow Deep, Prussian Blue, and Sap Green. We need a lot of the pinks to cover the background, so in one well mix the Quinacridone Magenta at about a 50% saturation and 10% in another well. Tape down your paper.

STEP 2

Starting on any of the agave segments, fill your brush with the Permanent Yellow Deep mixture and concentrate that near the tip. Without washing your brush, grab some of the Sap Green and fill in any areas near the top that the yellow didn't fill, plus about half of the middle and sides. Without washing your brush, grab some of the Prussian Blue and place that along any of the overlapping edges as well as the bottom of the segment. You want to work quickly and with lots of water and color in your brush so it stays nice and wet as you do this. If you have water pooling, dry your brush and then tap it on the puddle to suck up the extra water. Repeat this step on a few of the other segments that do not touch any of the ones you've painted. Let this dry or make it dry!

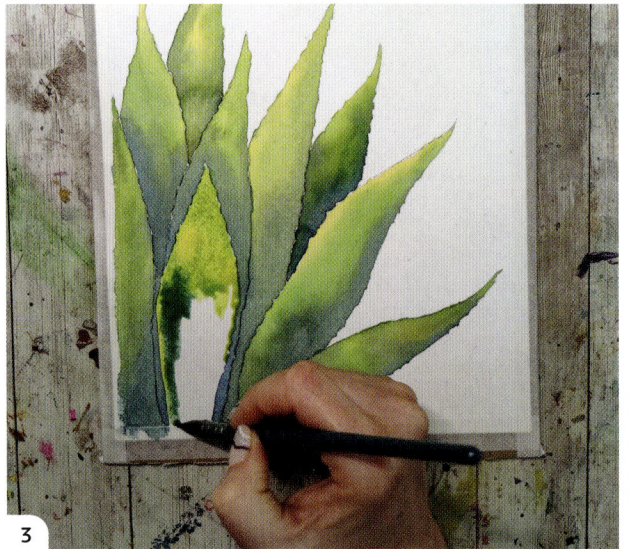

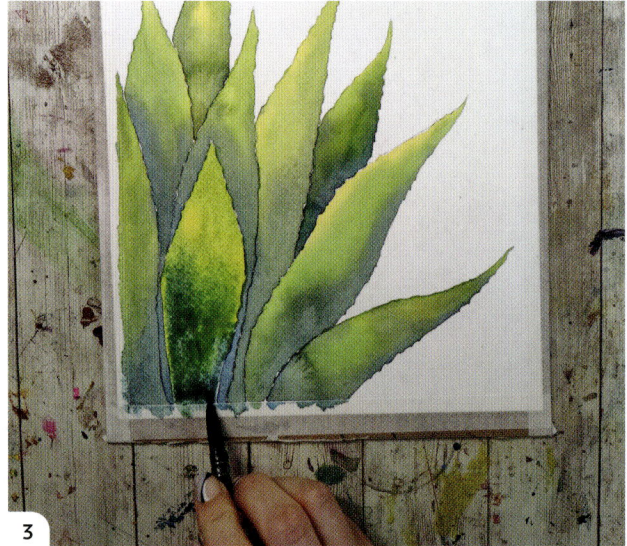

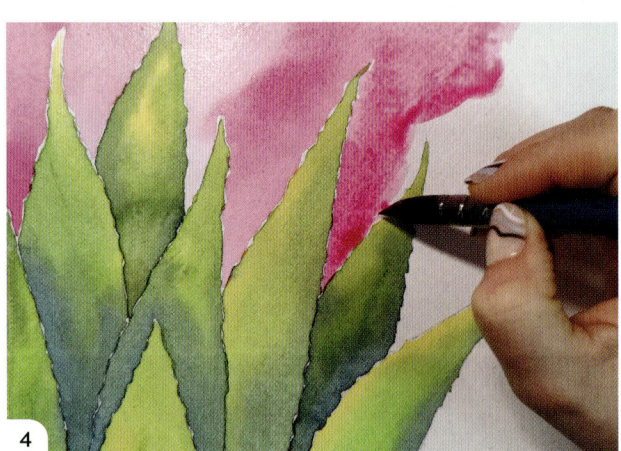

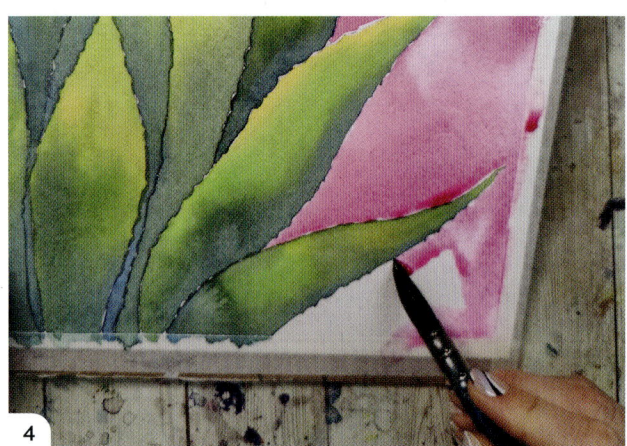

STEP 3

Repeat step 2 for each segment of the agave plant, ensuring that segments that touch are dry before you start painting. The placement of these colors doesn't need to be precise. In general, concentrate lighter colors near the top and darker colors near the bottom, or where they disappear behind another segment. Repeat these steps of filling in and drying until you've painted all the segments. Then let this dry or make it dry!

STEP 4

For the background we are creating a variegated wash—this creates some nice life and depth, and hides lines. To start, fill your brush with the 50% saturation of Quinacridone Magenta and begin painting around a segment of the plant. As you start to run out of color in your brush, dip your brush into the 10% saturation instead of the 50% and continue painting, refilling your brush in the lighter saturation, until you can see that the color has gotten noticeably lighter. Then start dipping into the 50% mix and begin the process again. Continue this until you have painted all the way around the plant. Let this dry or make it dry!

Supplies

Size 3 quill brush or
size 12 round brush

Color Palette

- Burnt Sienna
- Payne's Gray
- Permanent Yellow Deep
- Prussian Blue
- Quinacridone Magenta

Color Mixing

RED: 50% Permanent Yellow Deep and 50% Quinacridone Magenta at 40% saturation

Techniques

Charging, p. 21
Wet-on-Wet, p. 15

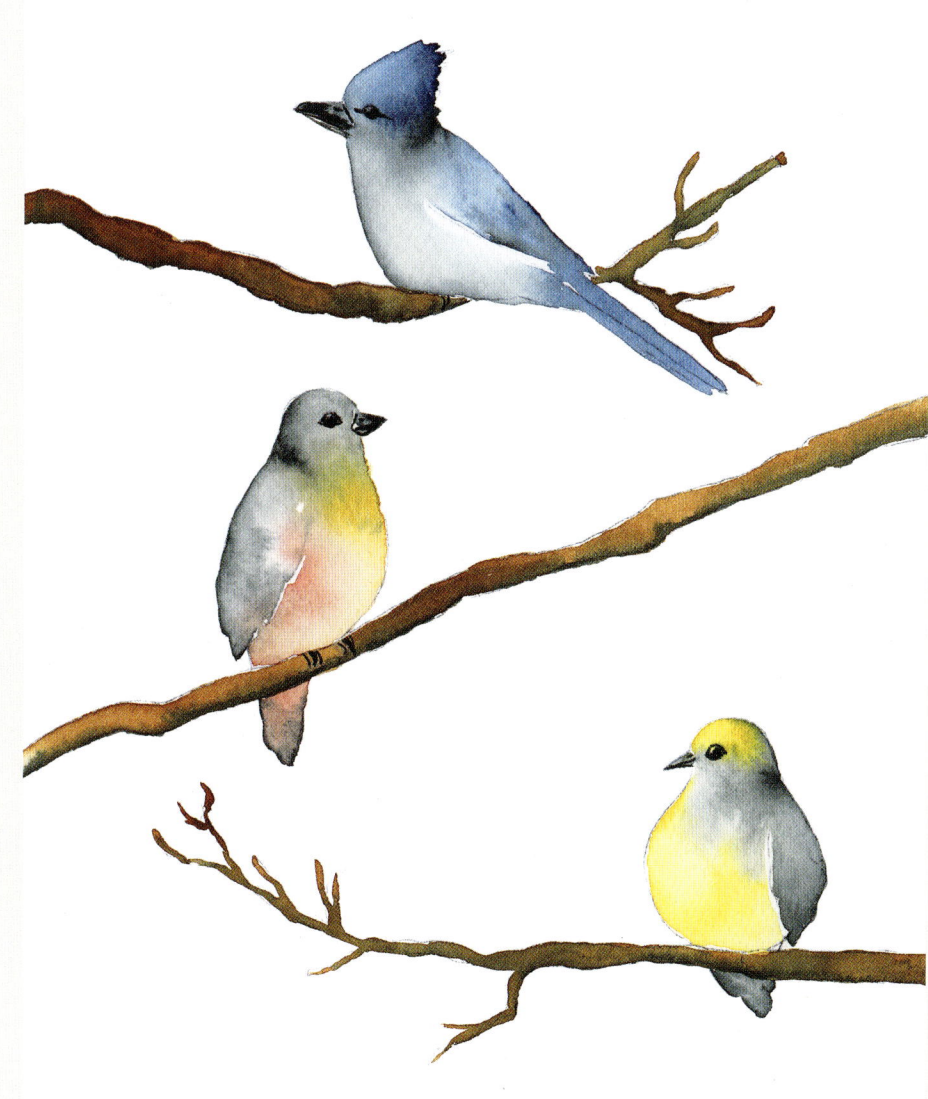

BIRDS OF A FEATHER

The older I get the more I enjoy watching the birds around me. I've even been known to carry some binoculars, just in case I see a particularly interesting bird. This newfound love of birds has collided with my love of watercolor—birds are so fun and easy to paint, you can just drop in a few colors and let them bleed together. There are so many different types of birds that you can really use your imagination with your color choices and placements—here I've painted a blue jay at the top and two imaginary birds below.

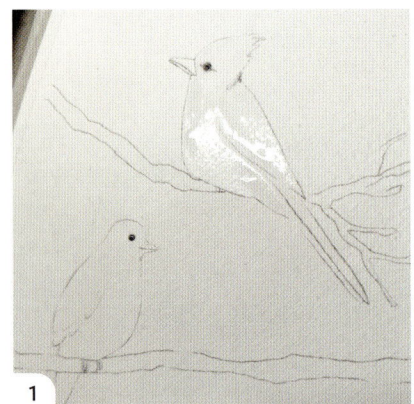

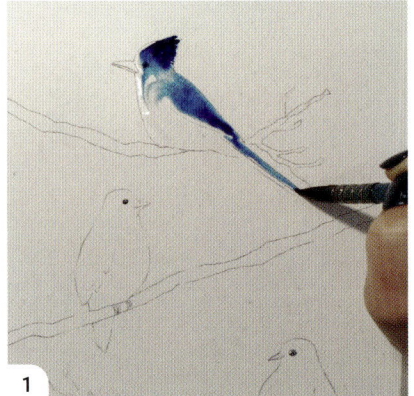

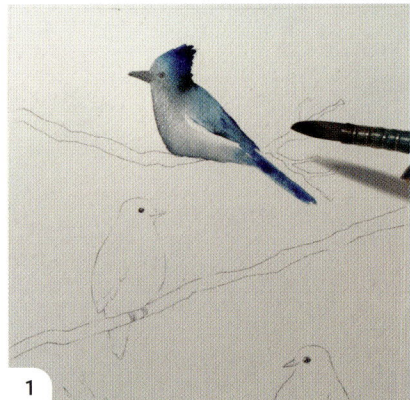

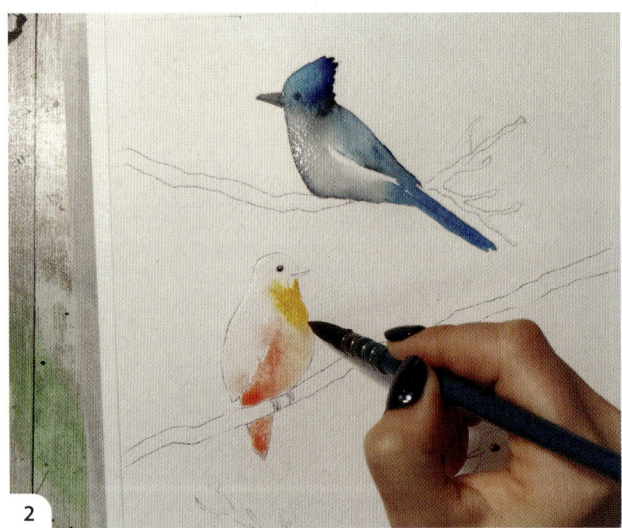

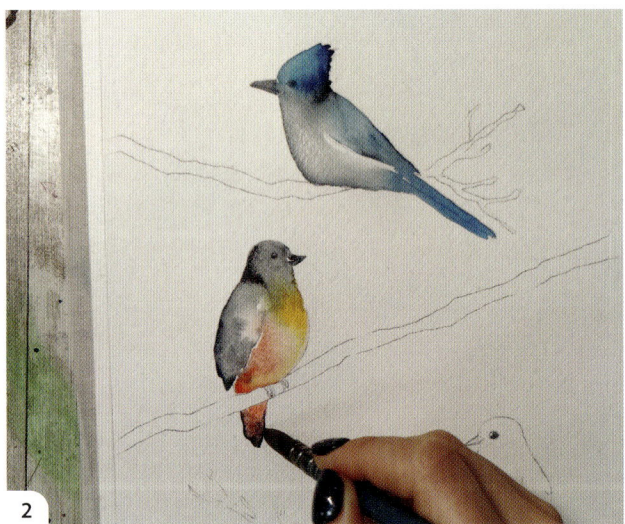

STEP 1

Start with the blue jay and wet the head, body, and tail with clean water at the Gloss or Satin stage, but leave a little gap of dry paper right under the wing. Then take Prussian Blue at a creamy consistency and drop it in at the top of the head, the base of the wing, and along the tail. Allow this to bleed into the rest of the wet area a bit. While you're waiting for the colors to move on the wet paper, fill the tip of your brush with a little Payne's Gray at a creamy consistency and drop this at the back of the neck. Then fill your brush with a little more water to dilute the Payne's Gray in your brush and place that in the beak and along the chest and belly. If too much flows in, dry your brush and lift out a little from the round part of the belly.

STEP 2

To paint the remaining birds, you can choose to use whatever colors you like; these are your fantasy birds. Wet the entire middle bird to the Gloss or Satin stage except a little line under the wing, leaving that area dry. I concentrated some of the custom Red and Permanent Yellow Deep on the belly and tail, letting that flow together while putting some creamy texture of Payne's Gray on my brush and concentrating that again on the neck, tip of tail, and wing. Place a little more water in the brush to dilute the Payne's Gray and fill it in a bit more on the beak, head, and wing.

STEP 3

I repeated similar steps for the final bird, wetting it with water then concentrating Payne's Gray on the tail and wing and Permanent Yellow Deep on the head and belly. Let this dry or make it dry!

STEP 4

For the branches, fill your brush with a watery Burnt Sienna at about 50% saturation and paint the entire branch. While it's still wet (around the Gloss or Satin stage), put a little Payne's Gray in the tip of your brush and lightly touch it along the bottom of the branch. This lets the color bleed into the branch but remain concentrated along the bottom, creating a bit of a shadow. Repeat on all branches and then let this dry or make it dry!

STEP 5

Once everything is dry, fill your brush with a paste consistency of Payne's Gray on just the tip with very little water. Then go over the beak, eyes, and feet of the birds to add in their final details.

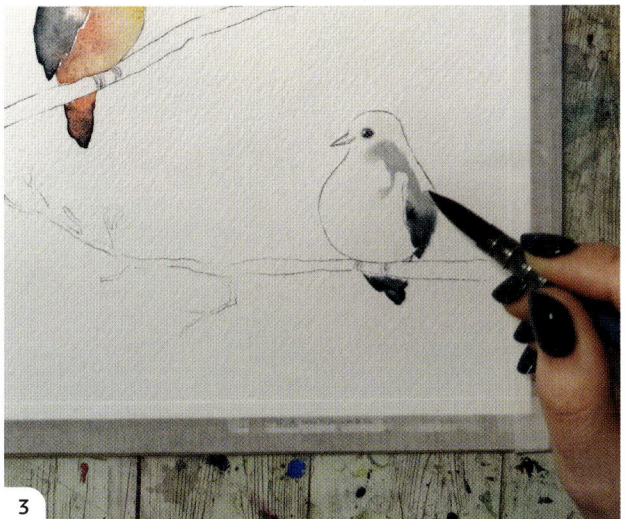

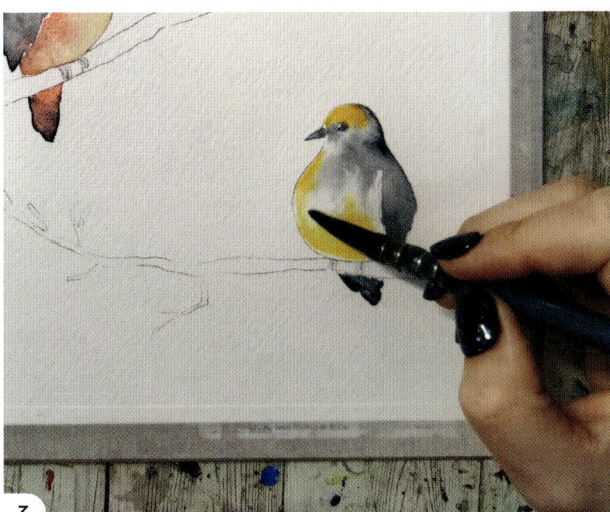

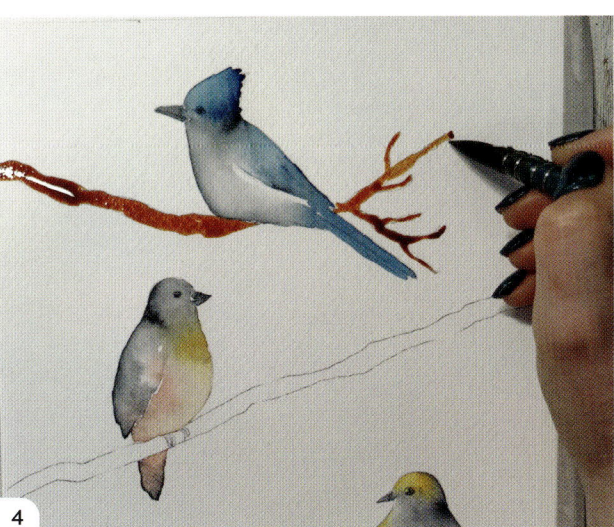

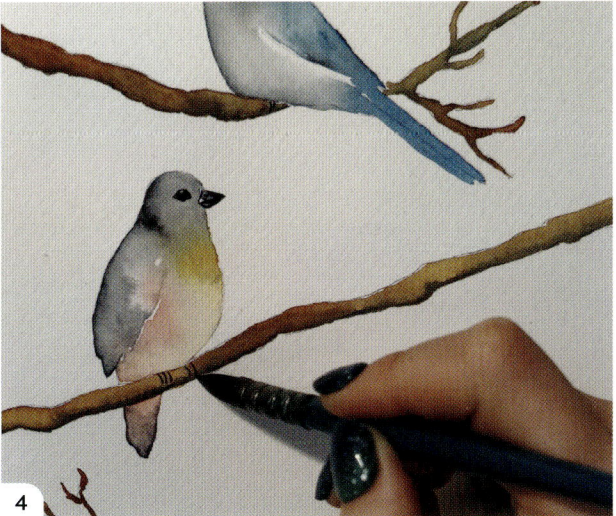

BIRD OF PARADISE

This painting is inspired by a bird of paradise plant I saw in a garden in California while visiting one of my oldest friends, and I think of them every time I see this flower. This painting will help us further explore wet-on-wet and wet-on-dry, and I promise it's easier than it looks.

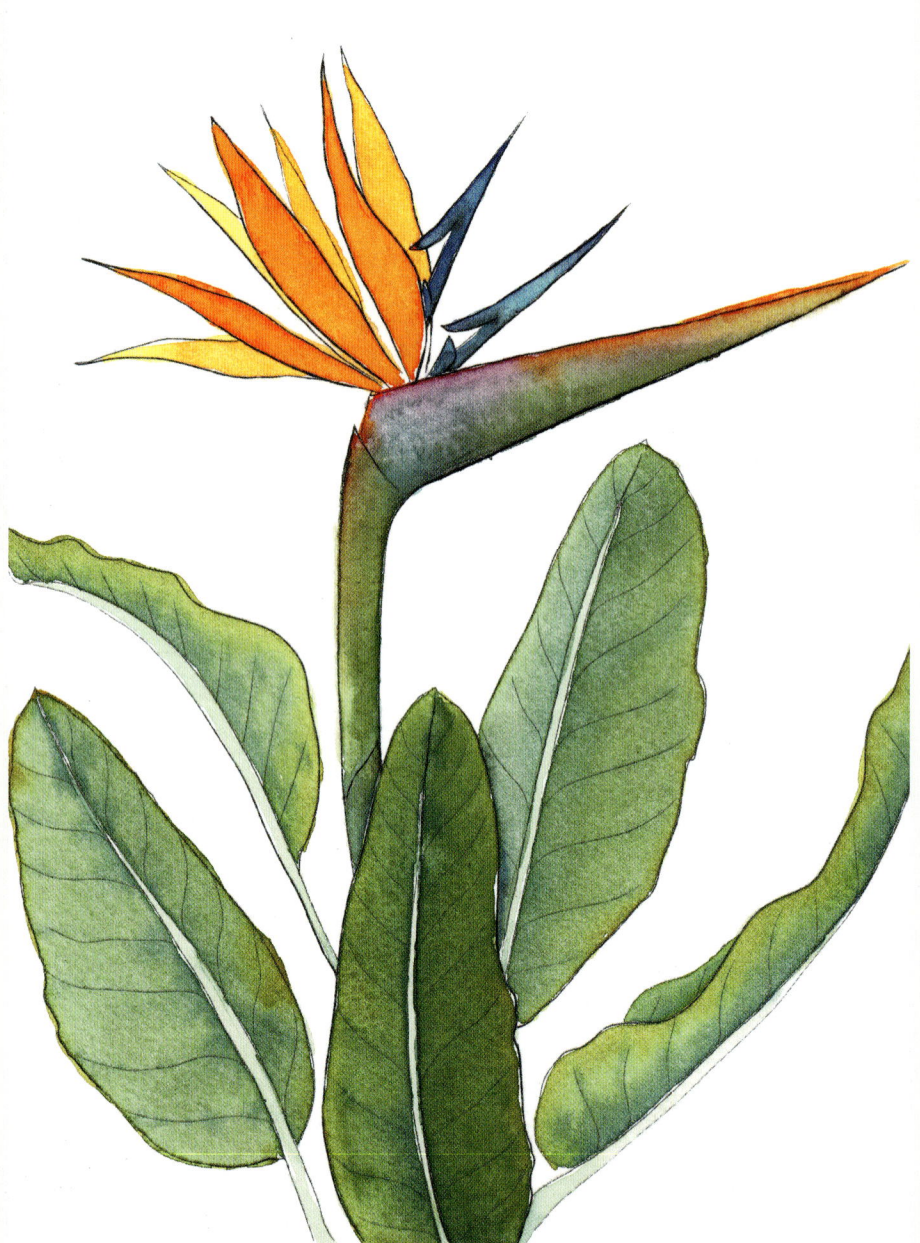

Supplies

Size 3 quill brush or
size 12 round brush

Color Palette

Burnt Sienna

Payne's Gray

Permanent Yellow Deep

Phthalo Blue

Quinacridone Magenta

Sap Green

Vermilion

Color Mixing

YELLOWY ORANGE: 60% Vermilion and 40% Permanent Yellow Deep at 60% saturation

LEAFY GREEN: 60% Sap Green, 20% Phthalo Blue, and 20% Burnt Sienna at 50% saturation

Techniques

Charging, p. 21
Wet-on-Wet, p. 15
Wet-on-Dry, p. 15

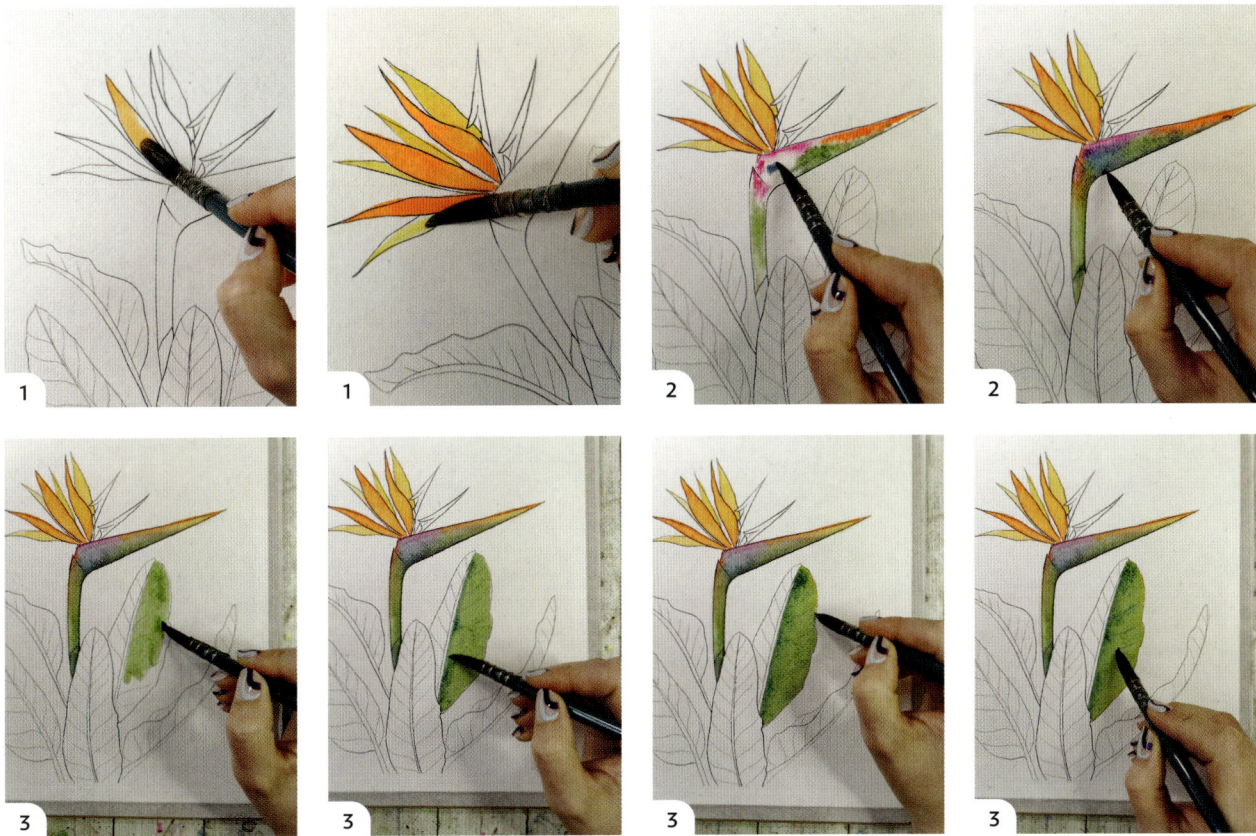

STEP 1

Load your brush with the custom Yellowy Orange color and paint the three sepals in the front wet-on-dry. Fill in the back four sepals with Permanent Yellow Deep with long brushstrokes—don't worry if the paint touches the wet orangey sepals; you want a little bit of bleeding together to occur to give the illusion of catching a bit of light. Let it dry or make it dry!

STEP 2

Fill the beak of the flower (called the spathe) and the stem with clean water to the Gloss or Satin stage. On the upper left side, place a little Quinacridone Magenta, on the point Vermilion, on the bottom and the stem Sap Green, and in the middle Phthalo Blue. Add enough until these colors start to bleed lightly together. If they're not combining, you can take a

clean, damp brush and lightly brush across the colors to encourage them to blend. Take a little Payne's Gray and place it on the bottom of the spathe and right hand side of the stem to create a bit of shading.

STEP 3

For wet-on-wet, you don't have to always pre-wet your paper with just water, you can do this with a color. Use the custom Leafy Green to paint half of the leaf that is the farthest back. The paint should reach a Satin stage of wetness. Then while it's still wet, place a little Phthalo Blue along the center stem, enough so that it starts to bleed into the leaf. On the outside edge, place some of the Permanent Yellow Deep so that it bleeds into the leaf. Once this is mostly dry, drag a light amount of the Phthalo Blue along the veins of the leaves.

STEP 4

Continue with the other side of the leaf, leaving the vein white. For this background leaf to appear as if it's behind the front leaf, add a few extra drops of Phthalo Blue along the left side border with the unpainted leaf to make it seem like it's in shadow.

STEP 5

Paint the remaining leaves except for the front leaf the same way. Once you have the other leaves painted, make sure they are dry before starting the front one. Painting this leaf slightly warmer and brighter will help to bring it to the front. To make the colors a little more vivid, add less water to your color mixtures and add a little Permanent Yellow Deep to the green to warm it up a bit.

STEP 6

Once everything is dry, it's time for finishing touches. Add a supersaturated mixture of Phthalo Blue to the remaining petals. Drop a little bit of Payne's Gray on the underside of these petals to give them more dimension. The final step is optional; you can leave the center stems white as they are or add a lot of water to your custom Leafy Green color and lightly brush that on the center stems.

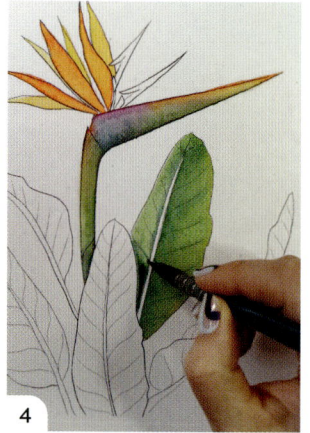
4

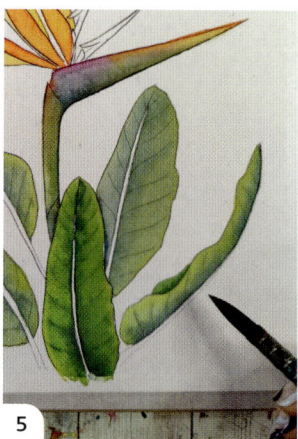
5

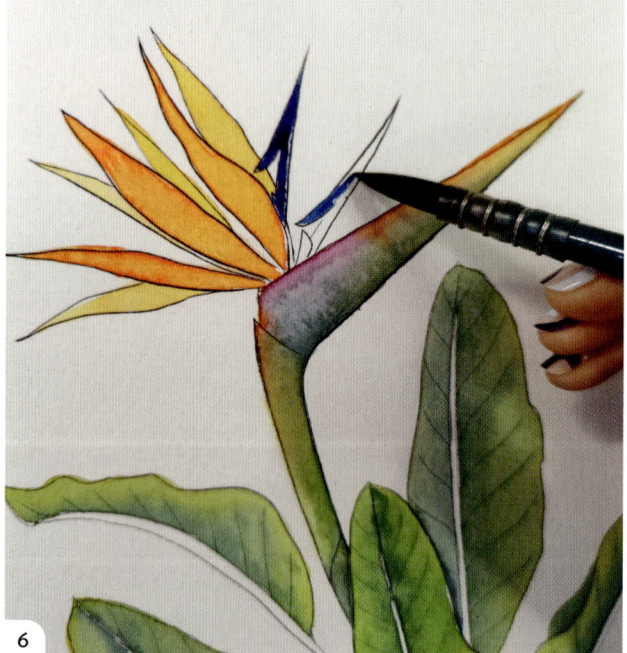
6

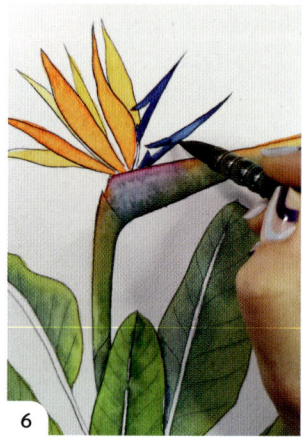
6

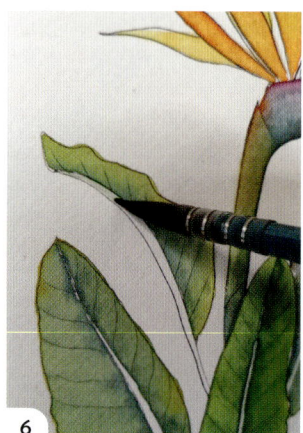
6

ANY SEASON WREATH

Supplies

Size 3 quill brush or size 12 round brush

Color Palette

■ Burnt Sienna

■ Payne's Gray

■ Prussian Blue

■ Quinacridone Magenta

■ Sap Green

Color Mixing

■ **BLUE GREY:** 60% Prussian Blue, 30% Quinacridone Magenta, and 10% Burnt Sienna at 70% saturation

■ **LIGHT BLUE:** 50% Sap Green and 50% Prussian Blue at 25% saturation

■ **CORAL:** 75% Quinacridone Magenta and 25% Burnt Sienna at 20% saturation

Techniques

Keeping White Space, p. 23
Wet-on-Wet, p. 15

Painting wreaths was one of the first types of paintings where I finally figured out how to work with a brush's movement. Plus, they are so versatile, wreathes can be used as a pretty seasonal painting, as a greeting card with a word placed into the center, or even a name plate. Once you have this brushstroke down, you'll be able to make freeform leaves.

I chose a blueish green and peachy pink color palette so that it can be painted at any time of the year, but you can customize the colors to make it more seasonal. If you are feeling spring, reach for bright greens, yellows, and pinks. If it's more sweater weather, you could substitute muted yellows, oranges, reds, and browns. This is a great painting to revisit throughout the year with different color schemes.

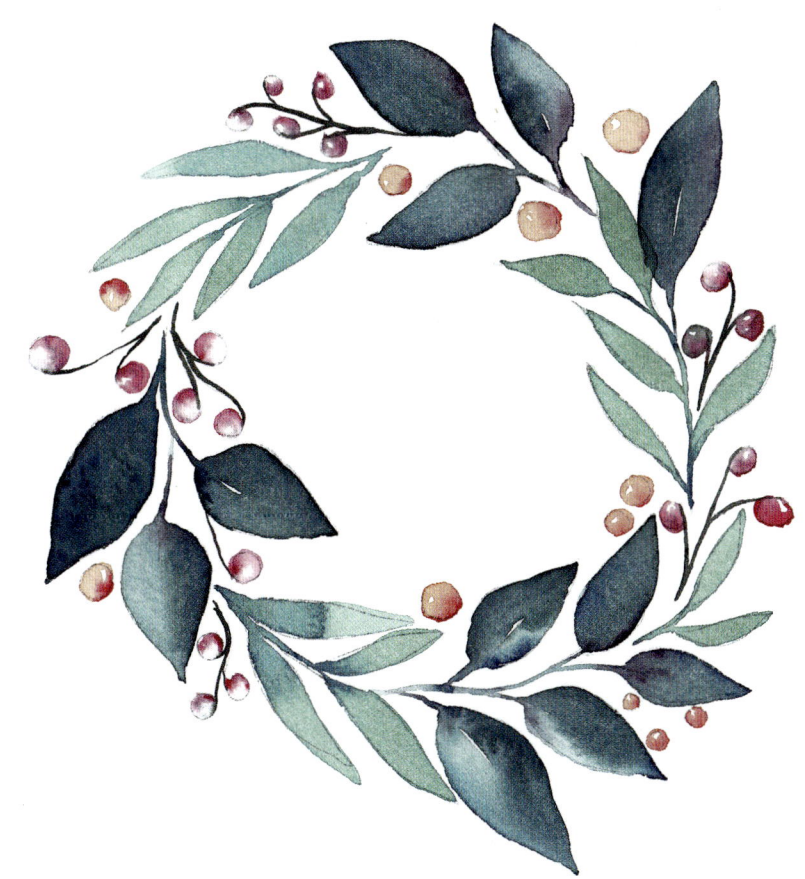

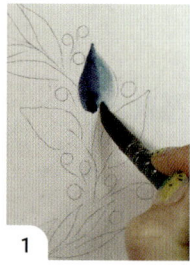
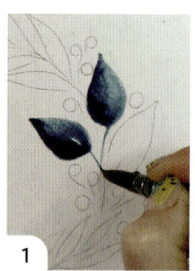

STEP 1

Mix the custom colors. Fill your brush with the custom Blue Grey. You'll paint the larger leaves in two strokes. On one half, take the tip of your brush and touch it to the tip of the leaf then start to press the brush down, spreading the bristles as you pull down the leaf. Once you're about two-thirds of the way down, start releasing the pressure and allowing the brush to reform its point. Then wash your brush, and while the first half is still wet, repeat the same brushstroke on the opposite side just with water, allowing the two halves to bleed together. If you happen to have a little white space between the two strokes, leave it be, it adds a highlight when dry. You'll be adding some more color to this but need to wait for it to be at the Gloss or Satin stage. While you wait, repeat these first two steps on several leaves, connecting the stems together.

STEP 2

Once your leaves are at a Gloss or Satin stage, clean your brush and grab some Quinacridone Magenta. Drop in a little where the leaf meets the stem. Drop in some concentrated Prussian Blue to one side of the leaf to add some more variation. This may not show up a lot while everything is still wet, but it will add some interest once everything dries. Repeat this process for all the larger leaves. Let this dry or make it dry!

STEP 3

Fill your brush with the custom Light Blue color and using one single stroke for each thinner leaf, touch the tip of your brush to the tip of the leaf and then press down as you drag across the leaf to allow the brush to fill the space, slowly reducing pressure as you near the edge of the leaf. You want each of these leaves to be filled with this color and at a stage of about Gloss wetness. Wash your brush and fill it with some concentrated Prussian Blue, drag the tip of your brush along the stem of the group of leaves to deposit some of this blue and let them bleed together. Repeat this process for all sections of these thinner leaves. Let this dry or make it dry!

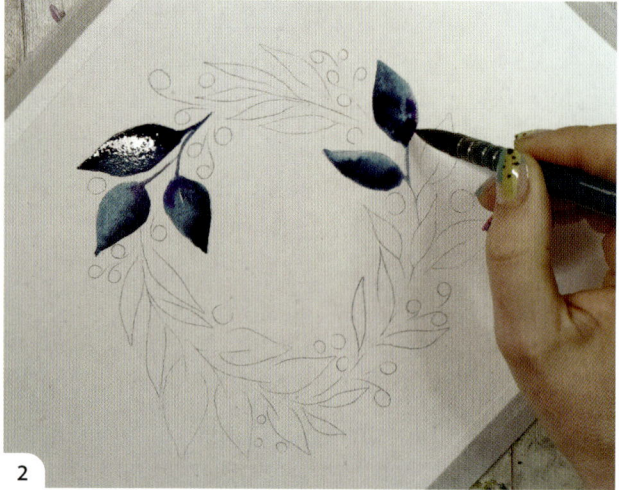

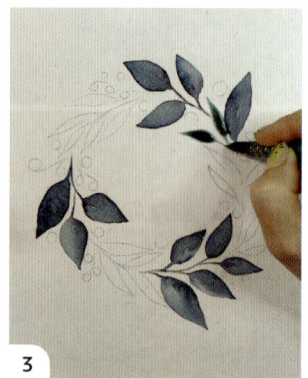
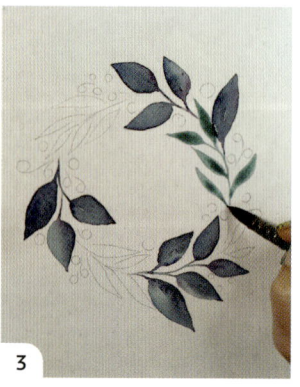

Brush control

If you're struggling with the single brushstroke for the leaves, it's okay to clean this up or use more than one stroke. I do encourage you to try with the one initially; the amount of brush control you'll gain by practicing this will be worth it.

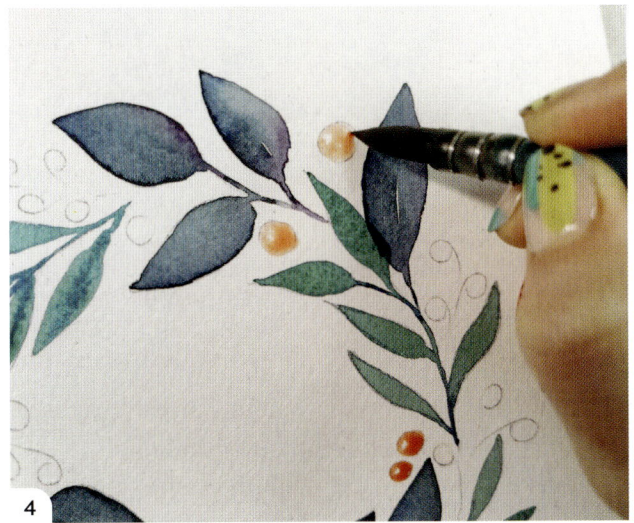

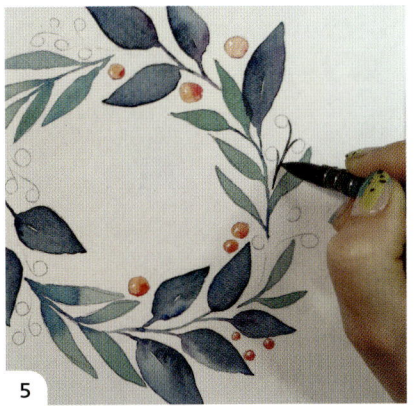
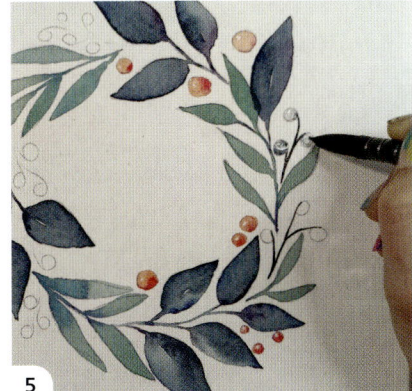
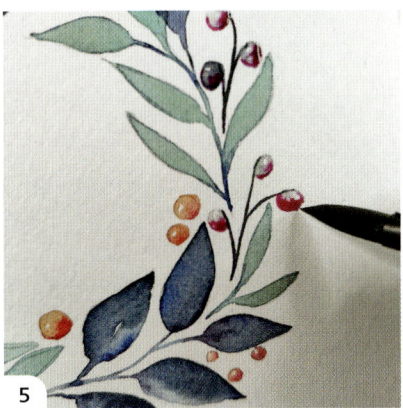

STEP 4

For the little round berries that are unattached, fill your brush with the custom Coral color and fill these in, leaving one spot open as a highlight. Fill several of these, then wash your brush and grab some concentrated Quinacridone Magenta and drop it in just a little along one edge of the berry. This will look pretty once dry. Do the same for all the unattached berries. Let this dry or make it dry!

STEP 5

To paint the little berries attached to the stems, fill the tip of your brush with a creamy consistency of Payne's Gray and using just the tip of your brush, paint on the stems. I like to work in groups of two or three bunches of these berries. Then wash your brush and wet the little berries, leaving a little spot of white space. The Payne's Gray will have appeared to have dried, but may still be a little wet and will lightly flow into the wet area. After each berry has been filled with water, wash your brush and put some Quinacridone Magenta into the tip of your brush and drop it in along the edge. Allow these to flow together and dry.

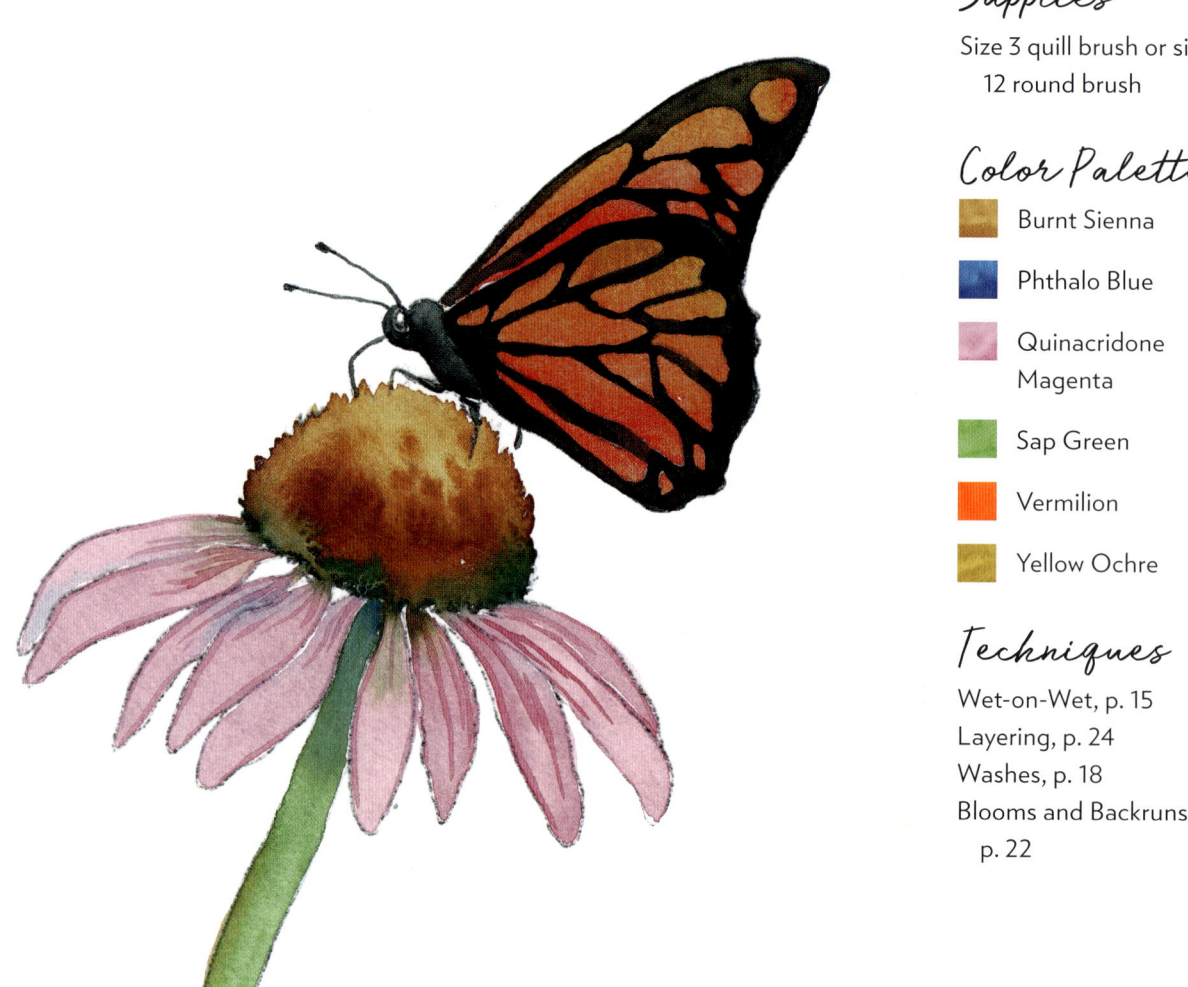

Supplies

Size 3 quill brush or size 12 round brush

Color Palette

- Burnt Sienna
- Phthalo Blue
- Quinacridone Magenta
- Sap Green
- Vermilion
- Yellow Ochre

Techniques

Wet-on-Wet, p. 15
Layering, p. 24
Washes, p. 18
Blooms and Backruns, p. 22

BUTTERFLY AND CONEFLOWER

Did you know that butterflies, bees, and hummingbirds all love coneflowers? I also love these humble daisy-like flowers and love to see who visits them every summer. This painting combines many of the techniques we've already explored like layering, shadows, color charging, and gradients. We'll be exploring how to create blooms with colors to give the cone texture without having to paint individual spikes.

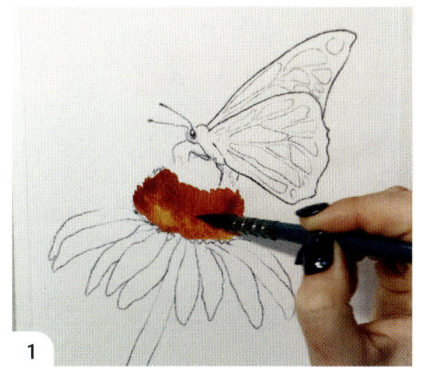

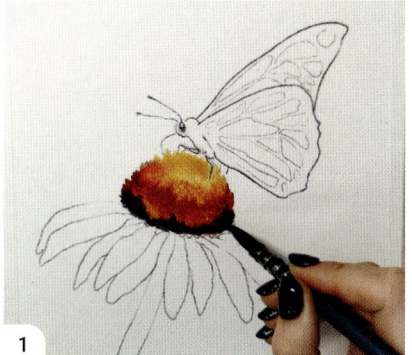

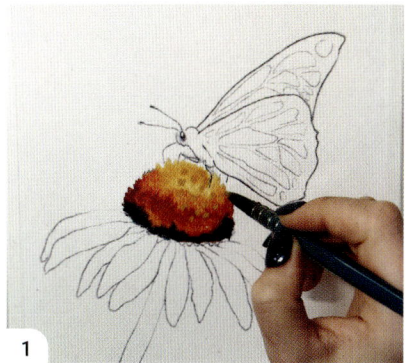

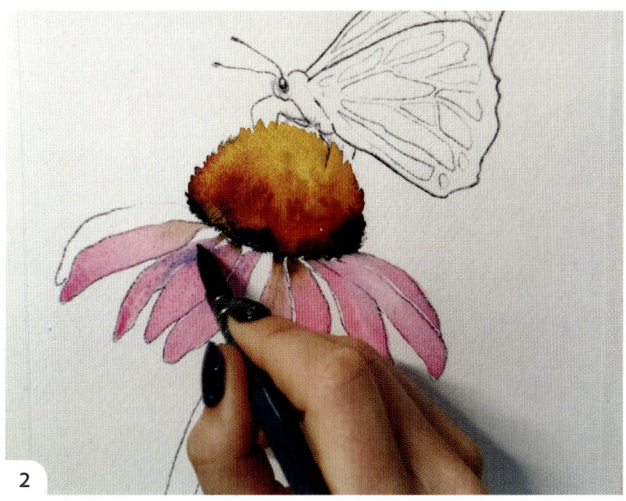

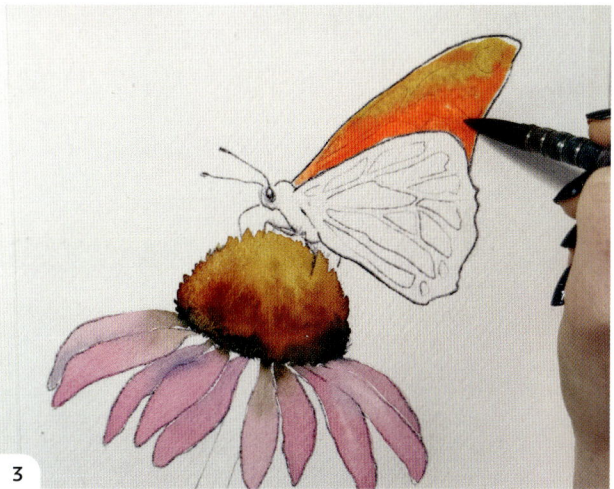

STEP 1

Fill the bottom two-thirds of the cone of the flower with watery Burnt Sienna, then wash your brush, and with just water in your brush, paint the top third of the cone. Wait until the cone has reached the Gloss or Satin stage and drop some Phthalo Blue at the bottom of the cone so it bleeds into the Burnt Sienna. Once the cone is at a Satin stage, fill the tip of your brush with a concentrated Yellow Ochre and place little dots across the top of the cone. This will push the other pigments to the side a bit and create yellow blooms and texture. Let this soak in until it's at the Satin or Damp stage before moving to the next step.

STEP 2

While the previous stage is soaking in, mix Quinacridone Magenta at about 20% saturation. Once the cone of the flower has gone to the Satin or Damp stage, start painting the petals with the light Quinacridone Magenta color occasionally lightly touching the petal to the cone so it softly bleeds into the petal. To add shadow to the petals that fall behind other ones, drop in a teeny tiny amount of Phthalo Blue to subtly push it back.

STEP 3

Paint the top wing of the butterfly starting at the top with Yellow Ochre and moving down to Vermilion. Let everything dry or make it dry! Once dry, paint the bottom wing in the same manner.

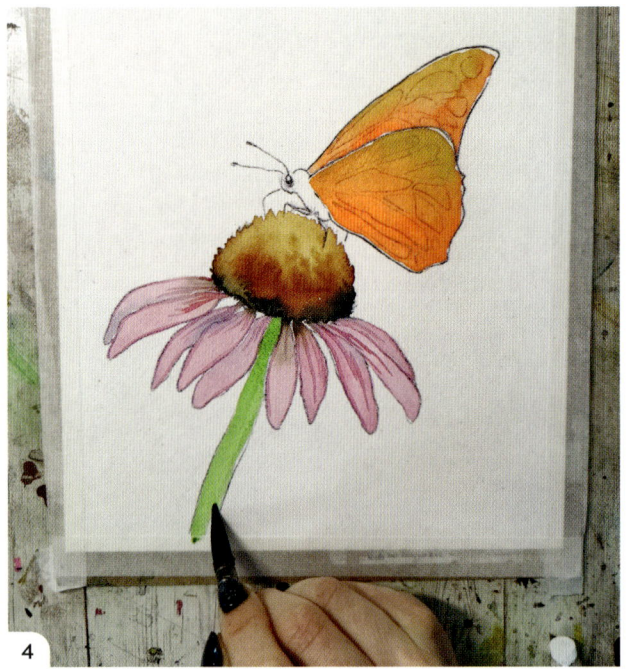

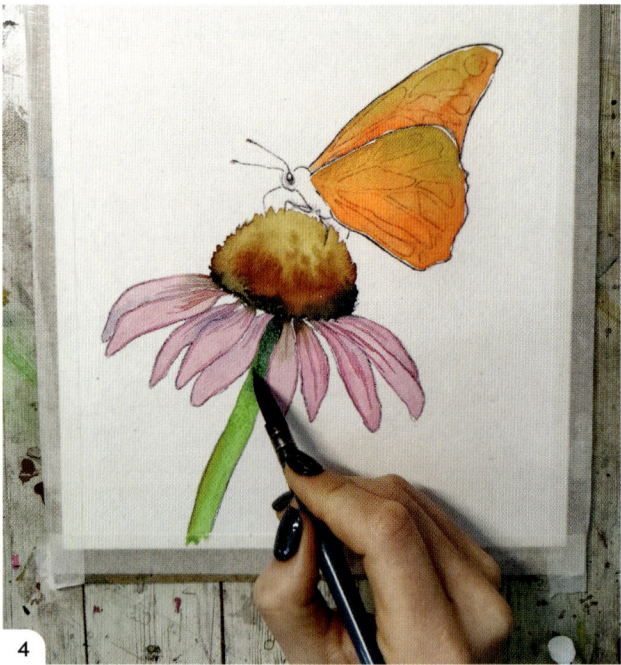

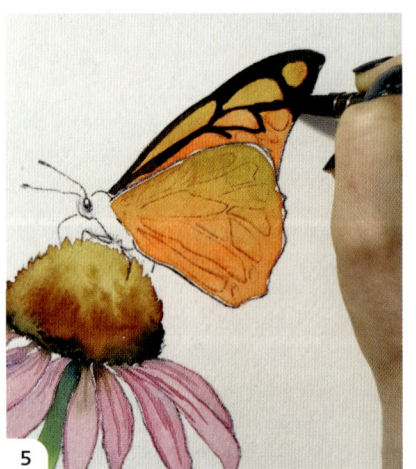

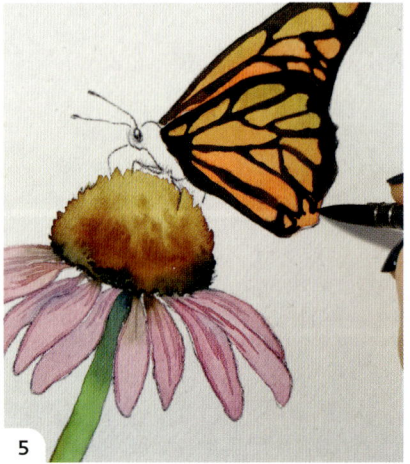

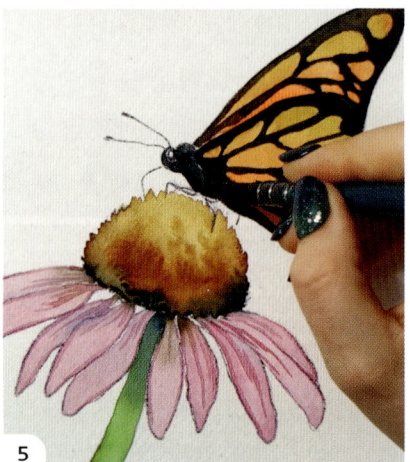

STEP 4

Paint in the stem of the flower with Sap Green at about 70% saturation. To add some dimension, drop a little Yellow Ochre on the left side of the stem and a little Phthalo Blue under the cone between the petals to create a shadow. Let this dry or make it dry!

STEP 5

Once everything is dry, paint around the shapes in the butterfly wings as well as on the body with Payne's Gray at an 80% or 90% saturation. Paint the antennas and legs. To give the body a bit more dimension, drop even more saturated Payne's Gray on the bottom of the body.

Supplies

Size 3 quill brush or size 12
  round brush
Masking fluid
Rag or rubber masking
  fluid remover

Color Palette

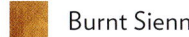 Burnt Sienna

Payne's Gray

Permanent Yellow
Deep

Prussian Blue

Quinacridone
Magenta

Techniques

Keeping White Space,
  p. 23
Washes, p. 18
Wet-on-Dry, p. 15
Wet-on-Wet, p. 15

FEATHERY FRIENDS

I love going for walks and finding feathers—the variety of shapes, sizes, colors, and patterns they have is always amazing. In this painting we'll explore using masking fluid as a way to preserve white space. You can do this painting without it, you'll just have to be more careful as you paint. Masking fluid allows us to freely paint over the masked area without worrying about getting color where we want it to stay white. There's one catch though, you have to let it dry overnight, so you may want to prep this painting ahead and then return to it. Feel free to use my color choices or choose your own.

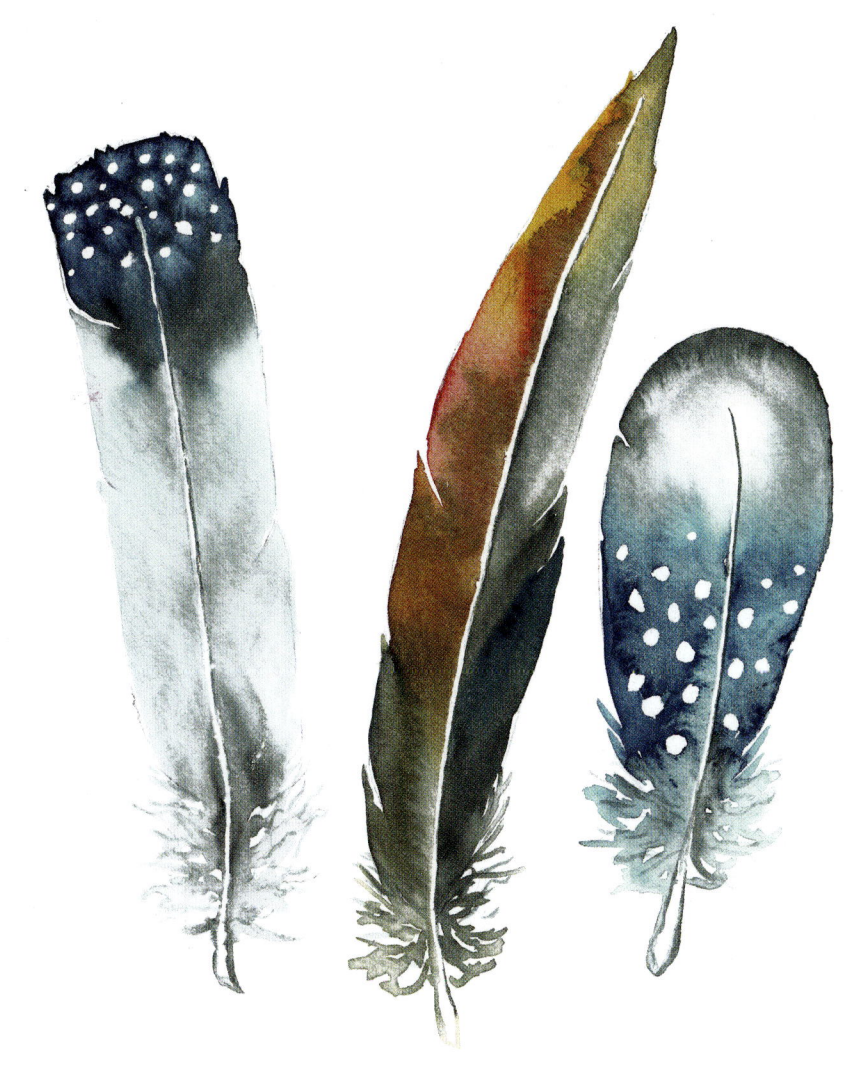

STEP 1

To prep this painting, paint masking fluid on the center line and quill of all of the feathers. Add some dots of masking fluid to the top of the left feather and middle of the right feather. Follow the drying instructions on your masking fluid, but it typically takes several hours to a full day.

STEP 2

Once your masking fluid is fully dry, start with the left feather. Paint Prussian Blue on the top segment. Paint a little concentrated Payne's Gray below this. Wash your brush and fill it with water and wash the grey down the entirety of the feather. Make some squiggles at the bottom for the fluffy bit of the feather. While it's still wet, drop a little more concentrated Payne's Gray on the bottom of the quill and along the center line.

STEP 3

For the middle feather, go with your gut and place colors next to each other on dry paper, but close enough that they bleed together. I painted Permanent Yellow Deep on the top, Quinacridone Magenta on the left, and then used a combination of Payne's Gray, Burnt Sienna, and Prussian Blue on the bottom, making it darker and more concentrated as I moved downward. Don't forget to squiggle your brush on the bottom around the quill to make the fluffy bit.

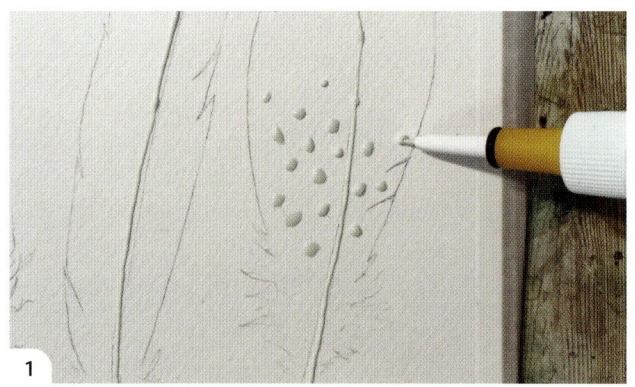

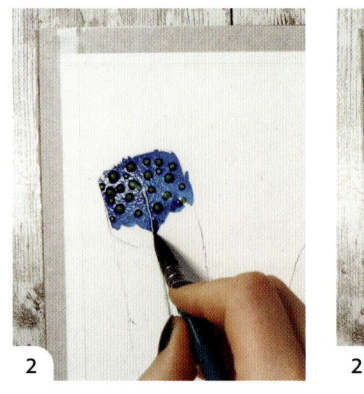
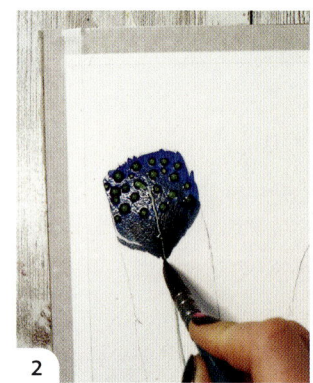

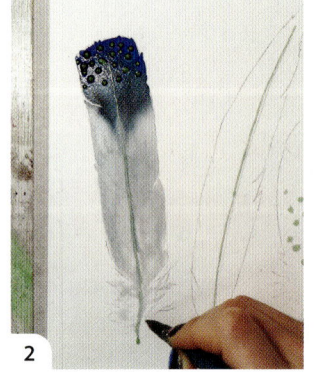
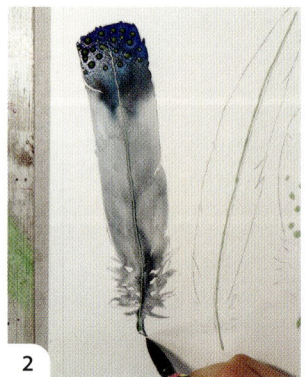

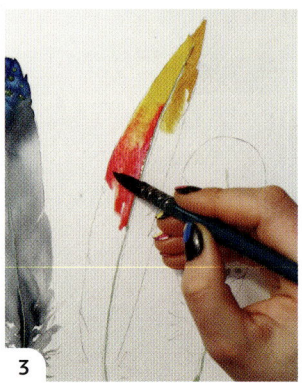
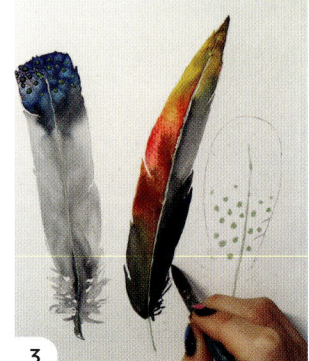

STEP 4

For the right feather, wet the top half of the feather with clean water. Paint Prussian Blue just below and barely touching the water, and then pull that down to the bottom of the feather and add the fluffy squiggles. Some of the Prussian Blue will bleed up into the water. While it's still wet, drop some Payne's Gray along the top of the feather and near the bottom along the center line. Let this dry completely. It's best to let this dry naturally instead of heating up the masking fluid. This is my one exception to make it dry!

STEP 5

Once everything is fully dry, remove the masking fluid. Note: If you try to remove the masking fluid before the paint is dry it will smudge your painting.

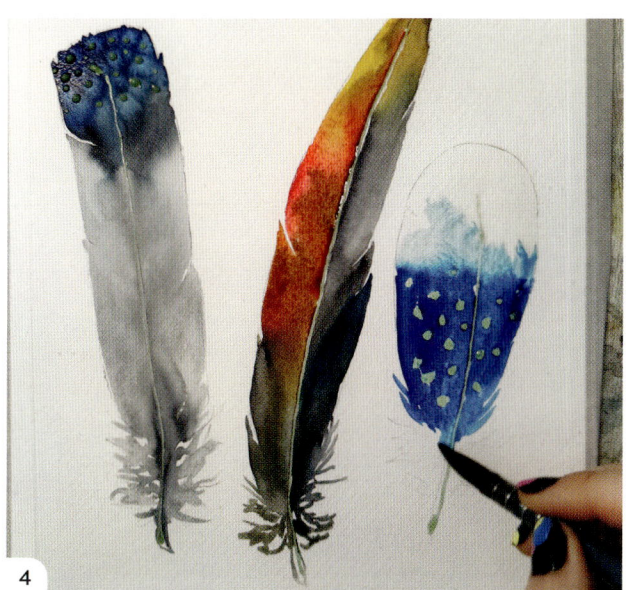

4

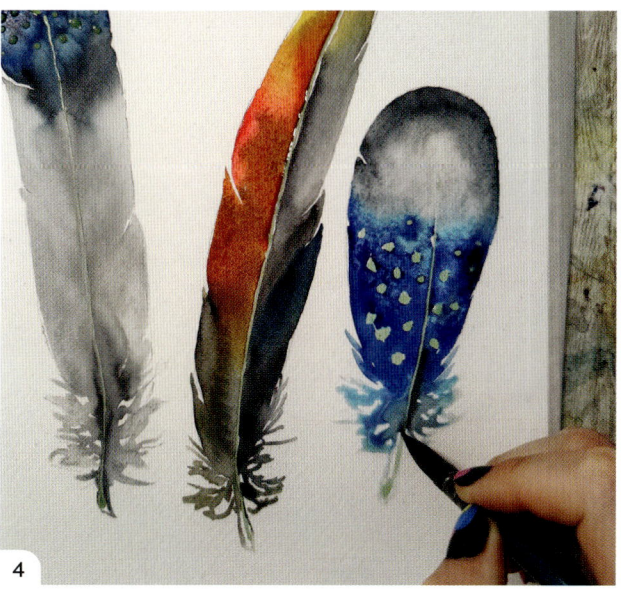

4

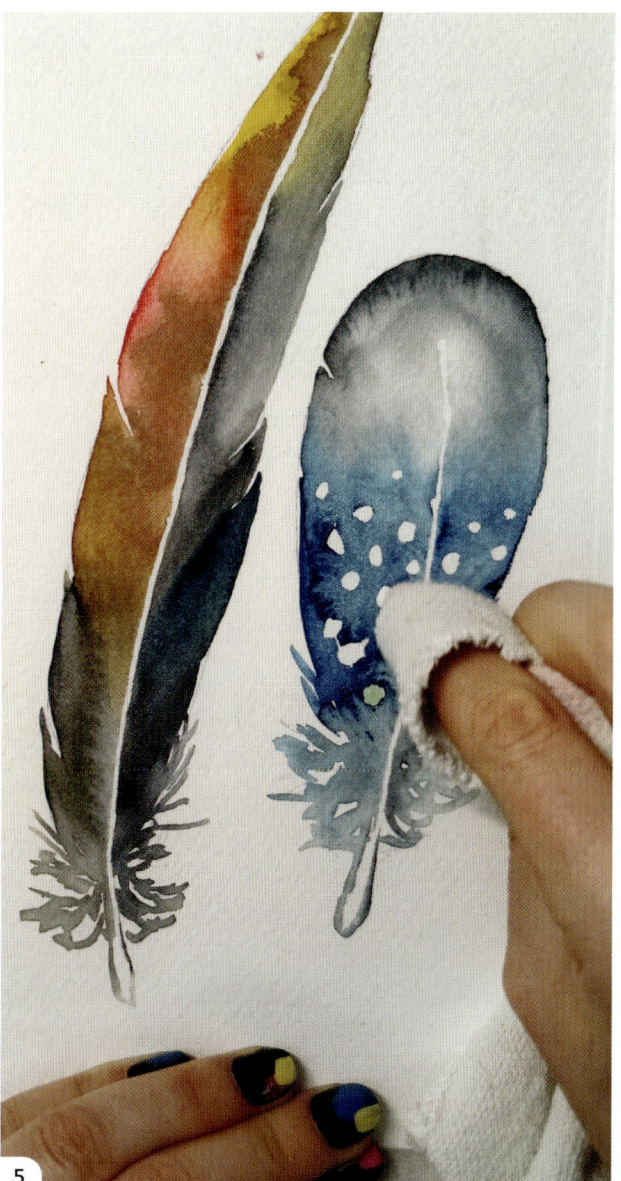

5

PUPPY LOVE

To say I love dogs might be an understatement. I especially love my dog, Moogie, who is the sweetest pup. I decided to include an ode to her in a cartoonish way that also combines one of the most interesting painting techniques called Negative Painting. You may have seen this technique demonstrated by my Jack-o'-lanterns or fall leaves in my social media videos. This painting technique is all about painting only the negative spaces. We will inadvertently be painting the subjects, but each layer isolates the subject and just paints the negative spaces. As you paint each layer, the previous one is revealed and pops from the page. Moogie is the pup on the right in this painting. She has one tip of her ear that flops down a bit and a ridiculously long neck.

Supplies

Size 4 quill brush or size 12 round brush
Felt tip pen

Color Palette

■ Burnt Sienna

■ Payne's Gray

Color Mixing

1ST LAYER: Burnt Sienna at 50% saturation

2ND LAYER: Payne's Gray at 30% saturation

3RD LAYER: Payne's Gray at 100% saturation

Techniques

Washes, p. 18

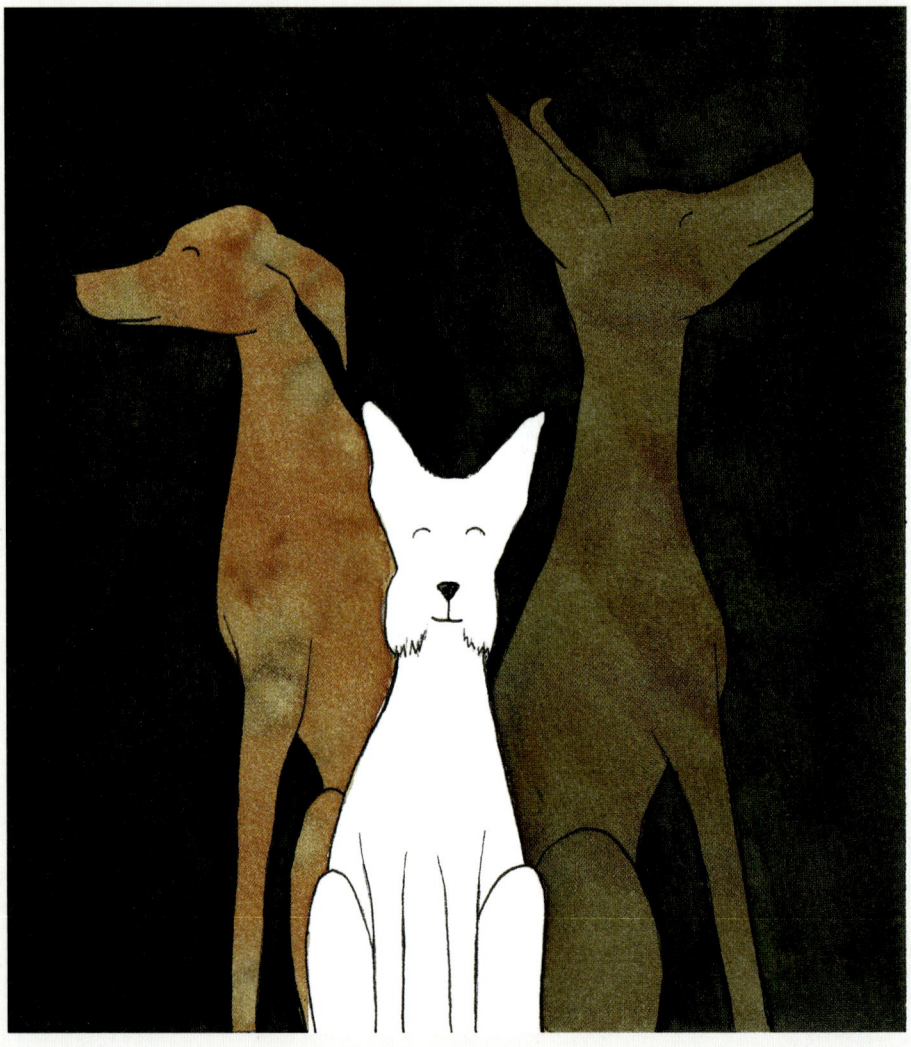

 Negative painting can be a hard technique to visualize if you've never tried it. Scan the QR code to watch a video where I demonstrate the negative painting techniques shown here.

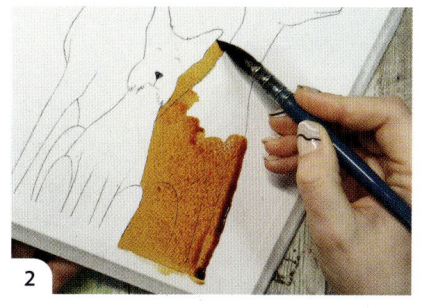
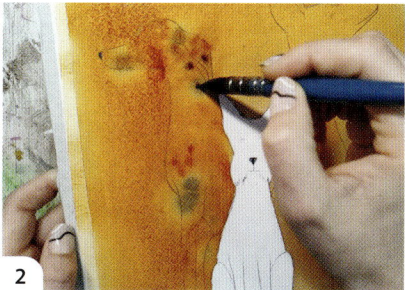
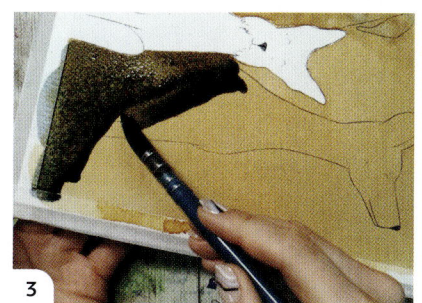
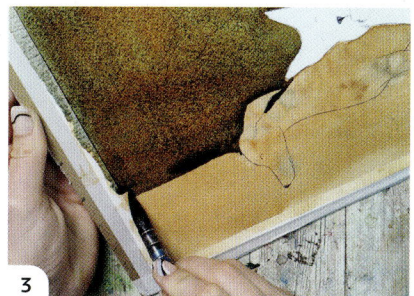
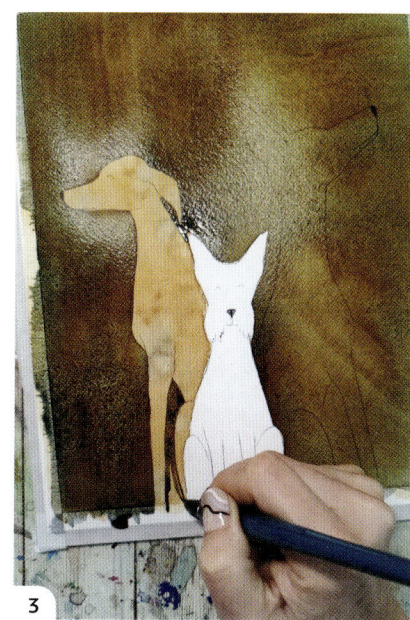

STEP 1

Mix up the custom saturations of Burnt Sienna and Payne's Gray. Each layer will require you to paint the majority of the page, so mix a lot. I filled each well of my muffin tin mixing wells about halfway with the water and color mixture. Also, choose the largest brush that you are confident in using. The less strokes you need to make, the better. Tape down your paper to a backing board because you will be moving the painting around.

STEP 2

Fill your brush with the first layer of Burnt Sienna and paint the entire page, except for the front middle dog, which will stay white. The key to getting even coverage is to work quickly and methodically while making sure your brush stays nice and full of color. If you run out of color, this can result in streaking. I used the drip line technique we explored in Washes, but it has to move around shapes. Because of this, I also rotate the page around to make it easier to get into the different areas and hold it at an angle to help preserve the drip line. The goal is to make sure all of the edges stay wet, so working back and forth, bottom to side, will help to make sure that happens. If your paper is still wet at the Satin or Gloss stage, you can drop in a few dots of Payne's Gray and a more concentrated Burnt Sienna on the dog on the left to give its coat a little texture. Let this dry or make it dry!

STEP 3

For the second layer we're going to be revealing the dog on the left. Fill your brush with the 2nd Layer of Payne's Gray and paint most of the page as you did in step 2. In this layer you're painting around both the center dog and the one on the left. The key to second layers is to quickly and lightly use the brush to place the water down instead of dragging your brush across the page. You can see in the third image there is some streaking on the right side. This was a result of using too much pressure on my brush and pausing while painting to take the photos. Even if you do get some streaking, it's fine because we'll be adding another darker layer that will help to cover this. Remember to paint in the area between the left dog's legs and belly. Let this dry or make it dry!

STEP 4

In the previous step we revealed the dog on the left and now it's time to reveal the dog on the right. Fill your brush with lots of the 3rd Layer of Payne's Gray and paint around all three dogs, making sure you also remember to paint inside the gaps between the legs and the bellies on both outside dogs. Notice that as each layer you painted, the dogs popped out more and more from the background. We didn't really paint any of the dogs, we just painted the entire layer as if it were a background for the dog in front. This is an amazing technique for building depth. Let this dry or make it dry, then repeat the third layer if you want to make the background even darker.

STEP 5

This last step is optional. Once everything is dry, use a felt tip pen to go over all the outlines on this painting to make them pop.

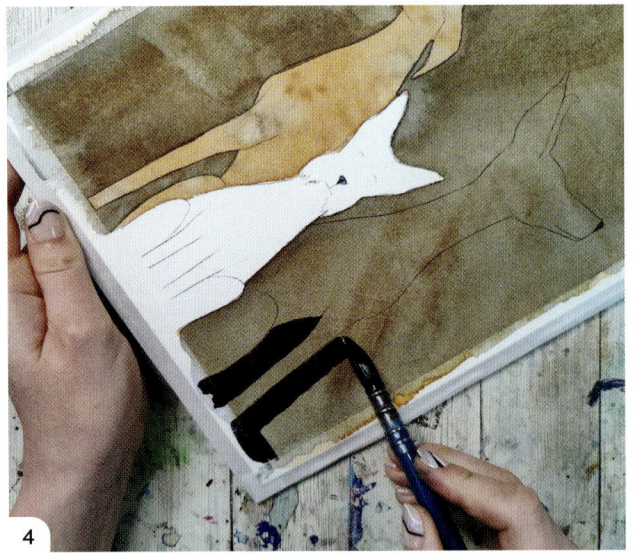

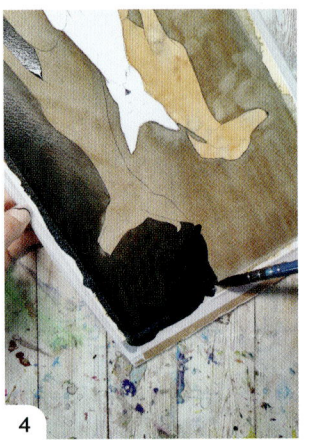

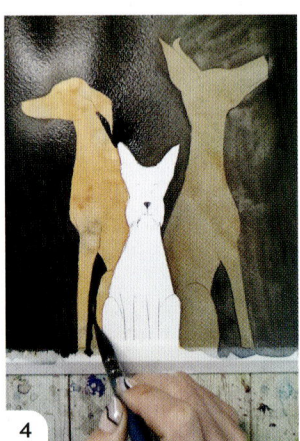

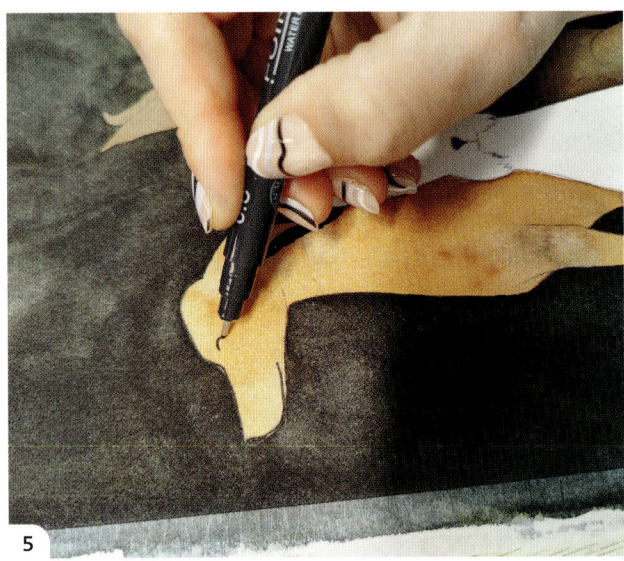

Supplies

Size 3 quill brush or size 12 round brush

Color Palette

■ Phthalo Blue

■ Vermilion

Color Mixing

■ **DEEP PURPLISH GREY:** 50% Phthalo Blue and 50% Vermilion at 80% saturation

■ **DEEP BLUE (80%):** 60% Phthalo Blue and 40% Vermilion at 80% saturation

■ **DEEP BLUE (20%):** 60% Phthalo Blue and 40% Vermilion at 20% saturation

Techniques

Wet-on-Wet, p. 15
Blooms and Backruns, p. 22
Layering, p. 24

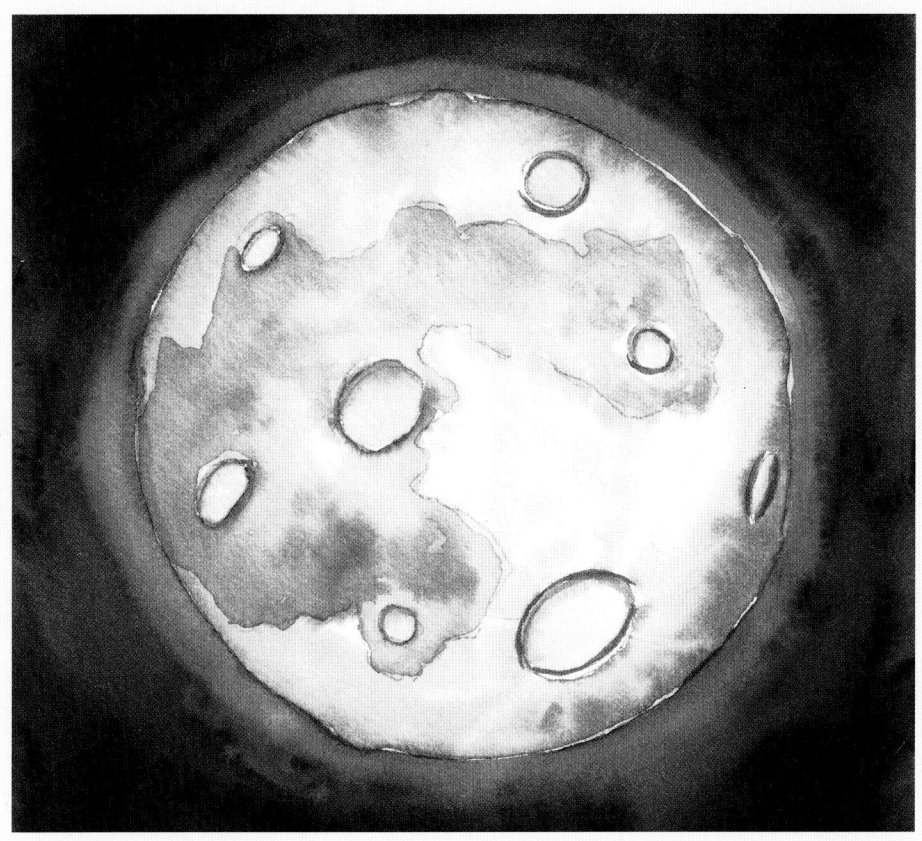

STARING INTO SPACE

I love space and have often wondered at the night sky. Watching the moon climb over the horizon and then dimly light the sky is just so magical. Not only is the moon a fun subject, but it's also a great way to learn about contrast and value. In addition to that, this painting will teach you how to achieve dark colors in watercolor.

Would you believe that this painting of the moon does not include Payne's Gray, the darkest of the colors I have in my recommended paints? This painting uses only two colors, and those two colors are mixed into three different combinations to give a little variety to the black and grey of this painting. Of course you could do this with Payne's Gray, but I encourage you to try mixing up your own grey and black. There are lots of different ways to mix up black and grey, but my absolute favorite way is to combine Phthalo Blue and Vermilion. The undertones of each of these colors work to mute each other and ultimately results in stunning blueish or purplish black colors. Watercolor dries a lot lighter than when it's wet, so even if you think you've gotten a super dark color, it will surprise you when it dries.

STEP 1

Mix a lot of each of the custom colors. In my muffin tin mixing wells, I mixed enough to fill each well a little over half way, and I even had to remix one color to add an additional layer. Tape down your paper to a hard backing board to prevent the paper from warping and to allow you to move it around.

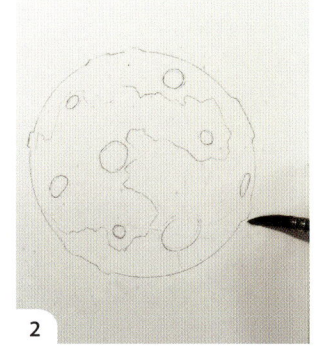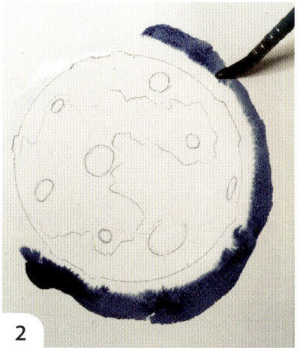

STEP 2

Fill your brush with clean water and wet one brush width directly around the moon. Then fill your brush with the 80% Deep Blue color and working in a ring that just kisses the wet edge of your previous ring, fill the background with Deep Blue. Work in rings and refill your brush often. Deep dark backgrounds often have streaking in them, so if we paint in rings, even if we get streaking it will mimic how light rings reflect around the moon in the sky. Fill the whole page with the Deep Blue and before it dries, wash your brush, dry it, and then go back and do a little cleanup right around the moon by lifting out any of the Deep Blue that's sneaking in too close to the moon. We want a light ring around this to help give it some glow. Let this dry or make it dry!

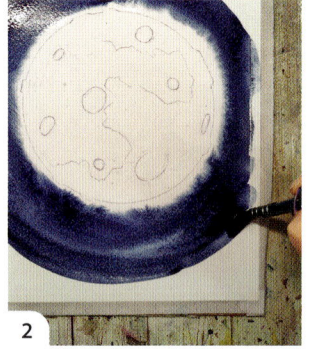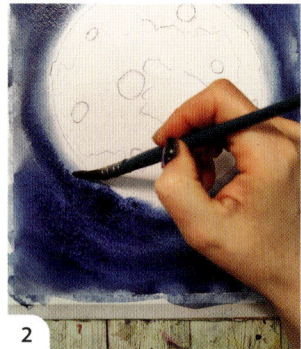

STEP 3

Fill your brush with the 20% Deep Blue color and paint a ring around the inside edge of the moon. Then grab more water, but don't wash your brush, and paint in the entire moon, avoiding the inside of the craters. Add more and more water as you move towards the middle of the moon.

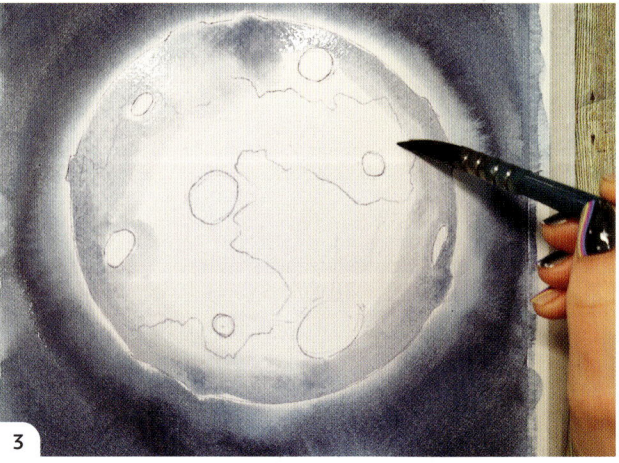

STEP 4

Moons have lots of texture, so you'll add some blooms while the moon is at the Satin or Damp stage. Fill your brush with some of the 20% Deep Blue and dot it in a few areas along the outer ring of the moon. While you still have the light color in your brush, dip the tip into the Deep Purplish Grey and dot that around. Do the same with some of the 80% Deep Blue. Then while it's still wet, add some of the Deep Purplish Grey

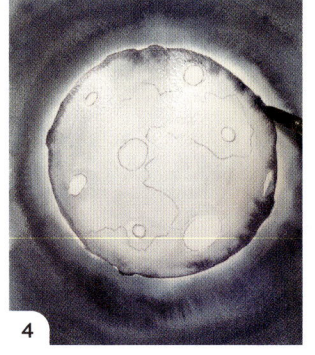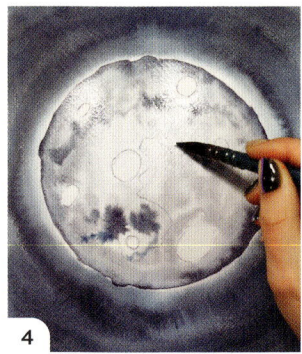

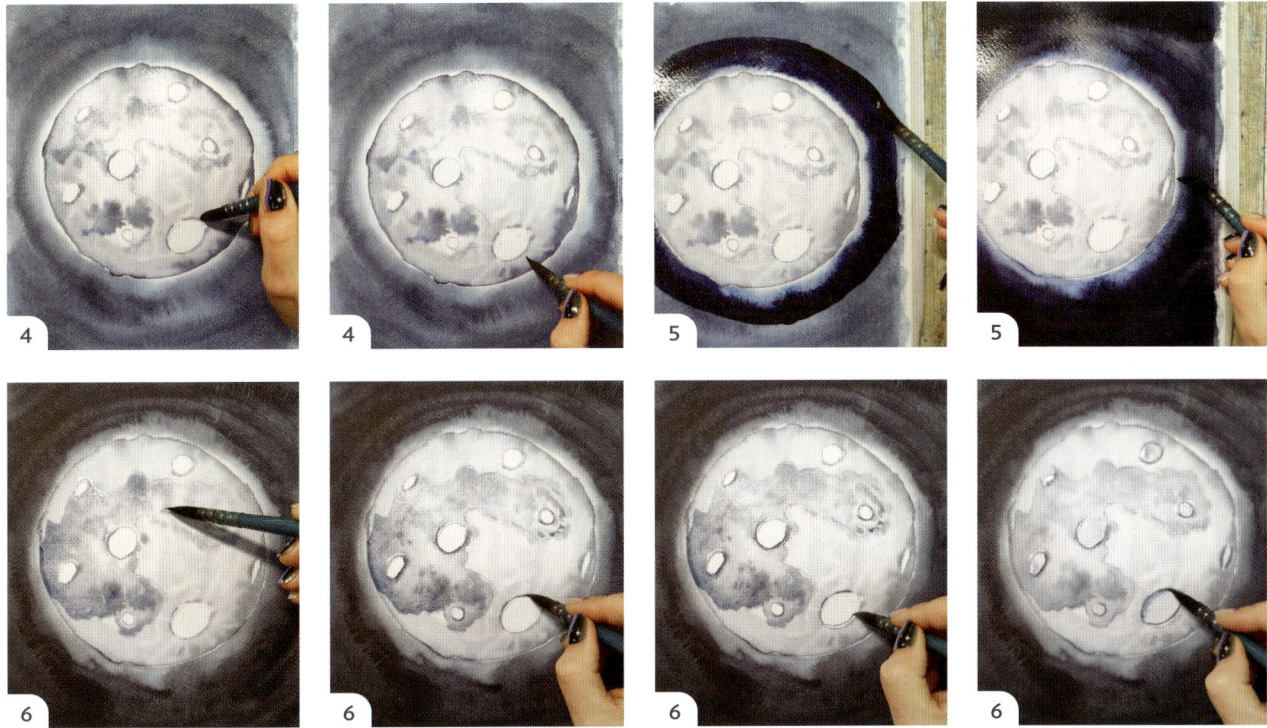

around the edges of the craters. Finally wash and dry your brush and lift the lines emanating out around the largest crater to give the impression of the impact. Let this dry or make it dry!

STEP 5

We need to darken that background to give it more contrast. This could potentially be your last layer on the sky depending on how dark you mixed your colors. Follow step 2, painting rings around the moon, but using the Deep Purplish Grey. When layering over a previous layer, a lighter touch is better. The harder you press the more brushstrokes you'll leave. Working with more water and color in your brush will help you keep a barrier between the brush and paper. Let this dry or make it dry!

STEP 6

For the final details on the moon, fill your brush with the 20% Deep Blue color and concentrate that along the side of the squiggly blob within the moon. Add

more water as you work across it. Fill your brush with some of the Deep Purplish Grey and make lines along the edges of the craters to help indicate the depth of the craters. The sides closest to the center of the moon will get a line around the outside of the crater. On the side farthest from the center of the moon, add a line on the inside of the crater. You could stop here, or repeat with another color to get more variation.

STEP 7

I mentioned in step 5 that your sky could have been done after the second layer, but I found mine too light. Decide if you want to darken the sky. Keep in mind that each layer you add risks adding more streaking, but each layer builds more depth so it's a high-risk high-reward. Repeat step 5 if you want to darken your background. Let this dry or make it dry!

WHAT A GEM

I was walking past a piece of labradorite in my studio and the shine just called to me. It made me wonder if there would be a simple way to capture the luminous nature of labradorite, one of my favorite stones. I sat down and started to play and once I figured out the basic "formula," each one I painted turned out to be unique yet beautiful. I bounced upstairs to show my husband, Nick, and he said "Wow . . . wow. But can a beginner really paint that?" I asked him to try and within about 15 minutes he'd painted two.

That is to say, this one might look complicated because of the way it mimics the light in labradorite, but if you go with the flow, you will succeed, in part because each stone looks different in nature.

Supplies
Size 4 quill brush or size 12 round brush

Color Palette
■ Payne's Gray

■ Permanent Yellow Deep

■ Prussian Blue

■ Quinacridone Magenta

■ Sap Green

Color Mixing

■ **GOLDEN YELLOW:** 75% Permanent Yellow Deep and 25% Quinacridone Magenta at 60% saturation

■ **STONE TEAL:** 75% Prussian Blue and 25% Permanent Yellow Deep at 50% saturation

■ **CHARTREUSE:** 50% Sap Green and 50% Permanent Yellow Deep at 30% saturation

■ **DARK BLUE:** 75% Prussian Blue and 25% Quinacridone Magenta at 80% saturation

Techniques
Charging, p. 21
Wet-on-Dry, p. 15
Wet-on-Wet, p. 15

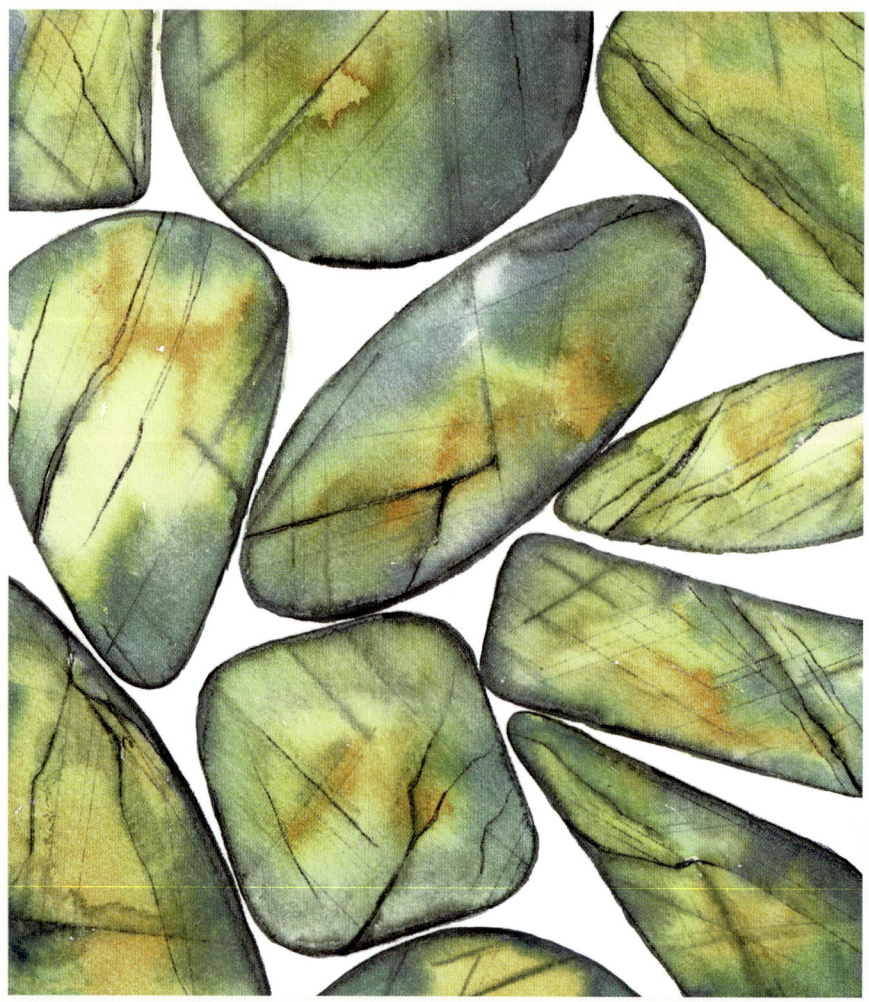

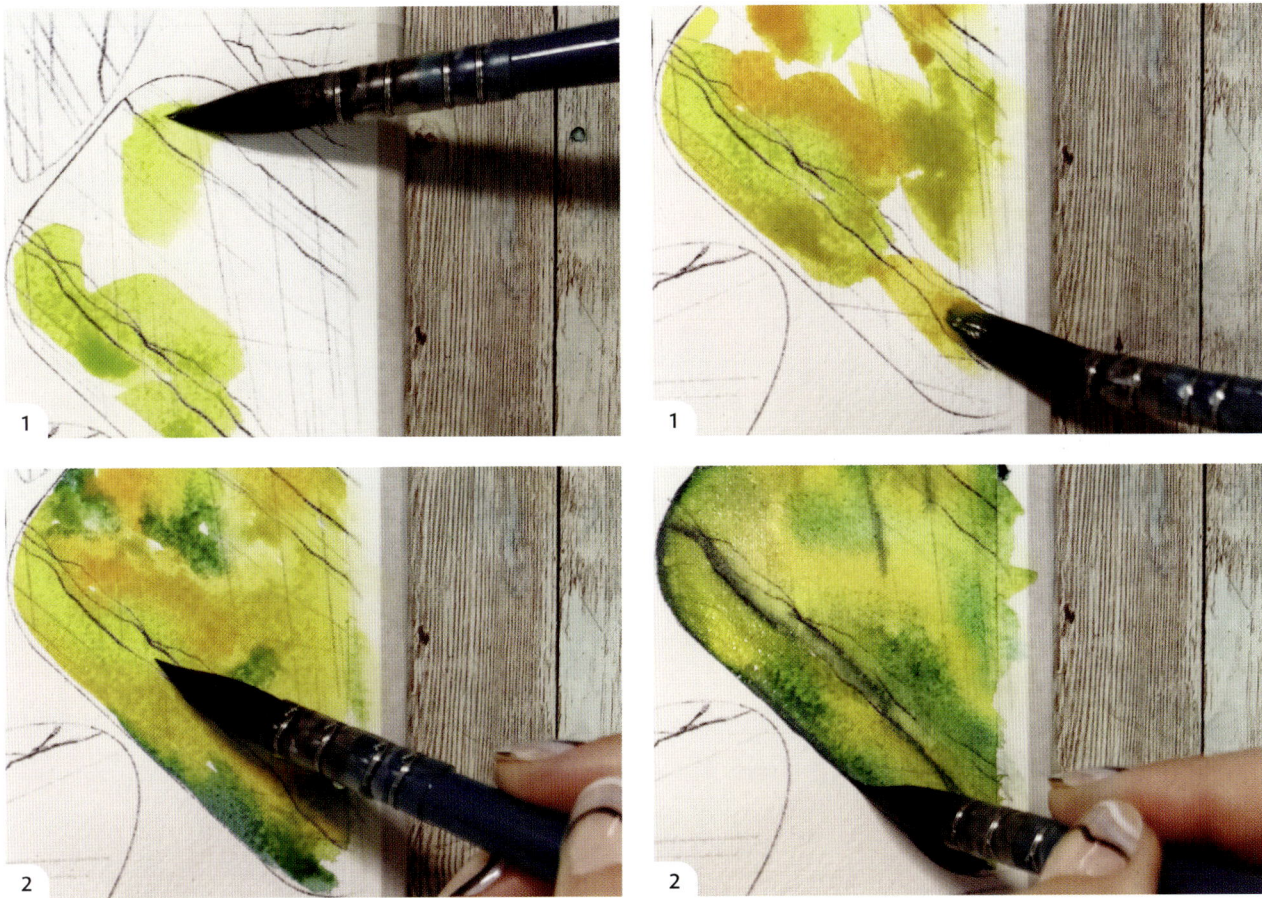

STEP 1

Mix your colors and tape down your paper. You'll want quite a bit of the custom Golden Yellow color. For each of these, we'll begin with our lightest colors, either the custom Golden Yellow or Chartreuse. Touch these in a couple random spots on the gem. Don't overthink this, just go with your gut but try to fill about 50–70% of the stone with these colors. Then wash your brush and wet together any painted areas that aren't already touching. Add some water to the edges of the stone.

STEP 2

Pick up the custom Stone Teal color and place it in a few areas along the edges or even a few drops within the stone here and there. Aim to cover about 15% of the stone with darker color. It will bleed in and take up more space as it sits. You could swap the Stone Teal for the Dark Blue, or even some Prussian Blue. Then while this is still wet, ideally at the Satin or Gloss stage, fill the tip of your brush with a super saturated Payne's Gray and drop it along the outside rim of the stone. This will create the shadow of the sides and bleed in a bit. Pick about three of the lines in the stone to run your brush over to deposit some of the Payne's Gray for emphasis. Let this dry or make it dry!

STEP 3

For the next stone, you'll follow steps 1 and 2 again. Fill your brush with one of your lighter colors—I started with the custom Golden Yellow—and make a couple random strokes. Next dot the same with Chartreuse. Then, fill your brush with water to soften those strokes together. Fill your brush with the custom Stone Teal and drop it along a few edges and inside in just a few places. Then grab either the Dark Blue or the Prussian Blue and drop those in the areas along the edges that are still lacking color. When the stone is at the Satin or Gloss stage, fill the tip of your brush with the concentrated Payne's Gray and line the outer rim and a few of the inside fracture lines.

STEP 4

Continue following the above steps until you've filled all the labradorite gems. Remember, they should all look a little different just as they do in nature.

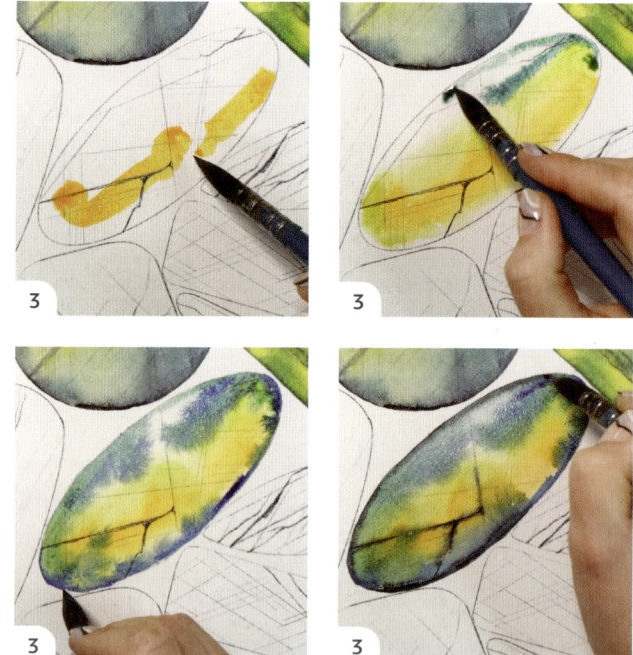

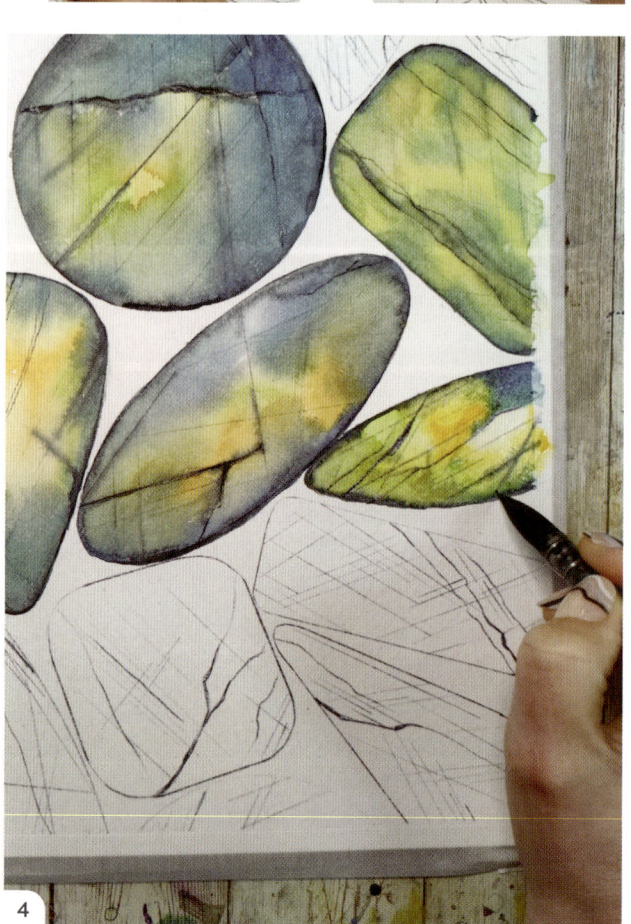

Here's Nick's version

My husband, Nick, wanted to try this painting after I showed him mine. He rarely paints with watercolor, and his turned out amazing!

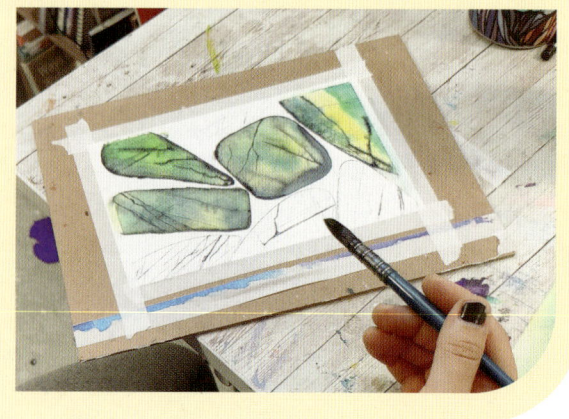

COASTAL CALM

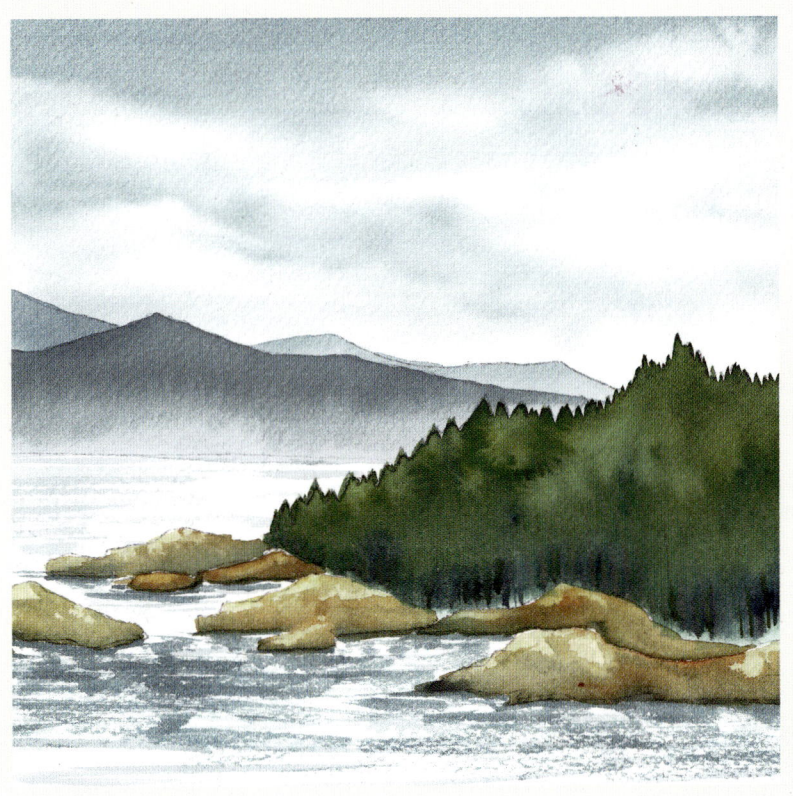

Many of my paintings are taken directly from my experiences and photos, but this one is from my imagination and is an experience I am trying to make reality. There's a beach in Oregon called Agate Beach where you can walk along and pick up agates. This painting encapsulates the feeling I hope to have while moseying along the beach and looking for treasures surrounded by the sounds of the ocean and the scent of the forest. Someday soon I'll be there.

There is a lot going on in this painting, but have no fear—remember that nature looks, well, natural, so your painting doesn't have to match mine exactly.

Supplies

Size 3 quill brush or size
  12 round brush
2-inch (5 cm) flat
  wash brush
Paper towel

Color Palette

Burnt Sienna

Payne's Gray

Permanent Yellow Deep

Prussian Blue

Vermilion

Color Mixing

FOGGY DAY BLUE:
85% Prussian Blue and
15% Vermilion at
50% saturation

FOGGIER BLUE: Foggy
Day Blue plus 10% Payne's Gray
at 60% saturation

FOREST GREEN
40% Prussian Blue,
40% Permanent Yellow Deep,
and 20% Burnt Sienna at 80%
saturation

SANDSTONE BROWN:
80% Burnt Sienna and
20% Prussian Blue at
30% saturation

Techniques

Wet-on-Wet, p. 15
Lifting, p. 17
Layering, p. 24
Blooms and Backruns, p. 22
Dry Brushing, p. 21

STEP 1

Mix all the custom colors except for the custom Foggier Blue. Make sure you mix quite a bit of these colors; it's always better to have too much than too little. Using the flat wash brush, wet the top half of the paper to the bottom of the distant mountains. Fill your brush with a generous amount of the custom Foggy Day Blue and place it randomly in the sky, getting a bit more sparing as you get closer to the top of the forest and mountains. The placement doesn't have to make a ton of sense, we just want some variation. Then dry your brush and lift out some areas. You want to keep these soft. Don't over think this part and stop the first time you think "have I done enough?" Let this dry or make it dry!

STEP 2

Fill your brush with the same custom Foggy Day Blue and place it along the top of the back layer of mountains; then wash your brush and soften that color down and into the trees with clean water. This doesn't need to be perfect as the colors we'll be adding later are darker, but we want to avoid super harsh edges.

STEP 3

Next we're going to be using some dry brushing on the ocean section, so fill your brush with Foggy Day Blue but then tap it lightly and repeatedly on a paper towel until when you tap barely anything comes off. Your brush will still have some color in it, but not enough to soak the paper. Touch the side of the brush very lightly to the page where the ocean is and drag it lightly along, allowing the bristles to skip across the page. The dry brushing technique creates texture with some white showing through, like little ripples. Repeat this a few times with different dry brushing strokes of different lengths, working in the ocean water and avoiding touching the rocks. Let this dry or make it dry!

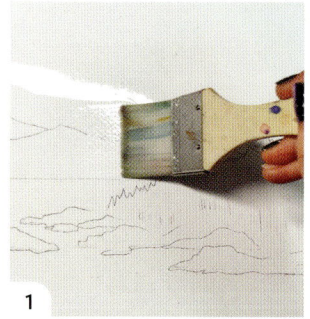
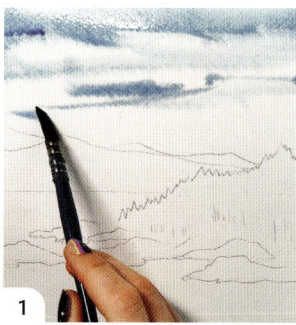
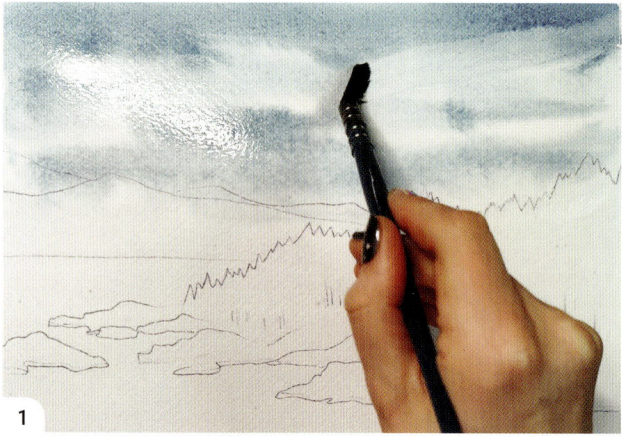
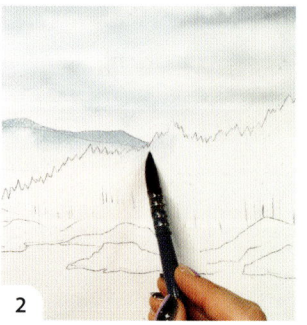
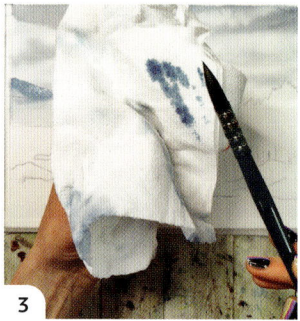
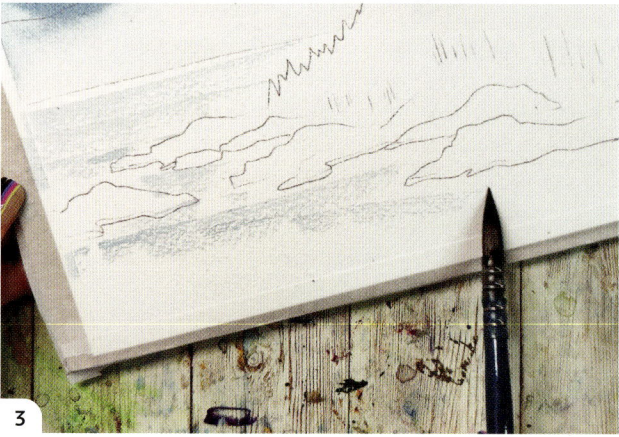

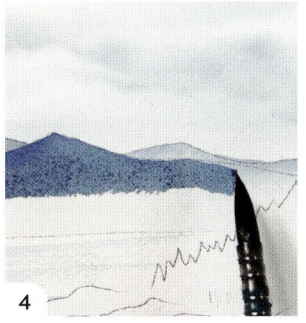 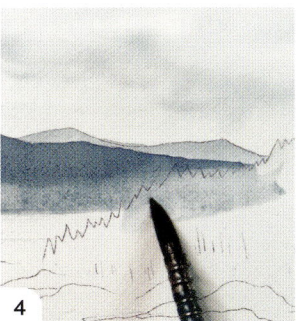 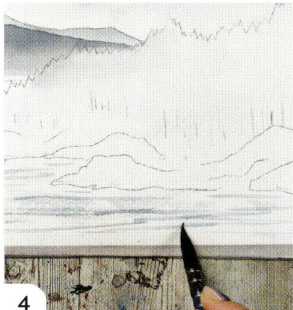 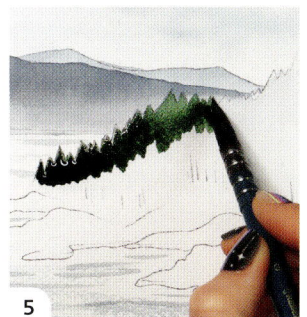

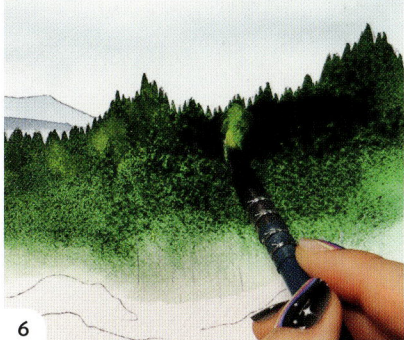 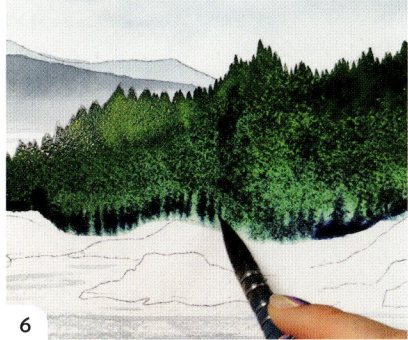 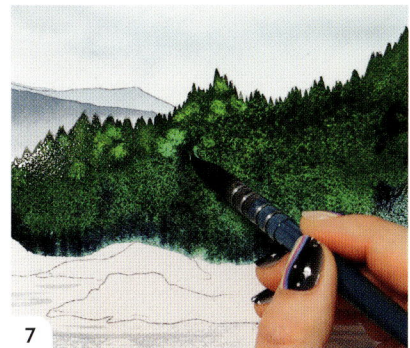

STEP 4

Take whatever is left of your custom Foggy Blue Color and add a little Payne's Gray to make a Foggier Blue color. Add this to the second layer of the mountains to about halfway down. Then wash your brush and soften to the horizon line into the trees to soften out that color so no harsh lines occur. Take this same color in the tip of your brush and add more horizontal lines sporadically around the water. Don't worry about making these perfect. This is just the texture of the water so if yours are thicker or more squiggly, it's just a rougher day at sea. Let this layer dry or make it dry!

STEP 5

Fill your brush with a generous amount of the custom Forest Green. Use up and downward strokes, taking advantage of the tip of the brush at the top to fill in the forest area. Refill your brush as needed—you want to make sure this stays nice and wet, so err on the side of too much color and water on the page.

STEP 6

Once you have filled in most of the forest area, fill your brush with water and wash it down to the bottom. While it's still wet, wash your brush and fill it with Permanent Yellow Deep and drop this in a couple spots along the top of the tree line to add the illusion of light. Then while it's still at the Gloss or Satin stage, wash your brush and fill it with Prussian Blue and drop this in randomly within the trees. Then concentrate it at the bottom by making up and downward strokes. These will bleed together a bit, but it alludes to the vertical nature of trunks and captures the forest shadow.

STEP 7

While things are still wet near the top of the forest, wash your brush and fill it with water. Drop some of this water near the top to create blooms where the water pushes the pigment away from areas and creates an interesting texture. Err on the side of just a few drops—these blooms might not seem like much at first, but they grow as they dry.

Observe your paper to see how wet it is. The top of the forest can remain fairly wet, but near the bottom it should be approaching the Damp stage. Notice on the photo to the right how it's a little shiny, and then near the bottom of the green and blue section you can't really see the shine? It should look a little like that. Add a little Payne's Gray to your brush and add vertical strokes along the bottom edge to allude to the tree trunks. The previous vertical strokes you added when it was wetter will have softened. These strokes will stay more or less in place and create a little more depth. Let this layer dry or make it dry!

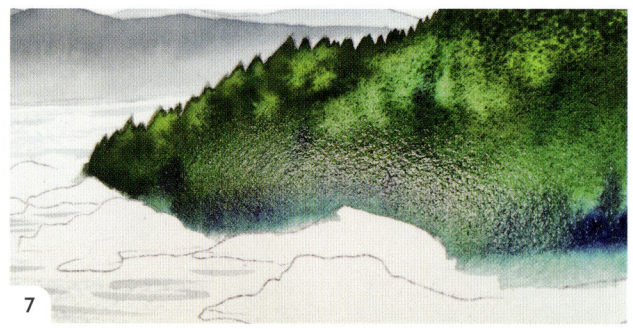

STEP 8

For the rocks, start by adding in some of the custom Sandstone Brown mixture along with Burnt Sienna on the majority of the rocks, aiming to keep it a bit lighter on top. Then lift color from the top using either a brush or a paper towel to show the highlights on the top of the rocks. While the brownish color on the rock is still wet, fill your brush tip with Payne's Gray and drag it along the bottom edge to create shadow. Feel free to add the shadow first and then lift color from the top; see what works best for you. Paint the segments that don't touch at first, and then dry them before working on ones that touch. Let this dry or make it dry!

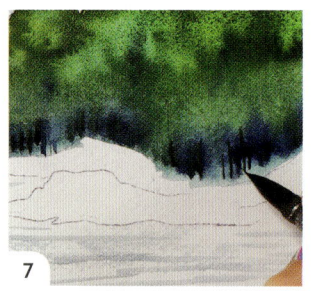 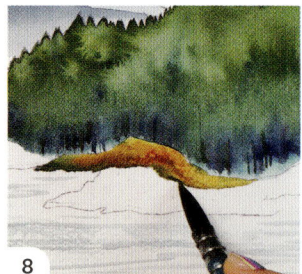

STEP 9

The final step will add a little more depth to the ocean and shadow from the rocks. Fill your brush with the remaining custom Foggier Blue and tap it off a bit on your paper towel so that you can do the dry brushing technique. Start by lining the border between the bottom of the rocks and ocean with the tip of your brush. Then lay the side of the brush on the page and swipe it from side to side so that the dry brushing texture is achieved. The key to the texture of the water is to stop while you still have some white space peeking through. It's easy to overdo this part, so go slow and observe frequently. Let this dry or make it dry and you're done!

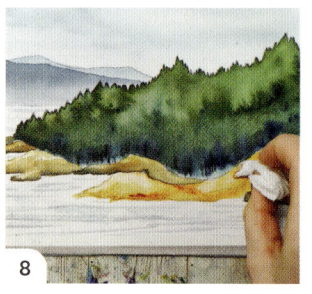 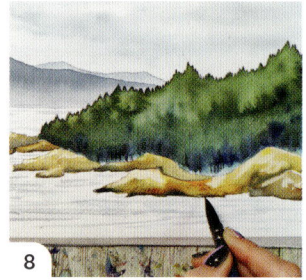

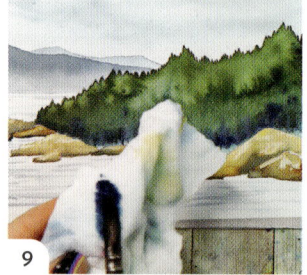 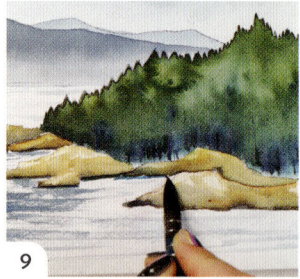

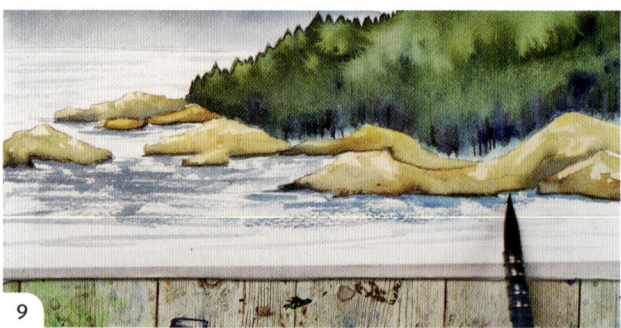

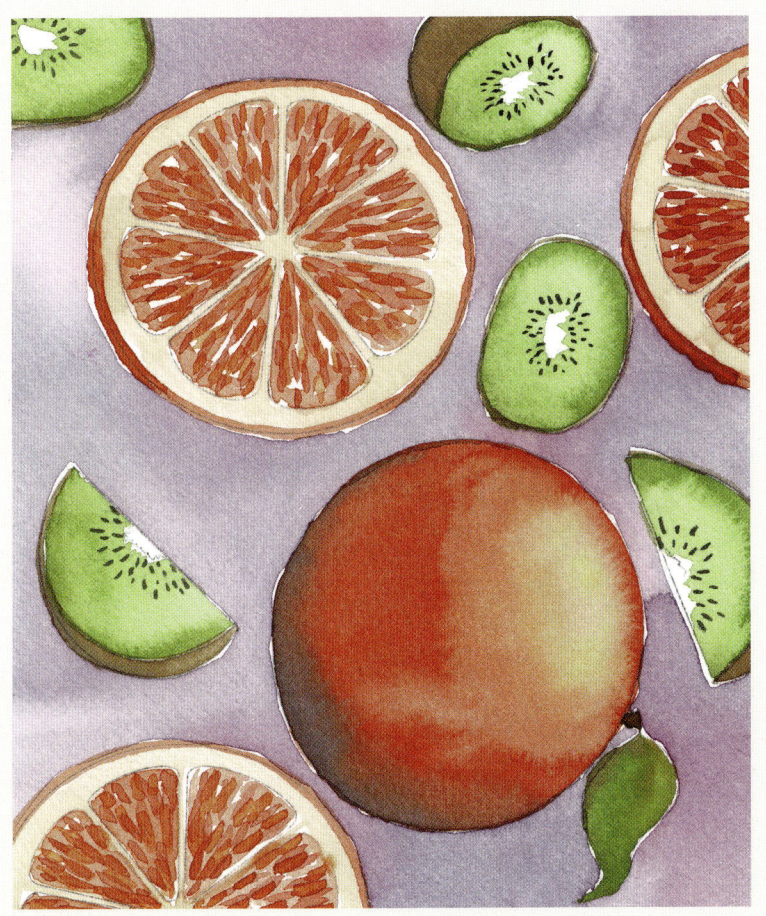

FRESH AND FRUITY

Oh how I love fruit. I love how juicy it is and I am a sucker for a sweet and tangy treat. Nothing says Christmas to me quite like a box of grapefruits. I look forward to this all year and often eat these in an unusual way that a roommate once taught me. I peel it like an orange and then peel open each individual segment so that I get all the juicy grapefruit goodness without any of the bitterness.

Get ready to mix up custom colors, and make sure you mix a lot. We'll also be working on modifying our mixes as we go, so don't get too attached to some of the colors. For this final painting, we'll be combining most of the skills in the book—charging, layering, shadows, leaving white space, and a variegated wash to top it off.

Supplies

Size 4 quill brush or size 12 round brush

Color Palette

- Payne's Gray
- Permanent Yellow Deep
- Phthalo Blue
- Quinacridone Magenta
- Sap Green

Color Mixing

GRAPEFRUIT: 70% Quinacridone Magenta and 30% Permanent Yellow Deep at 70% saturation

SHADOW PURPLE: 50% Quinacridone Magenta and 50% Phthalo Blue at 70% saturation

KIWI GREEN: 50% Permanent Yellow Deep and 50% Sap Green at 60–70% saturation

KIWI BROWN: 50% Quinacridone Magenta, 35% Sap Green, and 15% Permanent Yellow Deep at 60% saturation

Techniques

Charging, p. 21
Layering, p. 24
Washes, p. 18

STEP 1

Mix your colors and tape down your paper. Fill your brush with lots of the custom Grapefruit color and fill in the main grapefruit with a Satin Level of wetness, leaving an open unpainted area in the upper left. Then wash your brush and add water to the unpainted area, softening it into the surrounding areas. Drop a tiny bit of Permanent Yellow Deep to add some variation into the white area.

STEP 2

Wash your brush and fill it with the Shadow Purple and drop that along the edge of the grapefruit opposite the highlight. Wash your brush and refill it with the Grapefruit color and line the outer rim of all the grapefruit slices as well as messily within each segment of grapefruit. Leave some white space when you fill these segments in. Let this dry or make it dry!

STEP 3

For the kiwis fill a clean brush with the custom Kiwi Green and line the outside near the skin of the kiwi with the full value color. Then wash your brush and use water to soften in towards the center, leaving the very center outline white.

    Paint the leaf on the grapefruit using Kiwi Green on the bottom half, then add some Permanent Yellow Deep to the top, and add shadows along the bottom and middle with the Shadow Purple. Finally, drop a little of the Kiwi Brown onto the stem. Let this dry or make it dry.

STEP 4

Fill your brush with the custom Kiwi Brown and fill in the skin of the kiwis. Add a bit of Shadow Purple to the same side as you did on the grapefruit for the kiwis with rounded bottoms. Add a fine line of the Kiwi Brown to the edge of the kiwi slices.

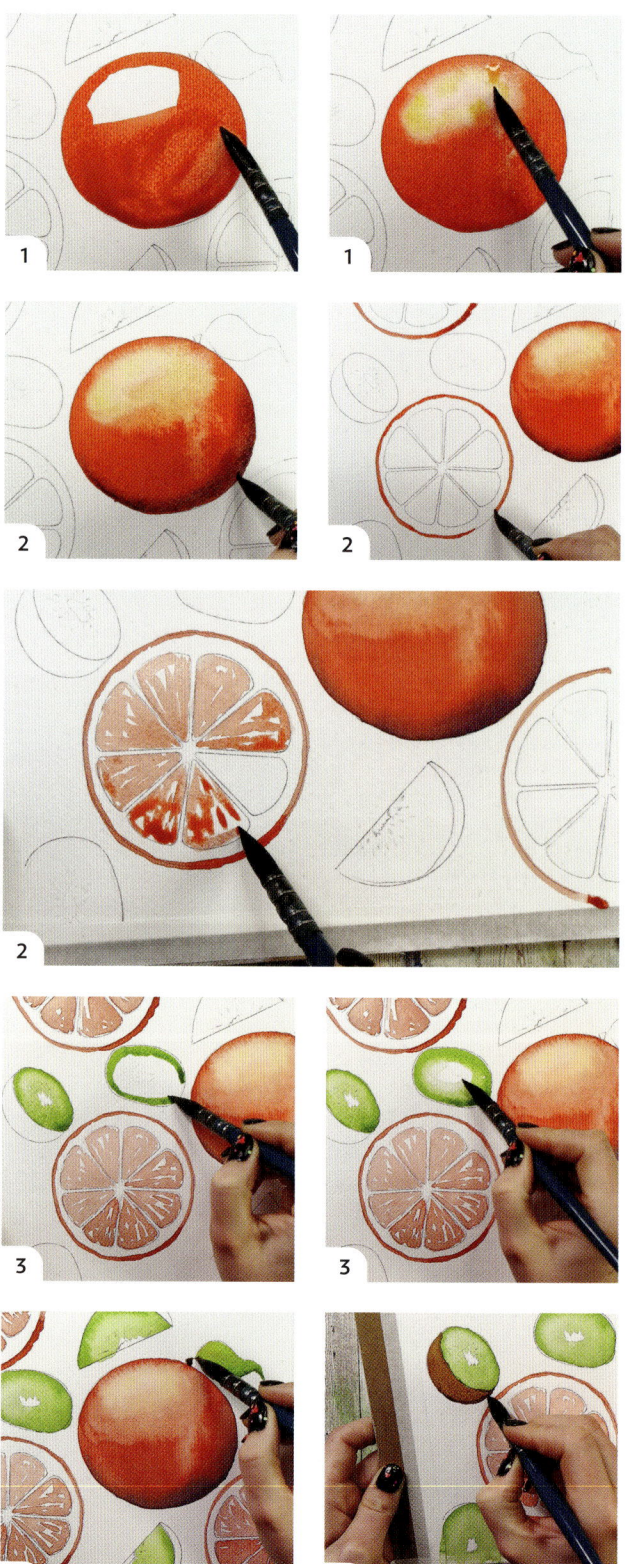

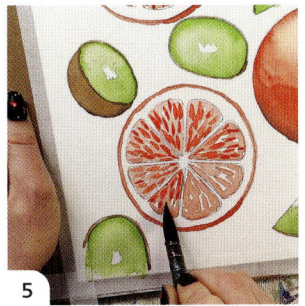
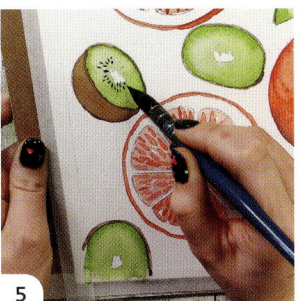
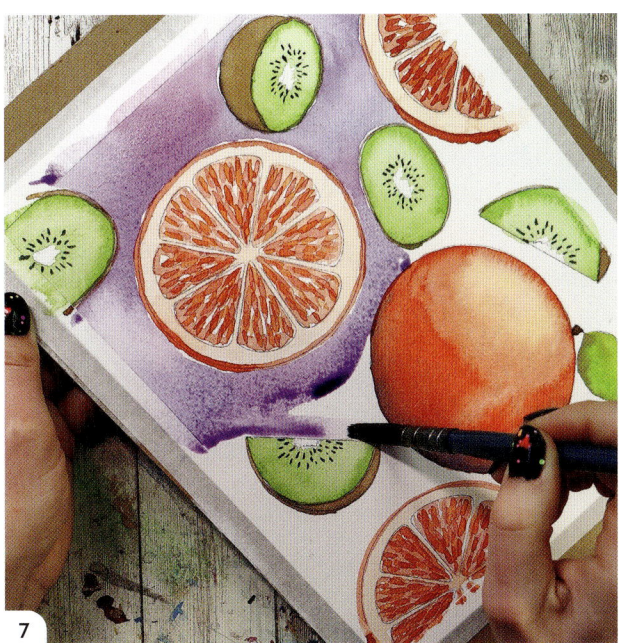
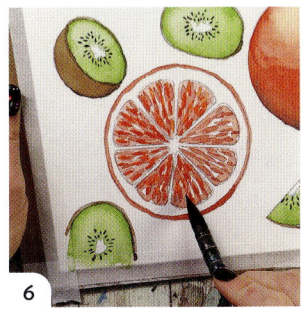
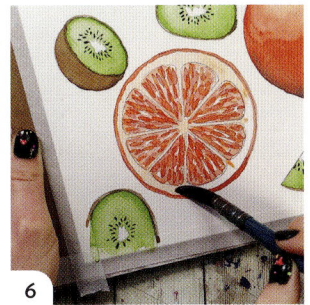

STEP 5

Modify the remaining amount of your custom Grapefruit color by adding a little more Quinacridone Magenta to give it more of a pink or red undertone. Then using the tip of your brush, dot this sporadically through each segment of the grapefruit. Keep the tip of your brush toward the center while doing this to orient the lines with the segments.

Wash your brush and then fill just the tip with concentrated Payne's Gray and dot little black seeds on the inside of the kiwi. Let this dry or make it dry!

STEP 6

Modify the new Grapefruit color by adding in Permanent Yellow Deep until the undertone of the color is more orangey yellow. Add it to the segments by making lines with the tip of your brush that radiate from the center.

Modify this same color by adding a bunch of water to desaturate it and fill in the white spaces of the grapefruits. This doesn't need to be perfect and can be done quickly and messily. Let this dry or make it dry!

STEP 7

For the background, create a variegated wash by first watering down your Shadow Purple until it's at about 30% saturation. For the wash, switch between filling your brush with Purple, then water, or even tapping a little onto some Quinacridone Magenta to get some variation. Don't worry if your background isn't perfect. Backgrounds are so easy to overthink, but the beauty of watercolor is that sometimes the best parts are the messy bits. Let this dry or make it dry!

How to mix bright colors

The first time I painted this, the colors were not as bright and vibrant as I wanted so I had to redo it. If you want to see how I mixed up the bright colors, scan the QR code and watch the video.

About the Artist

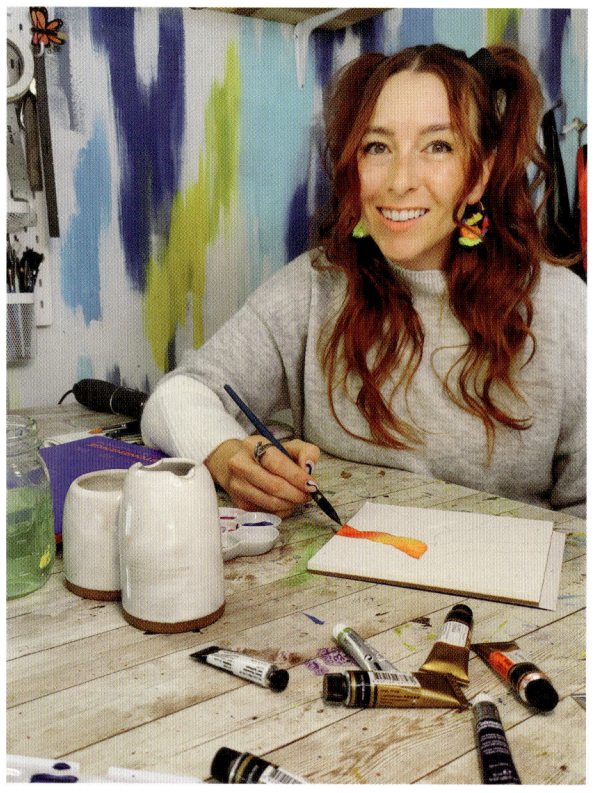

LACEY WALKER is the artist and creator behind Rebel Unicorn Crafts (www.rebelunicorncrafts.com) and her encouraging low-pressure painting channels on Instagram, TikTok, and YouTube @RebelUnicornCrafts. She has an unstoppable need to create, whether watercolor painting, drawing, crafting, pottery, or silversmithing. She is always thinking of new things to make and experimenting with new mediums. Guided by her belief that art and creativity are crucial to the world and essential for achieving happiness, she loves to spread knowledge and creativity through social media classes, her blog, and her shop.

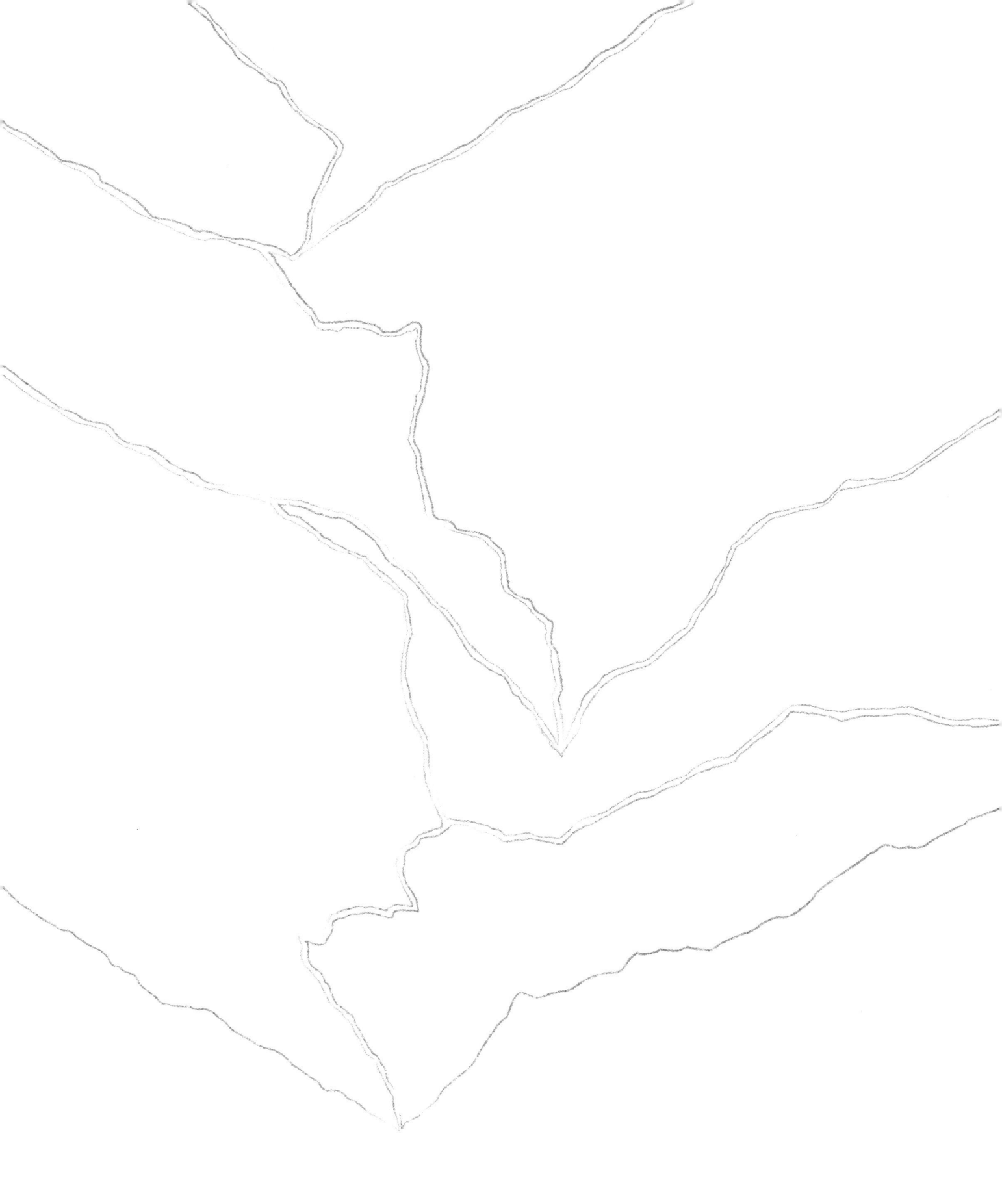

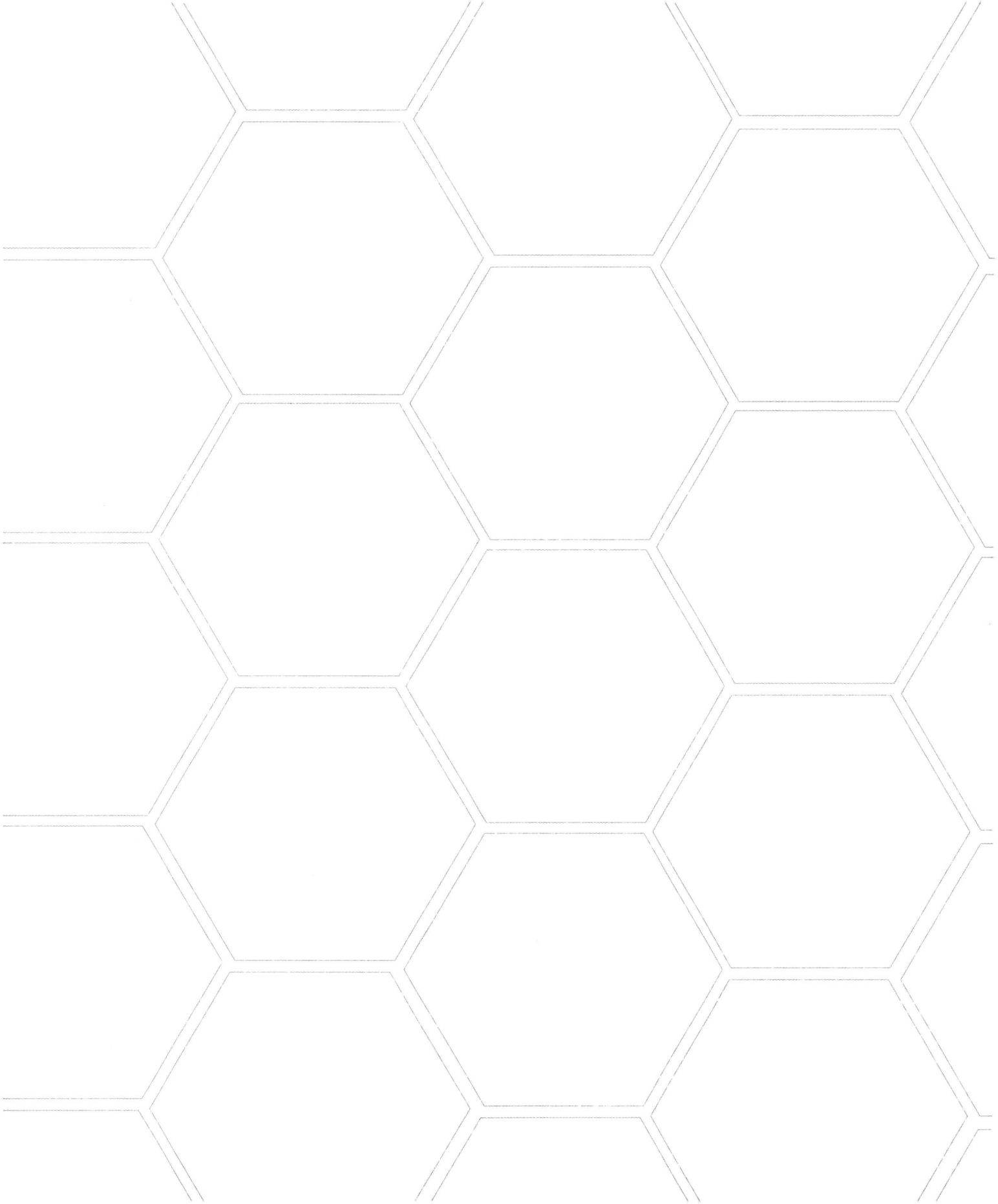

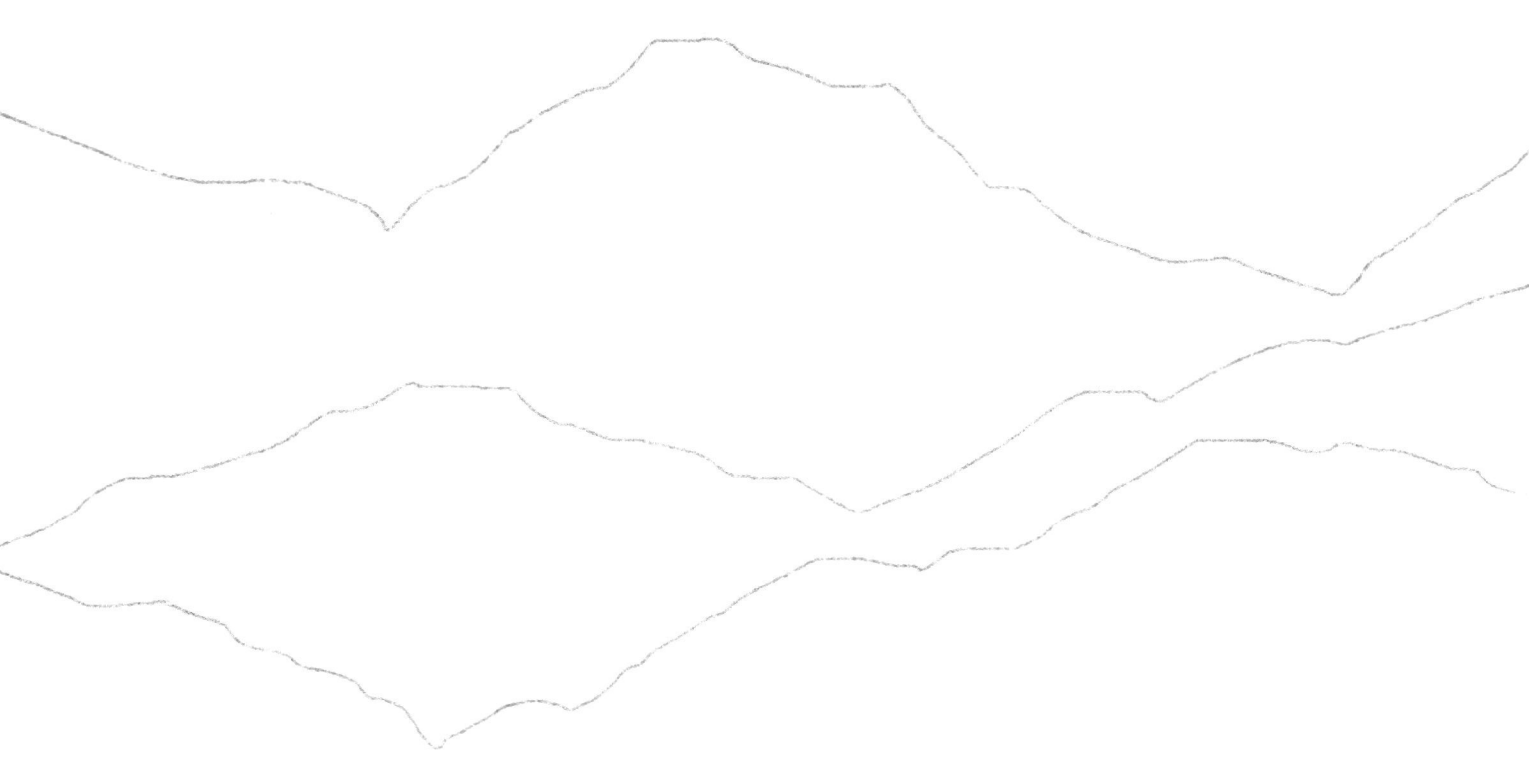

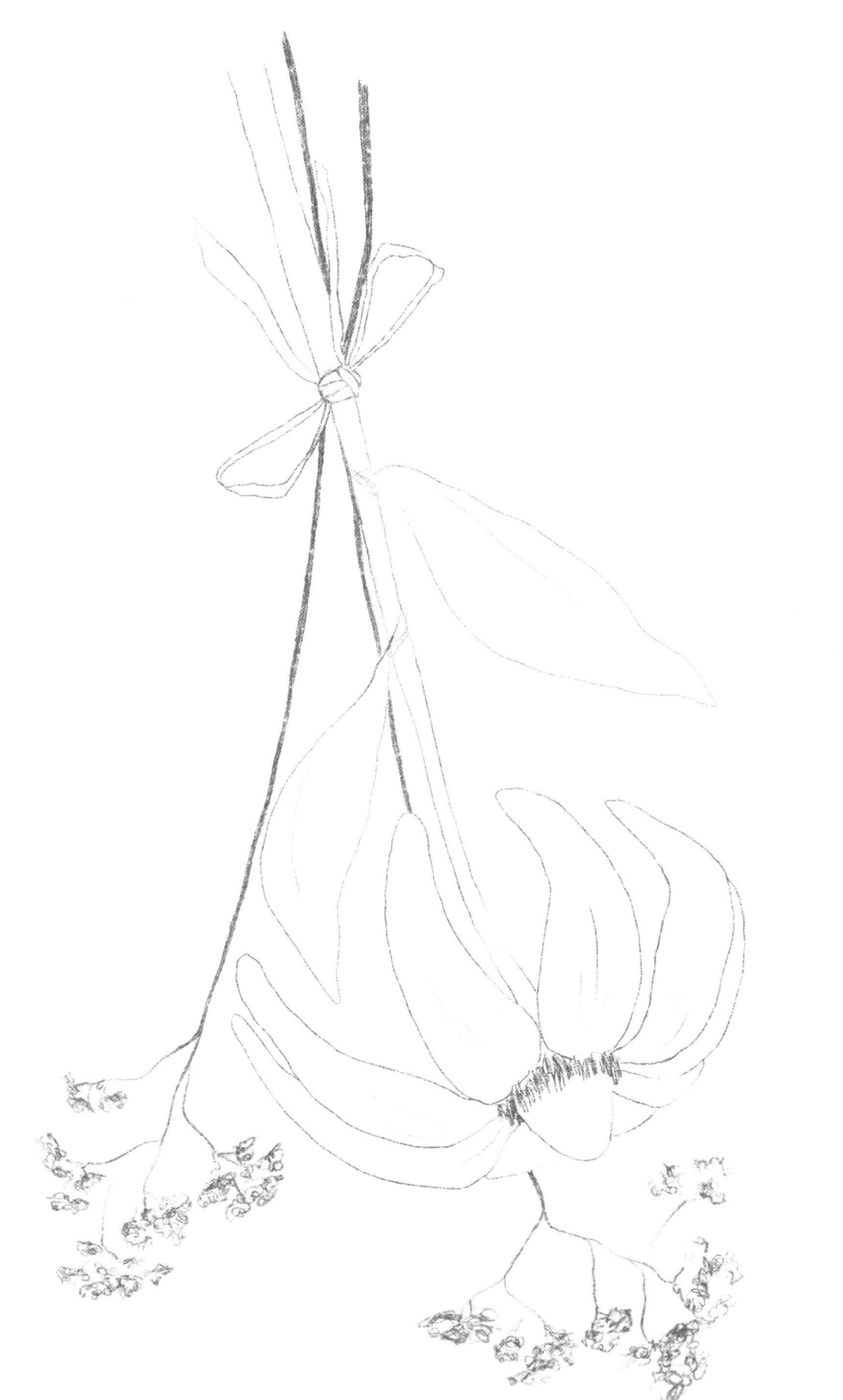

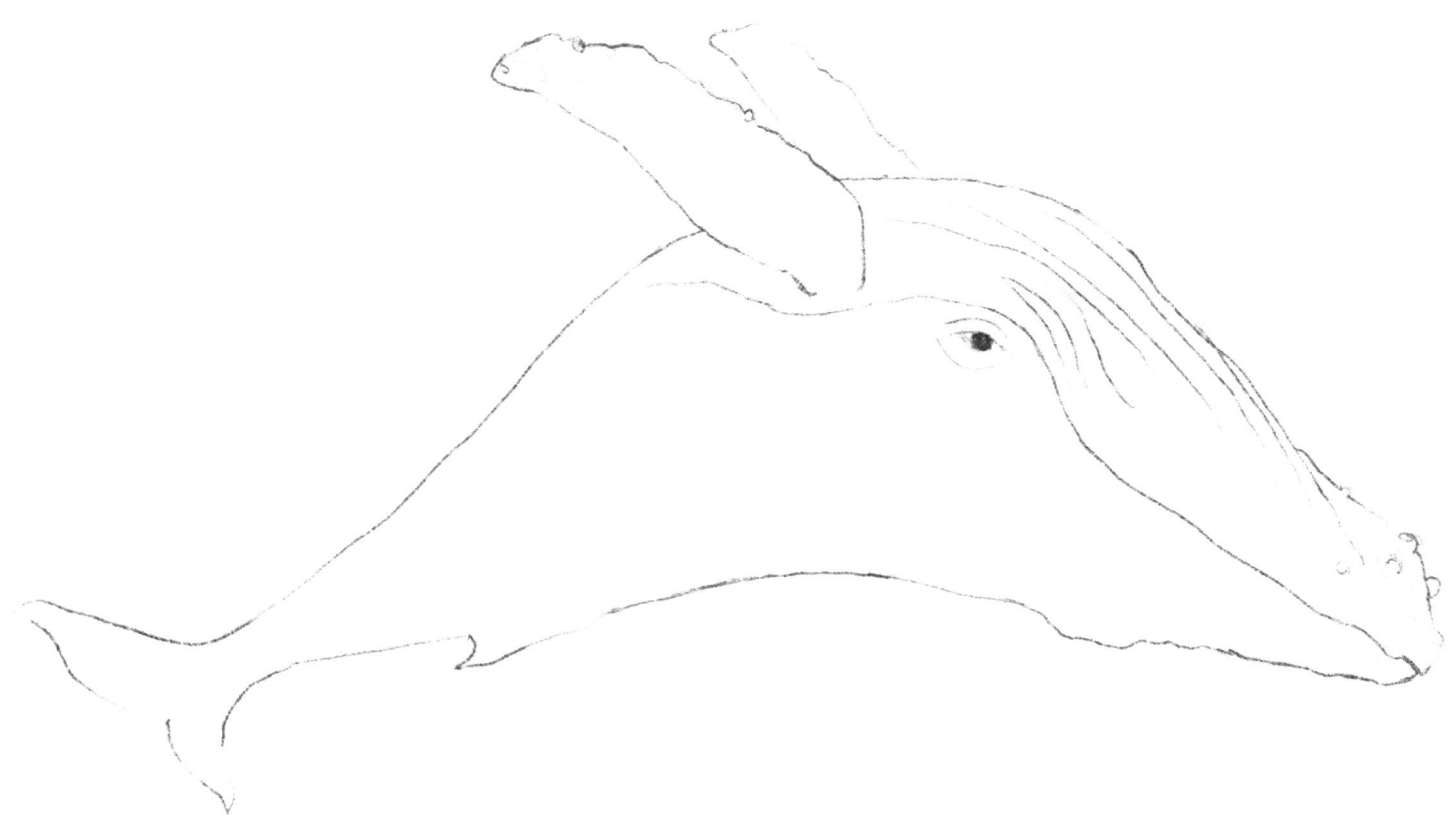

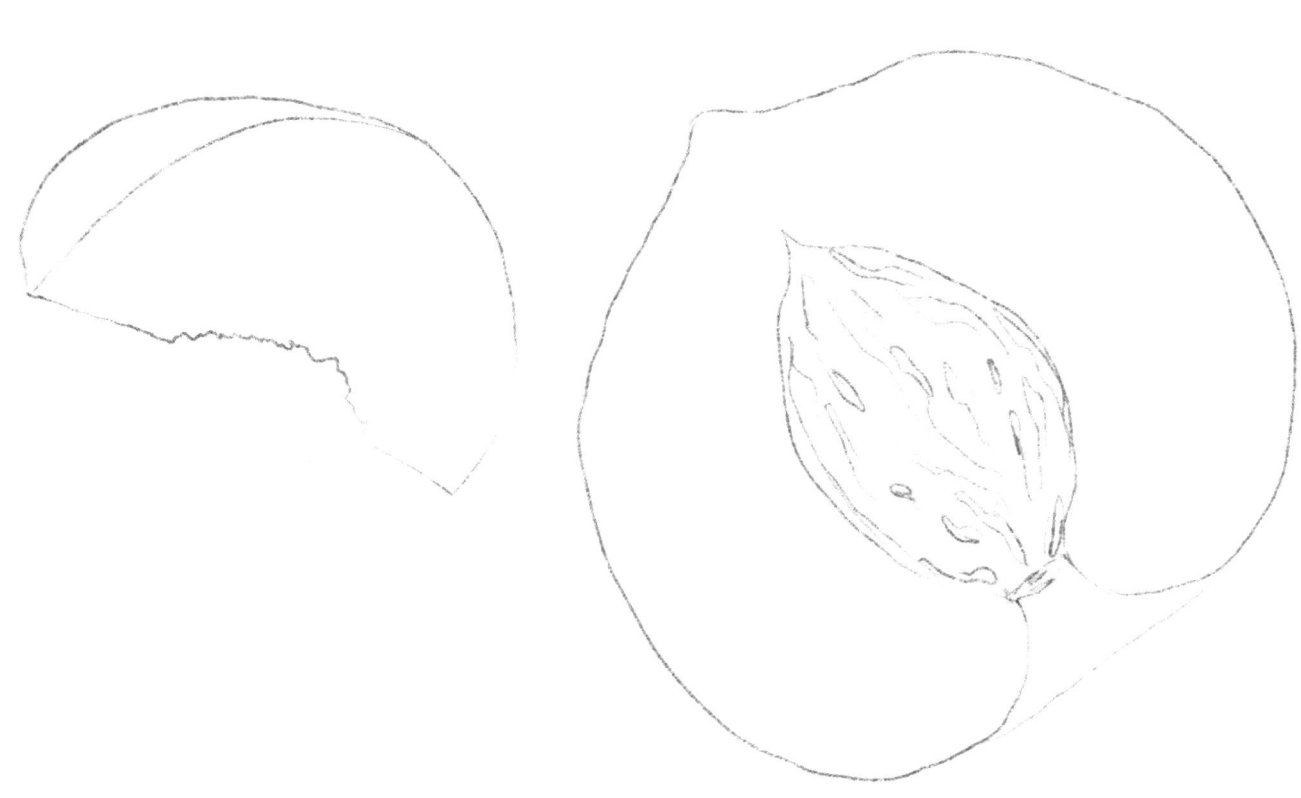

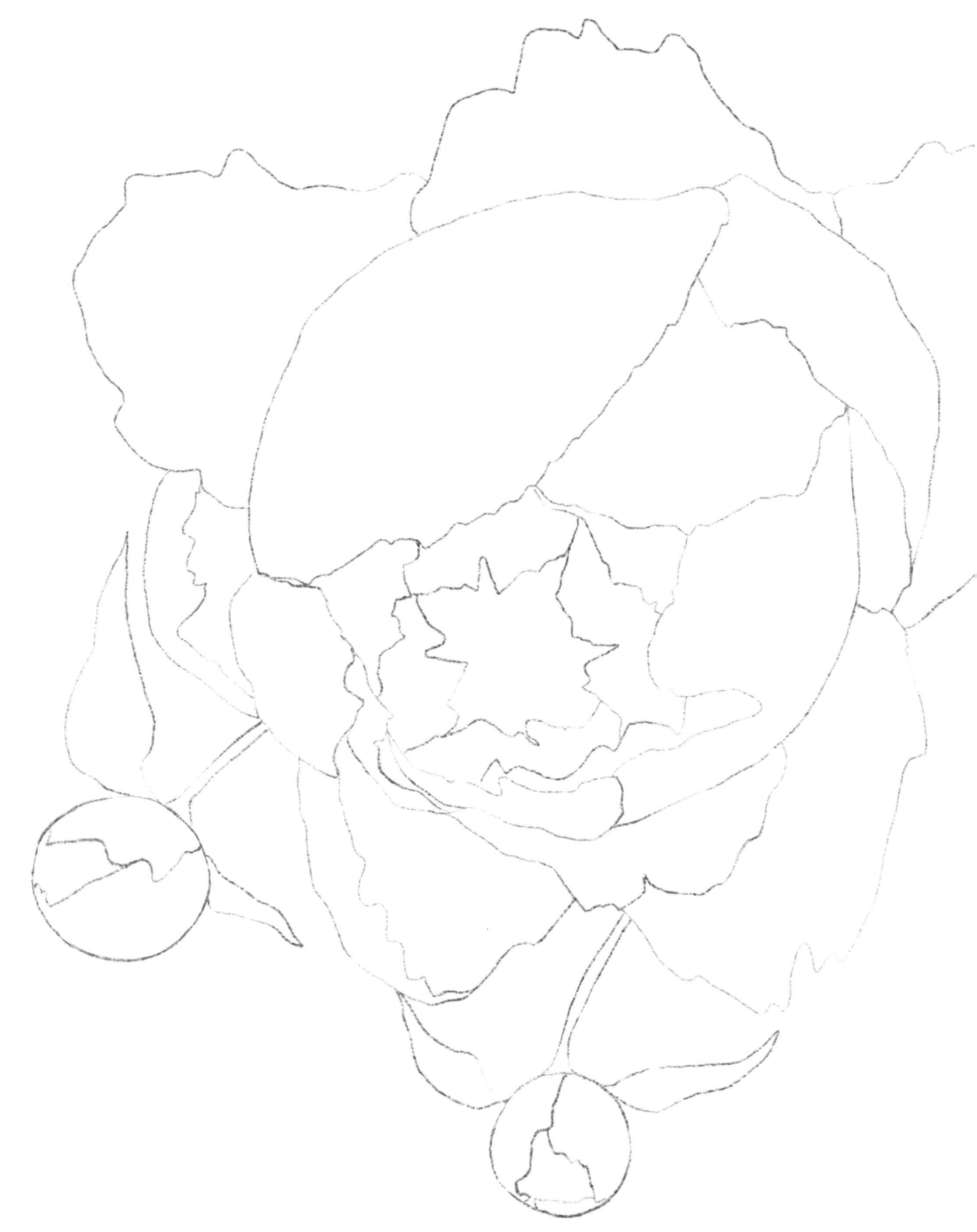

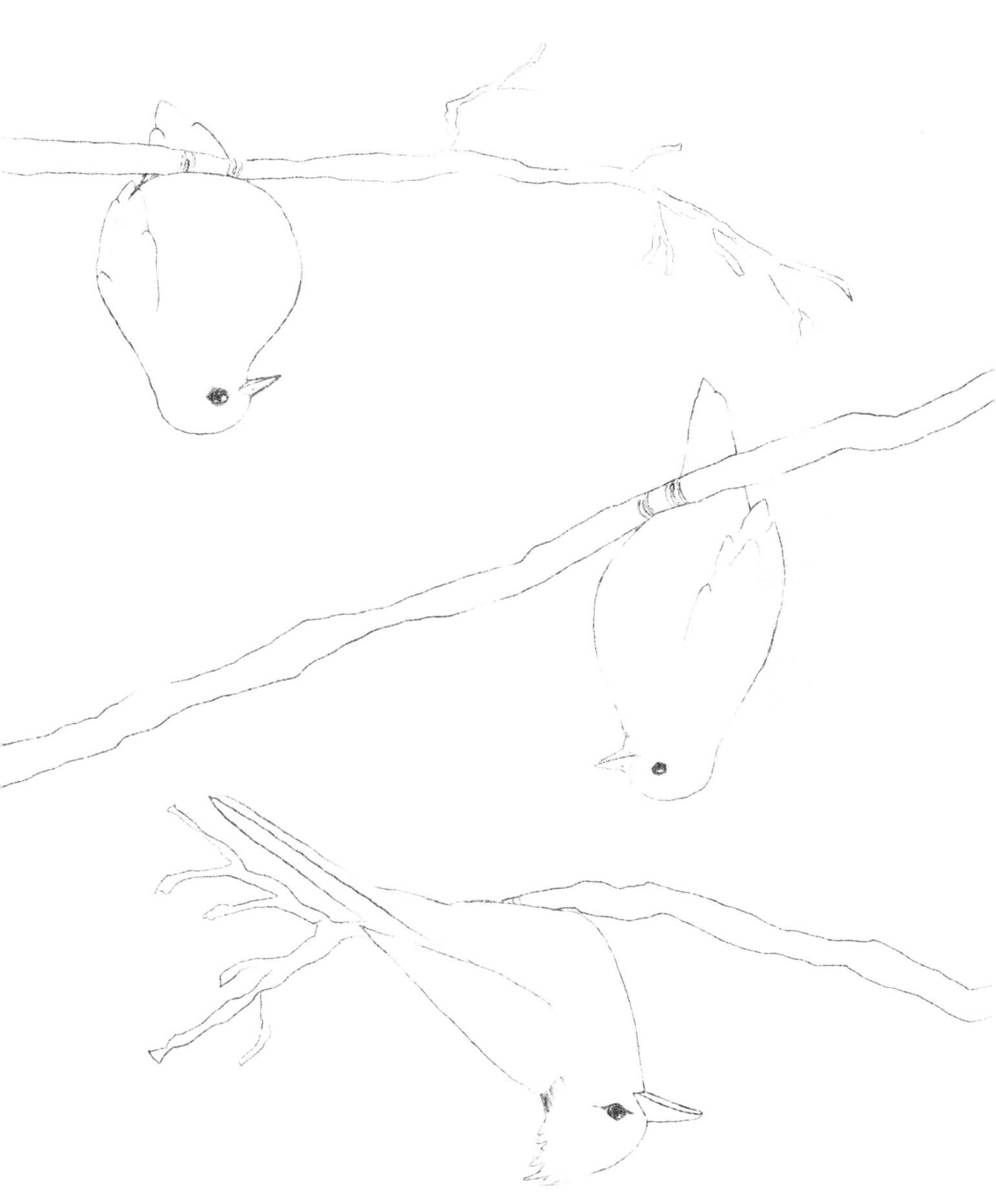

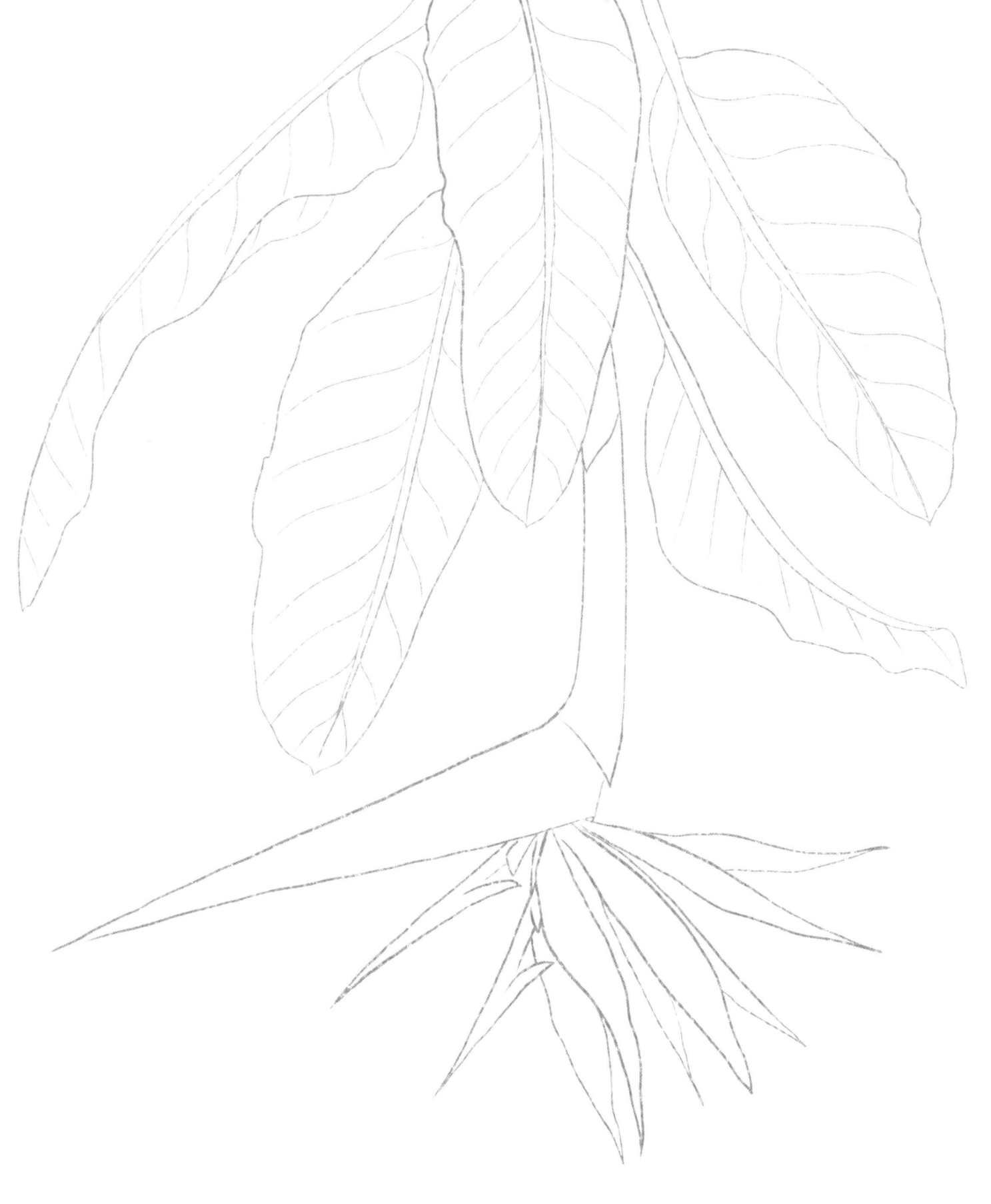

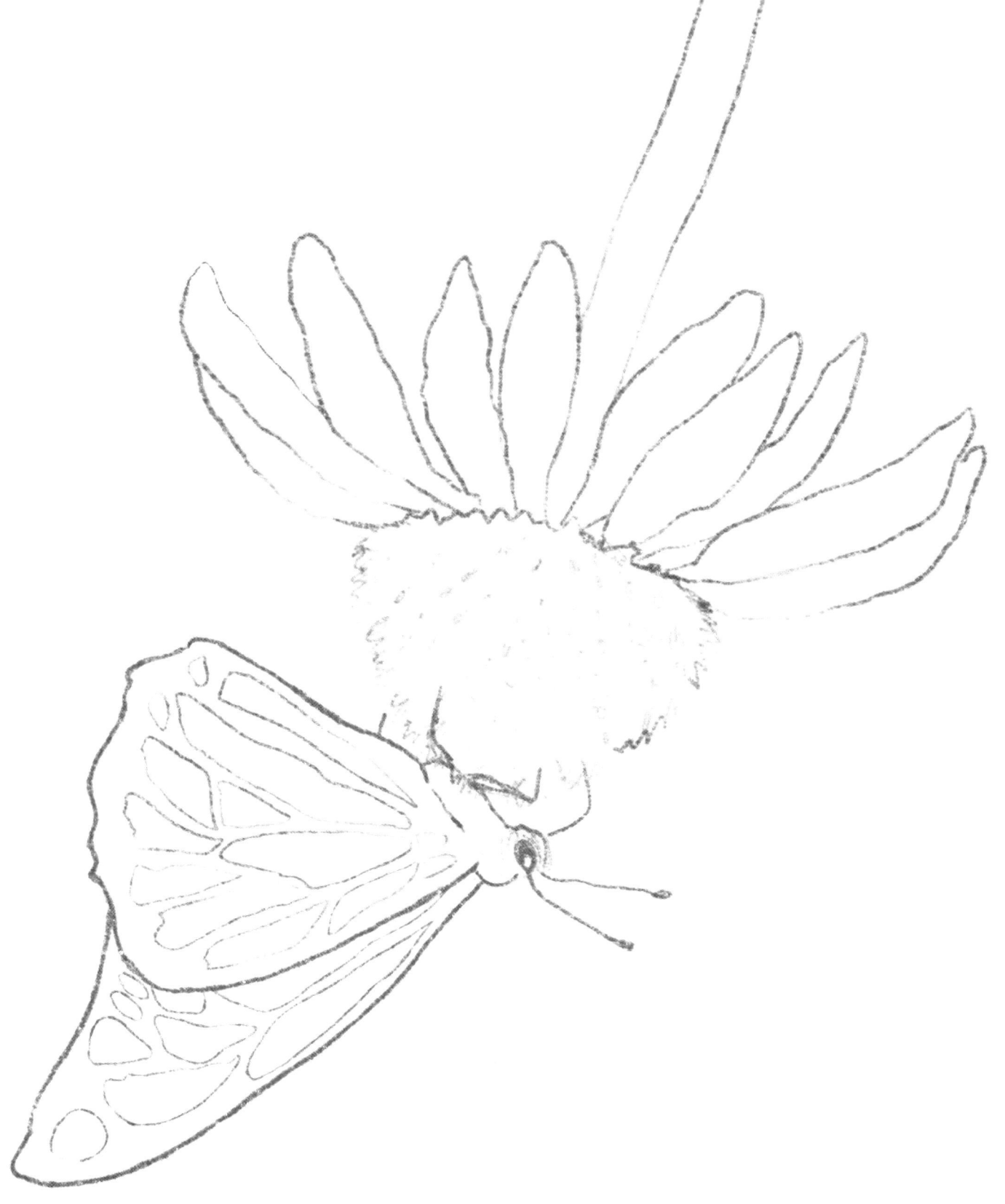

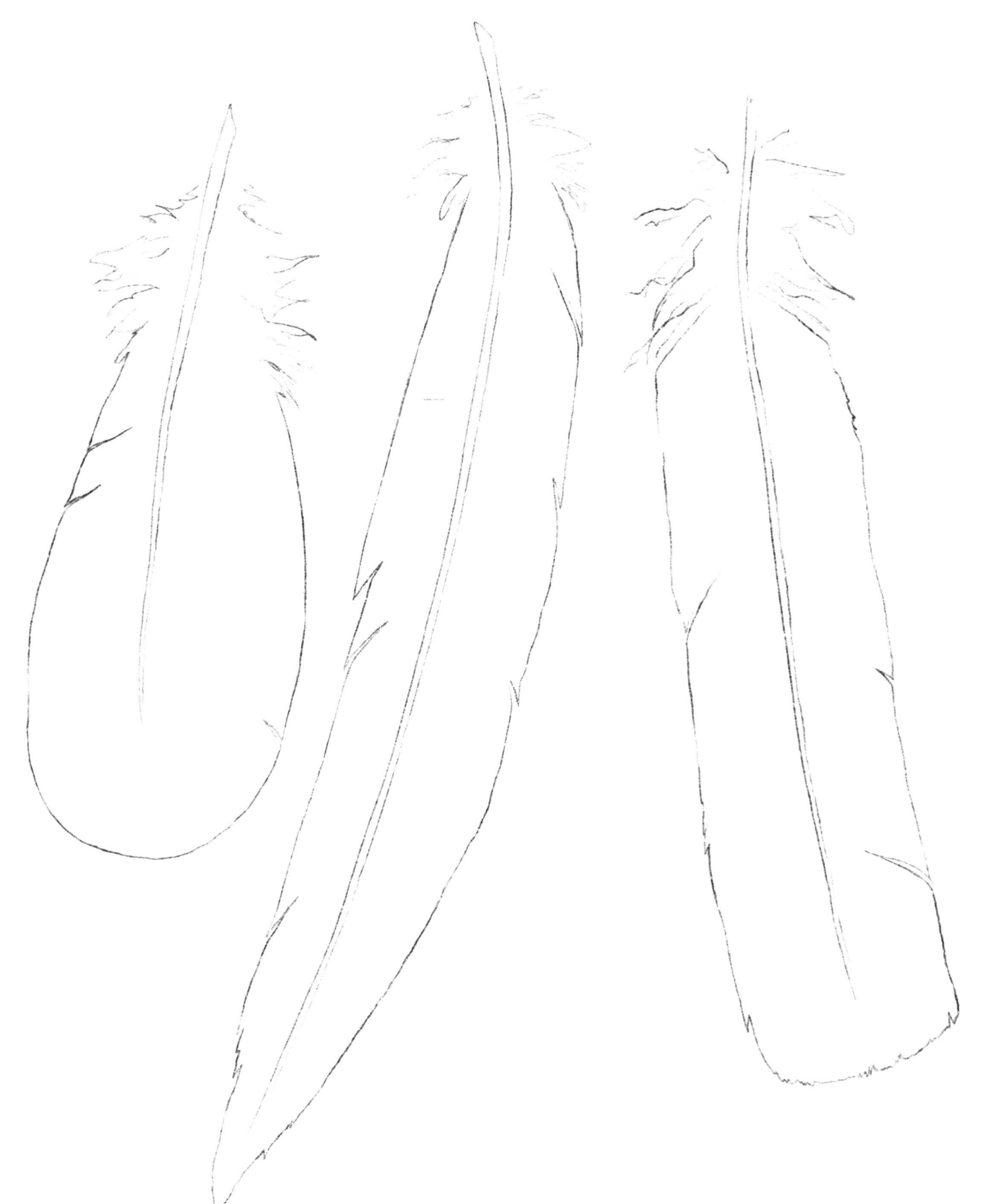

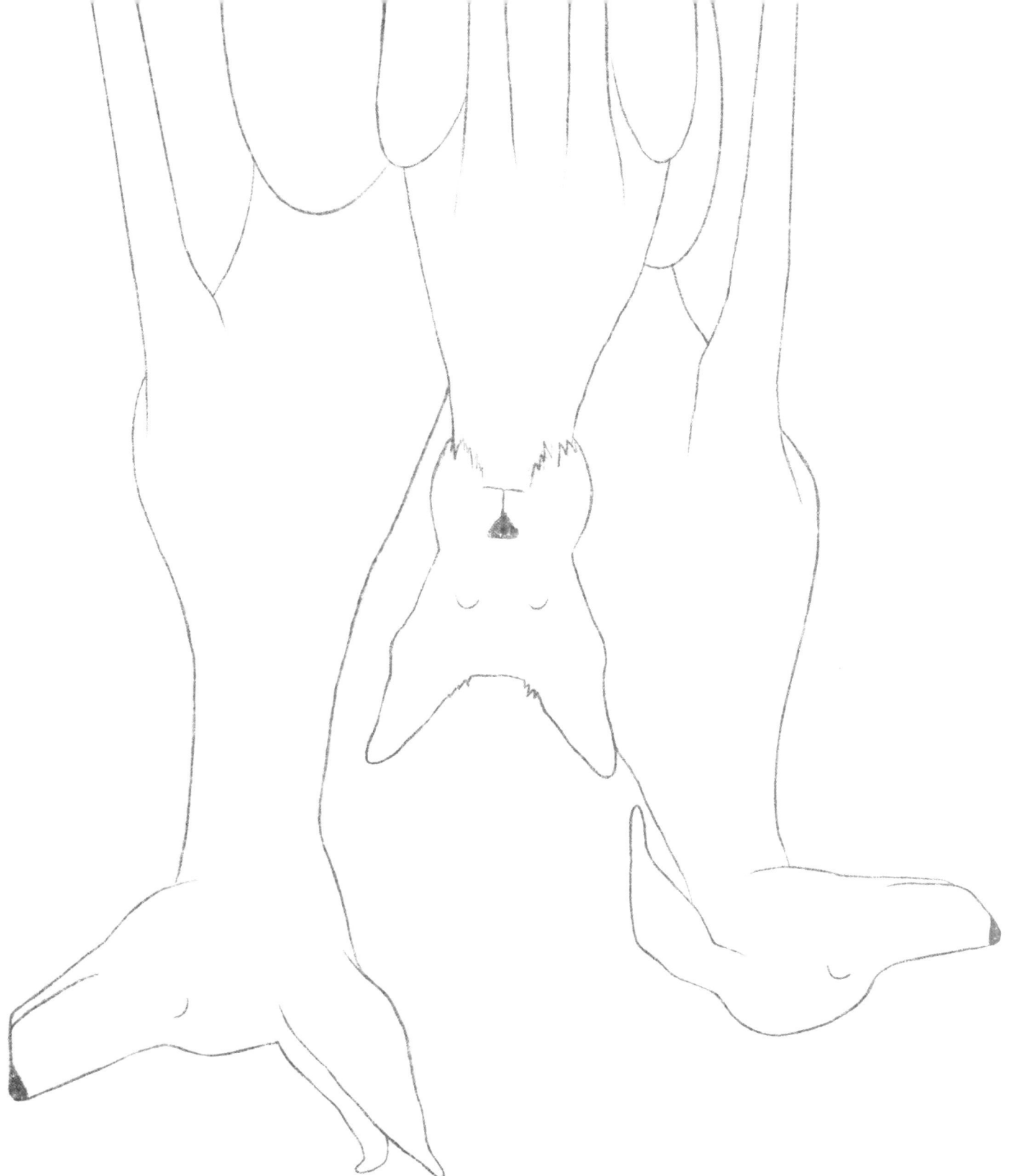

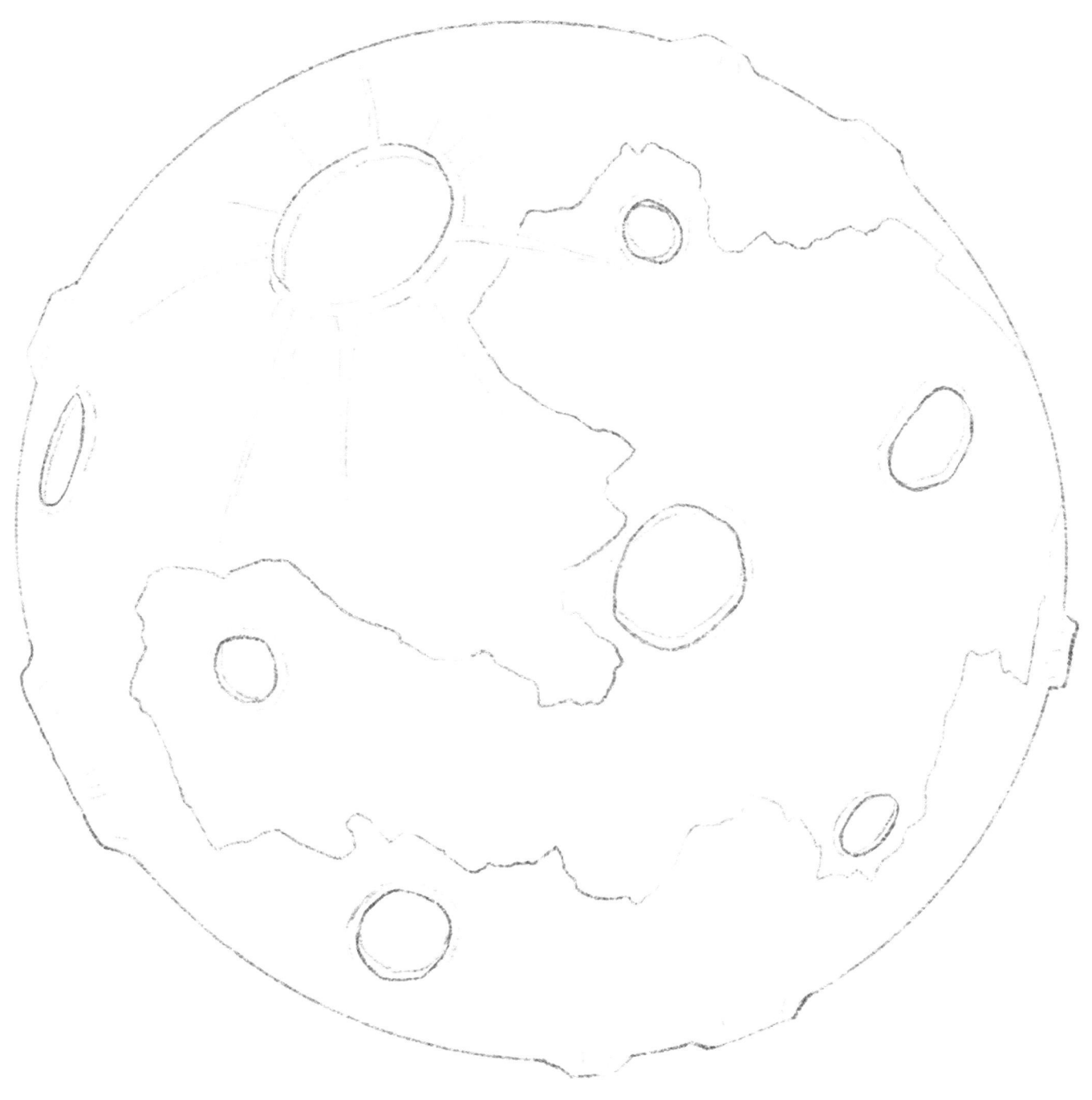

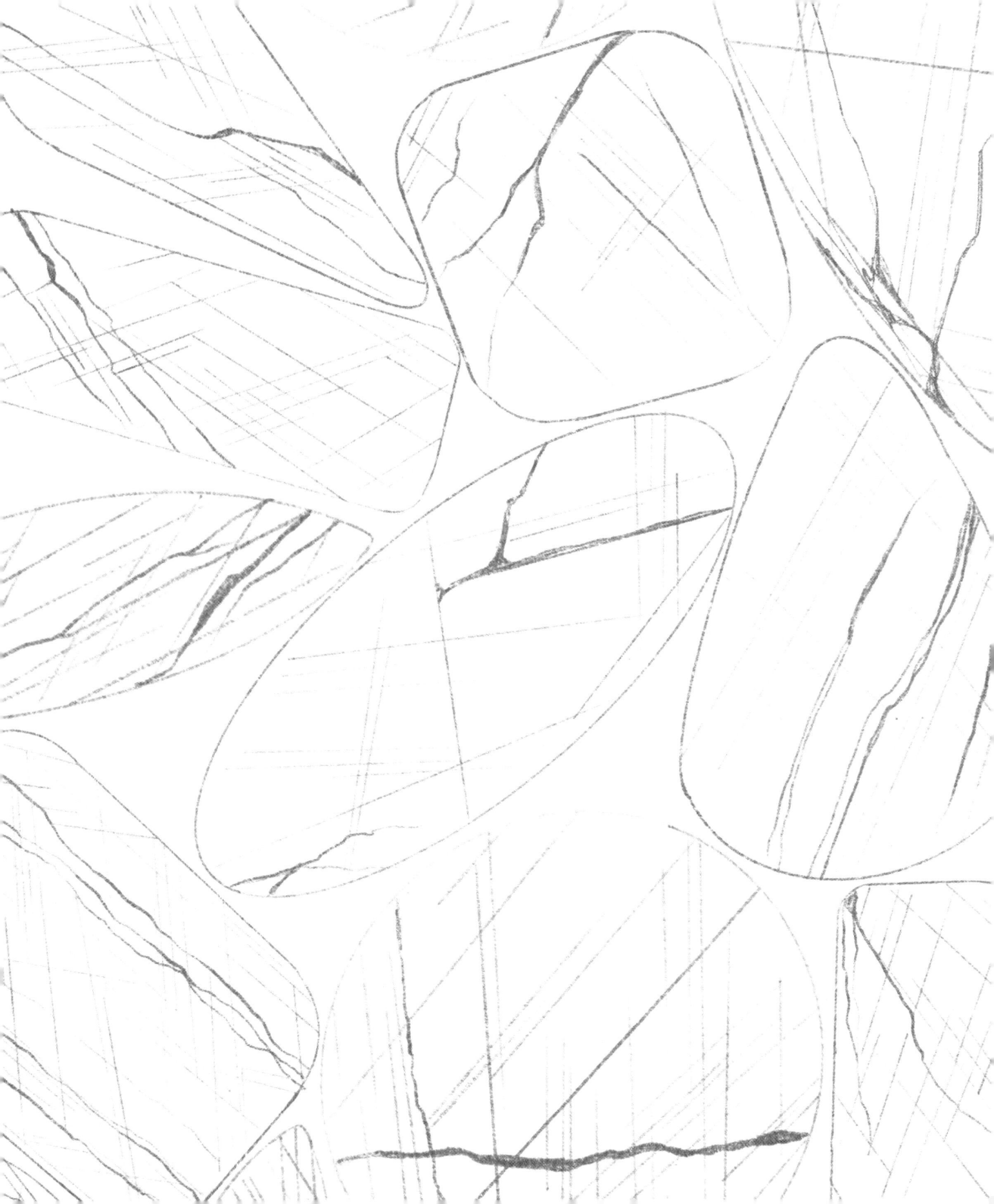

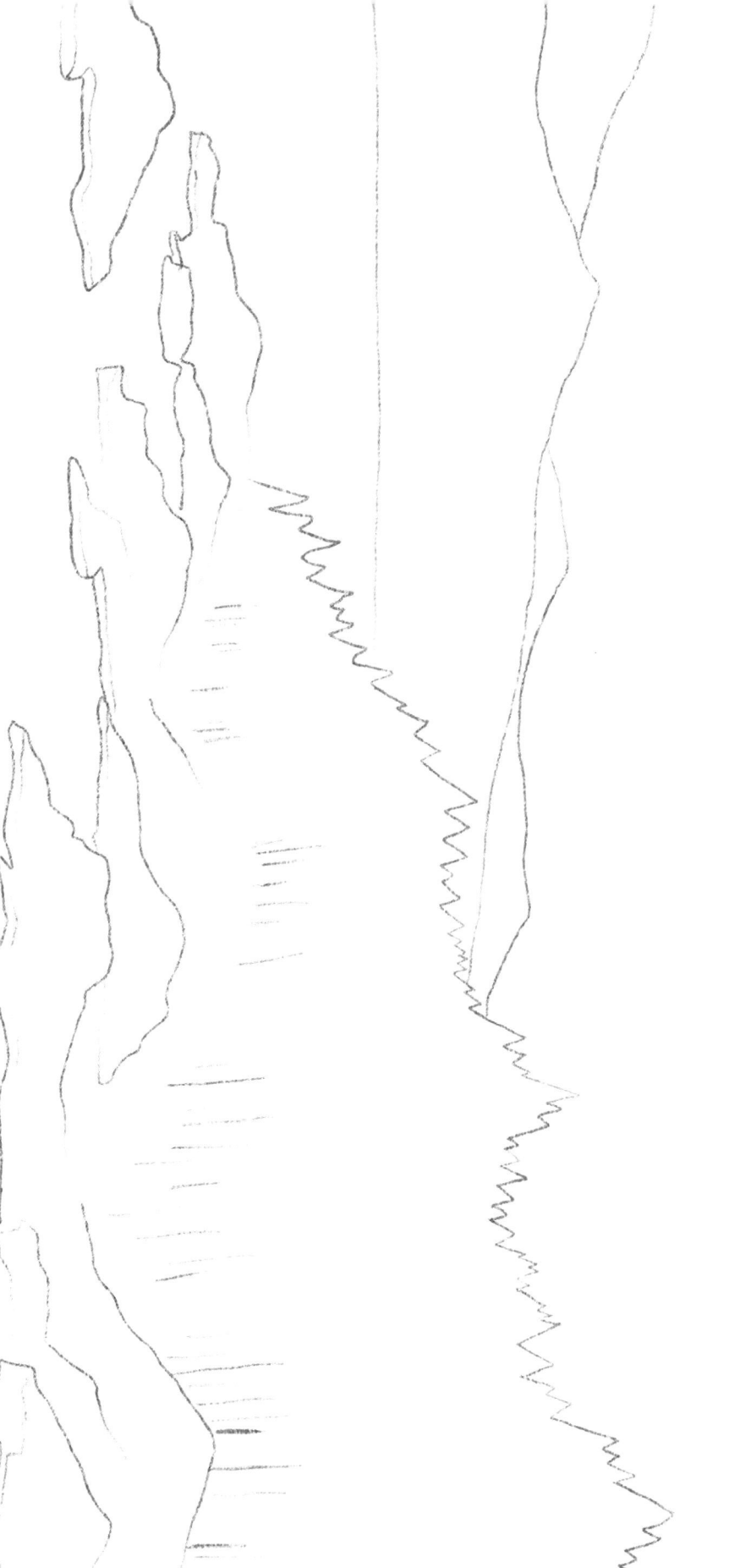